Sustainability and Peaceful Coexistence for the Anthropocene

The rapid industrialization of societies has resulted in radical changes to the Earth's biosphere and its local ecosystems. Climate scientists have recorded and forecasted worrying global temperature rises going back to the early twentieth century, while biologists and palaeontologists have suggested that the next mass extinction is on its way if the current rate of species loss continues. To avert further ecological damage, excessive natural resource use and environmental deterioration are challenges that humanity must deal with *now*. The human species has had such a significant impact on the natural environment that the present geological epoch can be referred to as the 'Anthropocene', the age of humans. The blame and responsibility for the prevailing unsustainability, however, cannot be assigned equally to all humans.

To analyse the root problems and consequences of unsustainable development, as well as to outline rigorous solutions for the contemporary age, this trans-disciplinary book brings together natural and social sciences under the rubric of the Anthropocene. The book identifies the central preconditions for social organization and governance to enable the peaceful coexistence of humans and the non-human world. The contributors investigate the burning questions of sustainability from a number of different perspectives including geosciences, economics, law, organizational studies, political theory and philosophy. The book is a state-of-the-art review of the Anthropocene debate and provides crucial signposts for how human activities can, and should, be changed.

Pasi Heikkurinen is a lecturer at the Sustainability Research Institute (SRI) at the University of Leeds, UK.

Transnational Law and Governance

Series Editor: Paolo Farah, West Virginia University, USA

In recent years the concepts of "transnational law" and "governance" have been explored by both scholars and practitioners with the terms taking on new meaning and significance, particularly in light of the ongoing economic crisis and a corresponding critical reappraisal of global institutional structures and governance. This multidisciplinary series aims to provide a home for research exploring these issues.

Transnational law covers a broad theoretical definition which includes studies emerging from disciplines such as international law, comparative law, international economic law and administrative law undertaken by legal scholars but also features extensive research undertaken by scholars from other disciplines, including but not limited to, political sciences, international relations, public administration, sociology, history, philosophy and geography. Governance in particular is now seen as important when we refer to the general stability of the markets, to good faith and other key principles which are fundamental to the notion of a fair market which is responsive to the needs of governments and citizens as well as businesses.

This series features cutting-edge works which critically analyse the relationship between governance, institutions and law from a variety of disciplinary perspectives.

Available titles in this series include:

A Radically Democratic Response to Global Governance
Dystopian Utopias
Margaret Stout and Jeannine M. Love

Forthcoming titles:

Administrative Appeals in EU Law
Giacomo Gattinara and Alessandro Di Mario

Corporate Accountability under Socio-Economic Rights
Jernej Letnar Černič

Sustainability and Peaceful Coexistence for the Anthropocene

Edited by
Pasi Heikkurinen

Routledge
Taylor & Francis Group
LONDON AND NEW YORK

First published 2017
by Routledge

2 Park Square, Milton Park, Abingdon, Oxfordshire OX14 4RN
52 Vanderbilt Avenue, New York, NY 10017

Routledge is an imprint of the Taylor & Francis Group, an informa business

First issued in paperback 2019

British Library Cataloguing in Publication Data
A catalogue record for this book is available from the British Library

Library of Congress Cataloging in Publication Data
A catalog record for this book has been requested

ISBN: 978-1-138-63427-5 (hbk)
ISBN: 978-0-367-88582-3 (pbk)

Typeset in Galliard
by Keystroke, Neville Lodge, Tettenhall, Wolverhampton

For the victims of the Anthropocene

Contents

Notes on contributors

Karl Johan Bonnedahl is a researcher and lecturer focusing on sustainability and the related needs for change, both in various parts of the economic system (production, consumption and organization) and in its underlying values and assumptions. He applies a system perspective and is interested in ethics and in conflicts between conventional economic approaches and issues of global justice and ecological sustainability. He works at Umeå School of Business and Economics, Sweden, but is equally committed to sustainability-oriented activity outside academia.

Pasi Heikkurinen (D.Sc. in Econ. & Bus.) is a lecturer in Business and Sustainable Change at the University of Leeds, Sustainability Research Institute (SRI). His current research focus is twofold. The first line of investigation deals with the role and responsibility of the corporation, as well as other forms of economic organization, for strong sustainability. The second investigation line scrutinizes the limitations of technology in the quest of ecological sustainability. In research, as well as in teaching, Pasi emphasizes transdisciplinary and holistic approaches as important means to gain understanding of the prevailing unsustainability, and the urgently needed alternative pathways for organising human activities.

Eeva Houtbeckers (M.Sc. Econ.) is a doctoral candidate at Aalto University School of Business, Department of Management Studies, Finland. Her Ph.D. dissertation focuses on mundane social entrepreneurship in Finland and the work of microentrepreneurs in emerging sectors. Her postdoctoral research interests relate to post-growth work practices in the Global North.

Tarja Ketola (Ph.D. in Econ., Imperial College, University of London) is Adjunct Professor of environmental management and Researcher of world history at the University of Turku, Finland. Her current research interests include past, present and future climate change migration (climigration), sustainable development, and responsible leadership.

Jessica C. Lawrence (J.D., Ph.D.) is an assistant professor in the Legal Studies Department at Central European University in Budapest, Hungary. Her research generally applies insights from critical legal studies, governmentality studies and contemporary social and political theory to analyse the relationships between transnational economic law (in particular in the contexts of the European Union, international investment and the World Trade Organization) and other areas of governmental responsibility, such as human rights, environmental protection and migration law.

Todd LeVasseur is Visiting Assistant Professor of religious studies and environmental and sustainability studies at the College of Charleston, South Carolina, USA, where he is also Director of their Quality Enhancement Plan on 'Sustainability Literacy as a Bridge to Addressing 21st Century Problems'. As an environmental humanist, his work explores intersections of religion, ethics and human treatment of the natural world, with a specific focus on sustainable agriculture, sustainability, radical environmentalism and global warming.

J. Mohorčich is a Ph.D. candidate in political science at Johns Hopkins University. He works on pragmatism, infrastructure and power relations. His dissertation draws on John Dewey, Michel Foucault and Shulamith Firestone to develop a problem-oriented, power-sensitive, purposeful relationship between politics and political theory.

Toni Ruuska (M.Sc. in Econ. & Bus.) is finalizing his Ph.D. on reproduction of capitalism at the Department of Management, Aalto University School of Business (Finland). In the study he argues that capitalism is unredeemable from the perspective of ecological sustainability. Moreover, the study is focused on updating the theory of reproduction of capitalism, as it seeks to theorize what capitalism is, how it functions, and which are the main social dynamics and structures needed to keep the dominant mode of production up and running. Toni is also an active member of civil society, and he is committed to finding alternative pathways to sustainable and peaceful coexistence beyond the prevailing capitalist rationale.

Tiina Taipale (M.Sc. in Social Sciences) is a doctoral candidate at Aalto University School of Business, Finland. In both practice and theory she strives to understand the political and moral underpinnings of making a living in the contemporary social and ecological conditions.

Marko Ulvila (M.Sc. in Sociology) engages with various aspects of society as a writer and an organizer. He takes special interest in democracy, ecological sustainability and global equity. Over the years he has been part of a number of civil society processes in Europe, East Africa and South Asia pertaining to environment and post-growth futures. The World Social Forum, the Green Party and the Vasudhaiva Kutumbakam Network are particularly dear to his heart. In 2009 he co-edited the book *Sustainable Futures: Replacing Growth Imperative and Hierarchies with Sustainable Ways* (Ministry for Foreign Affairs of Finland, 2009). Currently Marko chairs the Siemenpuu Foundation in Finland.

Colin N. Waters (Ph.D. in Geology) is a Principal Geologist at the British Geological Survey, working on modelling the UK geosphere. He has diverse research interests in Carboniferous geology, which have direct resource implications. As Secretary of the Anthropocene Working Group (AWG) of the Subcommission on Quaternary Stratigraphy, and as Honourary Professor at the University of Leicester's Department of Geology, he investigates the broad aspects of the Anthropocene concept, helps to coordinate AWG activities and also has a significant role in the process of developing a formal proposal for the Anthropocene as a geological time unit.

Kristoffer Wilén (M.Sc. Econ. & Bus.) is a Ph.D. student at Hanken School of Economics (Helsinki, Finland) within the fields of political ecology and socio-ecological economics. His research interests include the political dimensions of human-environmental relations, the post-political climate and neoliberalization of environmental debates, subjectification and power within consumption and work and the commodification and economization of everything in market(ing) society – and some of the alternatives to this: degrowth, commons, solidarity economy, environmental justice. As a hobby he is happily participating in debunking the myths surrounding the promises of the so-called 'green', 'circular', 'sharing' and 'bio' economy.

Mark Williams is Professor of Palaeontology at the University of Leicester, UK. He is interested in the evolution of the biosphere over geological time scales, with a particular emphasis on the Cambrian Period, when animals become widespread in the fossil record. He uses his knowledge of deep time changes in the biosphere to inform a better understanding of current, anthropogenically induced changes to biodiversity, and this has also influenced the two popular science books he has authored with Jan Zalasiewicz, *The Goldilocks Planet* (OUP, 2012) and *Ocean Worlds* (OUP, 2014).

Jan Zalasiewicz is Professor of palaeobiology at the University of Leicester, UK. In his early career he was a field geologist and palaeontologist at the British Geological Survey, working to decipher the lowlands of eastern England and then the mountains of central Wales. Now, he teaches geology and Earth history to undergraduate and postgraduate students, and studies fossil ecosystems and environments across over half a billion years of geological time. Over the last few years he has been involved in helping develop ideas on the Anthropocene, the concept that humans have changed the course of this planet's geological history.

Paolo Davide Farah teaches at West Virginia University, John D. Rockefeller IV School of Policy and Politics, Department of Public Administration, USA. He is Director of gLAWcal (Global Law Initiatives for Sustainable Development, UK (www.glawcal.org.uk)) and Senior Fellow at the Institute of International Economic Law (IIEL), Georgetown University Law Center, Washington DC, USA. He is an expert in the interaction between trade, economic globalization and non-trade concerns, such as sustainable development, energy, environment and human rights. He is also Editor-in-Chief for the gLAWcal book series published by Routledge Publishing (London/New York) on 'Global Law and Sustainable Development' and on 'Transnational Law and Governance'. He holds a dual Ph.D. in International Law from Aix-Marseille University (France) and the University of Milan (Italy), an LLM in European Legal Studies from the College of Europe in Bruges (Belgium), a Maitrise in International and European Law from Paris Ouest La Défense Nanterre University (France).

Foreword

Paolo Davide Farah

> I used to walk to school in a nearby village along a cart track through the fields and, on the way, see on the horizon a huge smokestack of some hurriedly built factory, in all likelihood in the service of war. It spewed dense brown smoke and scattered it across sky. Each time I saw it, I had an intense feeling of something profoundly wrong, of humans spoiling the earth.
>
> (Vaclav Havel, Politics and Conscience)

These words from 1984 of Czech statesman and philosopher Vaclav Havel are of great topicality in the age of Anthropocene. What in the mid-80s sounded like a final warning or a bad premonition has in our time gradually acquired the quality of an established fact: humans have become agents of global geological change and a major driving force behind processes that were, in the past, vested solely in the realm of nature. The crucial role of human beings and their activities in the multiplicity of crises in the current world – ranging from ecological to economic and socio-cultural – cannot be disputed, but their complex character requires the adoption of a holistic approach to the problematic issues and challenges facing us, including climate change, soil and water depletion, environmental degradation and loss of biodiversity. Bringing together the topics of peaceful coexistence and sustainability is an articulation of such an approach, acknowledging the interdependence of a variety of issues related to the Anthropocene.

In its *Climate Change 2007: Synthesis Report* the Intergovernmental Panel on Climate Change (IPCC) has referred to climate change as:

> a change in the state of the climate that can be identified . . . by changes in the mean and/or variability of its properties, and that persists for an extended period, typically decades or longer. It refers to any change in climate over time, whether due to natural variability or as a result of human activity.

The wording is slightly different from that used by the United Nations Framework Convention on Climate Change (UNFCCC), which, as noted in the IPCC report (p. 30), refers to climate change as 'a change of climate which is attributed directly or indirectly to human activity that alters the composition of the global atmosphere and that is in addition to natural climate variability observed over comparable time periods'. What is important to note here is that the IPCC is more cautious than the UNFCCC in terms of blaming humans for climate change.

The introductory words of this book indicate that the topic of 'Anthropocene' is part of a larger narrative, which is shedding light on the underpinnings of the problem: human beings and their value systems. The concept of 'narrative' is crucial in this regard. Narratives convey certain values, translate complex rational or irrational theories and policies into comprehensible forms and contribute to their acceptance by the public at large. The limits of the narrative of constant growth, never-ending economic and technological progress and the dominance of humans over nature is slowly being confronted with its limitations. According to Vaclav Havel, it is a paradox: humans in the age of science and technology believe they are improving their lives by mastering the laws of nature and exploiting nature. However, the contrary is the case: these natural laws prevail over humans and will penalise them for wrongdoing. Humans wanted to conquer nature, and as a result they destroyed it. There has to be a change in the narrative: civilization needs to be based on a revived and recreated responsibility of humankind, respecting the boundaries of the natural world. The narratives of science need to serve this cause as well, otherwise even the bold visions of Elon Musk and other visionaries of colonising Mars would only be escapes from the primary task, which is taking responsibility for our lives and the lives of future generations on the planet.

Principle 7 of the Rio Declaration can be seen as a step towards responsibility and accountability for human actions, as it importantly considers the needs and specific features of developing countries. It is indeed the poorest, most exposed, and most vulnerable who cannot leave their destroyed livelihood, but will have to stay and eventually perish.[1] This declaration refers to the 'Common But Differentiated Responsibilities' (CBDR), where the developed countries acknowledge the responsibility that they bear in the international pursuit of sustainable development in relation to the pressures their societies place on the global environment, as well as on the technologies and financial resources they command. Trying to face these issues in the fastest and most effective way should be the aim of all state representatives and policy makers in the Global North. The time for more negotiations has passed, and it is now time to take firm action with both strict mitigation and adaptation measures. While the mitigation measures should come in the form of technological change and substitution that reduce resource inputs and emissions per unit of output, the adaptation measures must take place through the adjustment of natural or human systems in response to actual or expected climatic stimuli or their effects, which are moderating harm or exploiting beneficial opportunities.

1 IPCC (2014). *Climate Change 2014: Impacts, Adaptation, and Vulnerability*. Working Group II. Geneva: Intergovernmental Panel on Climate Change.

But, of course, many developing countries and the least-developed countries would need assistance in solving sustainability, collaboration, and financial support issues from the developed countries in order to acquire or domestically obtain the best means towards sustainable development.

For instance, Chapter 34 of Agenda 21 identifies the most controversial dimensions of technology transfer:

> Environmentally sound technologies are not just individual technologies, but total systems which include know-how, procedures, goods and services, and equipment as well as organizational and managerial procedures. This implies that when discussing transfer of technologies, the human resource development and local capacity-building aspects of technology choices . . . should also be addressed. Environmentally sound technologies should be compatible with nationally determined socio-economic, cultural, and environmental priorities.

Of course, the successful completion of the Paris Agreement in December 2015 dealing with the mitigation of greenhouse gases, adaptation, and finance is a stepping stone towards this needed paradigm shift.

To add another piece to the puzzle, it is relevant to remember that according to the conclusions of the Stockholm Resilience Centre in Sweden, the crossing of planetary boundaries – especially climate change and the deterioration of integrity of the biosphere – will eventually drive the Earth and its ecosystems to the point of no return, gradually turning the planet into a less and less hospitable place. While more apt technologies can help to address the challenges of satisfying the growing needs of an increasing number of countries and the populations that come out of poverty and have their basic needs met, the ecological problems are not about a techno-fix. To slow down this undesired development and to alleviate the severity of its consequences – if not reverse it – more than technology is needed, namely broad-scale social change at both micro and macro-levels.

At the micro-level, philosophies, human behaviour, and social models advocating simplicity of life need to be reconsidered and fostered as alternatives compatible with the finite character of the planet. The radical change in the behavioural patterns driven by consumerism — mainly in developed countries and fast-growing economies – represents a necessary precondition for any wide-ranging social change. A paradigm shift is certainly needed to try to fight the inevitable end of our existence. It is unavoidable that developed nations must change their priorities and lifestyles, whilst developing countries and least-developed countries should try to avoid repeating the same series of mistakes in their run to 'develop', but instead search for new alternatives to achieve a sustainable society.

The narrative of social change opens the door to a broader discussion about the redefinition and restructuring of the existing global and good governance models. One of the leading and most influential ideologies behind the contemporary governance models worldwide and globalization principles is neoliberalism, which advocates a crucial and decisive role of markets when it comes to regulating affairs in the public and private sector. The application of models based on the market logic in the public sector, such as New Public Management and Value for Money, might serve as an example of neoliberalism in practice. Despite some undeniable benefits of such models for society derived from more effective public governance, better budget management and constraints ruled by the market, questions arise whether these models are still apt in the age of the Anthropocene where a greater account needs to be taken of aspects that do not have an explicit monetary value. Arguably, the Anthropocene should oblige us to reconsider our values and priorities, to ignite social change, and to rethink the definitions and the concepts of public goods, as well as the global commons and the related limits of the use of shared resources. In the Anthropocene, the fundamental human values must certainly include the Earth, its nature, and the environment.

For the social change to also be socially sustainable, it should not be a result of a revolutionary overthrow happening overnight. It remains a hope that the age of Anthropocene will come to represent a period of new enlightenment in the field of governance and policy-making. The aim should be the transformation of the existing governance models into sustainable ones that recognise the complexity of relations between the human and non-human worlds. Actually, there is little new to discover. Modern societies should simply learn from the past and implement in a practical manner the fundamental principles and concepts of philosophies from the West and the East that aimed at and envisaged a good balance between humans and nature. Environmental philosophy, environmental ethics and ecology also have roots in Eastern philosophies with concepts coming from Confucianism and Daoism. It has to be remembered that there are also more recent examples in other Asian countries, such as the works of Gandhi in India, yoga lifestyles and the virtues of non-violence, self-sufficiency and simplicity.

When addressing social change, one must take into account the thin line between a call for radical change pursuing noble ideas and a revolution eating up its own children. The same idea is applicable to the use of the words 'modernity' and 'innovative' as opposed to 'obsolete'. It is not always the case that modern society should simply proceed with fashionable and constantly new visions and methods. Sometimes it might be wiser and more innovative to use the old-fashioned and previously used principles that worked, and which were more appropriate than the present mainstream conformity. Indeed, the age of the Anthropocene requires that humankind questions and redefines its established behavioural patterns and social models and considers reintroducing the positive methods and ideas of the past and blending them with the present ideas and world of opportunity.

In fact, the current narrative of social change might be seducing and introducing a form of social engineering so concentrated on the achievement of desired objectives that it will neglect and undermine the democratic fundamentals of society. To prevent any form of totalitarianism, the elites in their ivory towers need to reconnect with the public at large. The Anthropocene calls for a spirit of cooperation highlighting the interdependence of the human and non-human realms. At the same time, coherent philosophies derived from in-depth combinations of the present and past theories of Western and Eastern tradition and revised concepts of ecology that might serve as the underpinnings for life in the Anthropocene are needed. These philosophies could accommodate the aspects of deep ecology and lead consequently to the reconsideration of anthropocentrism, but at the same time would not have to be hostile towards humanity, technology, development, and modernity as a whole. These philosophies could be based on the idea of peaceful coexistence in the world of humans, as well as between humans and non-humans.

The first Peaceful Coexistence Colloquium: 'Genders, Natures, and Technologies in the Anthropocene' and this book are important contributions to a new Anthropocene philosophy and narrative that looks at the world and the social change needed from the perspective of various scientific disciplines. Even though this book is a scholarly piece, it also has the potential to outline a more inclusive narrative for the age of the Anthropocene beyond the academic audience. On one hand, it is a narrative recalling the visions of a Mad Max-like dystopia but, on the other hand, it is a story of hope, providing theoretical and practical visions for imagining alternatives to the current system.

In the Post-Paris Agreement debate and the ongoing UNFCCC negotiations, this book will find momentum. States and their representatives must find more and more innovative ways to meet the targets through their Intended Nationally Determined Contributions (INDC) and to shape their policies towards degrowth and then post-growth societies. The use of these new theoretical and philosophical concepts to evaluate and reconsider the relations between humans and the Anthropocene Earth may be the lenses necessary to lead us towards a progressive and successful implementation of the Paris Agreement, not only in legal terms, but also so that they are accepted by the people. It is clear that there has been too much emphasis on growth and industrialization as measures of progress in national and worldwide geopolitical relations. This book attempts to reverse this trajectory. This kind of scholarship is increasingly necessary and timely.

Paolo Davide Farah is the Editor-in-Chief of the gLAWcal series 'Transnational Law and Governance' published by Routledge.

Acknowledgements

First of all, I would like to thank the matter-energetic basis of the world. Not only has it enabled the evolution of all species but it has also provided plenty of inspiration and hope for evolving human cultures, as well as memorable moments for those in decline. Your nature and nurture have been truly invaluable to all of us. Thank you for these beautiful gifts that shine as the brightest lighthouses in the dark times of the Anthropocene.

Second, I wish to express my deepest gratitude to all the people who take part in imagining and forming sustainable societies of peace. My special thanks go to the students, faculty and staff members of the University for Peace who helped in organising the first Peaceful Coexistence Colloquium in April 2014. The roots of this book are in this conference held in El Rodeo, Costa Rica. I am immensely grateful to Jan Breitling, Laura Shillington and Brian Dowd-Uribe from the Faculty of Environment and Development for their genuine collegiality and joyful spirits; Sara Sharratt, the Dean of Academic Affairs, for her support; Distinguished Professor Toh Swee-Hin for his great keynote speech; and the colloquium session chairs: Jan Breitling, Jimena Alvarado, Laura Shillington, Leon Berdichevsky, Mihir Kanade and Toni Ruuska. I also wish to express my gratitude to the presenters and co-authors of the conference papers: Anu Valtonen, Brian Dowd-Uribe, Christian Michelsens, Jan Breitling, Jan Hessbruegge, Jenny Rinkinen, Jessica C. Lawrence, John-Andrew McNeish, Joseph Mohorčich, Juan M. Amaya-Castro, Laura Shillingon, Mumbua Simon, Paolo Davide Farah, Pasi Heikkurinen, Pikka-Maaria Laine, Piritta Parkkari, Robert Flecther, Ross Ryan, Saija Katila, Susan Meriläinen, Takuo Namisashi, Tarja Salmela, Todd LeVasseur, Toh Swee-Hin and Virginia Cawagas, as well as all the other participants and discussants.

I am similarly grateful to people at the University of Leeds for new ideas on sustainability and their encouragement to edit this book. Special thanks go to colleagues at the Sustainability Research Institute (SRI), particularly to the Institute Co-Director Professor William Young and Professor Jouni Paavola for their support. I also want to express my gratitude to my colleagues Sebastien Nobert, Cécile Cam, Dan O'Neill, Marco Sakai Diaz, Paola Hernandez Montes de Oca, Beth Stratford, Elke Pirgmaier, Thomas Smith, Matthew England, James Van Alstine, Pablo Muñoz, Martin Dallimer, Stephen Hall and Lucie Middlemiss for their friendliness and openness that have led us to stimulating discussions on sustainable development and beyond.

The greatest thanks certainly belong to the authors of the book. Thank you for believing in this project and for your precious contributions! I also wish to acknowledge the important work of the anonymous reviewers on the book chapters. Your help with developing the content was irreplaceable. Thank you very much!

Finally, I wish to acknowledge to Paolo Davide Farah who open-heartedly welcomed the book to the Transnational Law and Governance series. I am also indebted to the knowledgeable reviewers of the book proposal who provided significant and constructive feedback on the manuscript, the Routledge Editorial Board who kindly accepted the proposal and Olivia Manley for her superb editorial assistance.

Thank you all for your remarkable contribution to open up this radically inclusive dialogue on the Anthropocene.

Pasi Heikkurinen
Weetwood, Leeds
September 2016

Introduction

Pasi Heikkurinen

The debate on the Anthropocene is largely about old problems illuminated with new evidence. Humankind is an overly dominant species on Earth. The Anthropocene discourse highlights the severity of the anthropogenic ecological and socio-cultural crises on the planet, and pleads for authentic responses from the human species. While the natural science behind the Anthropocene findings has emphasized the extra-human species level of analysis (the human species vis-à-vis the rest of 'nature') and the inter-species level of analysis (species vis-à-vis other species), the humanities and social sciences have emerged to complement the discourse with an intra-human species level of analysis (humans vis-à-vis other humans). The latter level of analysis critically shows that humans do not cause destruction equally, but that the high-consuming ones are particularly blameworthy for the ongoing violence towards other species and the natural environment. That being so, a more fine-tuned allocation of blame and responsibility has been proposed for the Anthropocene epoch.

As local ecosystems continue to collapse, they take the whole human civilisation closer to its end point; one micro-collapse at a time. On the one hand, the degree of urgency to change the violent modes of human beings increases, but the rush to transform organisations and societies, on the other hand, fades. That is, as the crisis deepens, the window of opportunity for sustainable change closes. This signifies that it is always more worthwhile to change the direction now rather than later. In other words, the closer the human species gets to its own extinction, the poorer the chances of human survival become.

In terms of space, this means that the human modifications in the non-built environment continue to set spatial limitations on what can actually still be done to enable even a partial recovery of the ecosystem. The more the local ecosystems, as well as their species, are taken over by human-built environments, the fewer the possibilities for the necessary reorientation. Every transformation of a non-human-made entity or process to a human-made version beyond the sustainable level is a step nearer to the tipping point. State shift theory suggests that once critical thresholds are passed, ecosystems will undergo unanticipated and irreversible changes to radically altered biotic states, which are unlikely to be habitable for the species living in the Anthropocene, including most or all humans.

Furthermore, the more humans build and dwell in their built environment, the more locked in to their thoughts and actions they seem to become. It appears almost as if there is no alternative but to continue the march of human dominance in the world. For instance, because of the reinforced energy path dependencies in housing, mobility, and food consumption, it is extremely difficult to imagine and practise alternatives to the conventional, violent modes of being. Moreover, being embedded in this human-made frame (including technological thinking and urban lifestyles), the basic skills needed to find and prepare food, as well as to obtain shelter without access to modern means, are becoming increasingly distant to the contemporary human.

In addition to the spatial and functional challenges of turning towards sustainable and non-violent human cultures, the temporal dimension sets limitations on what can still be done or, in the case of the Anthropocene, undone. As the critical thresholds for human survival are transgressed, the social change that may emerge will have a limited effect on altering the course of those natural forces already set in motion by humans. The answers to the challenges of the Anthropocene would be quite simple, if the problem were only about the wealthiest 1 per cent of human individuals, or only about the recent developments in Western culture. Unfortunately, however, it may well be that the will to acquire power – to destroy, create and control others – runs much deeper in the history of our species.

While non-human processes in the so-called natural environment demonstrate extraordinary levels of recovery and resilience, much of the damage caused is irreversible. A lost species will never return. Hence, in the biosphere and its ecosystems, limits to disturbance and disruption *do* exist. Despite the gloomy present of biological, as well as cultural, diversity loss and habitat destruction, it is both interesting and important to remain open to a metamorphosis in human culture, and consequently, to a radical reorientation in the way human activities are organized now and tomorrow. Every act of peace towards the world and its beings, including its human and non-humans inhabitants, enhances the quality of life and moves the extinctions further: to another place and time. Hence, for the aspiration to sustain life, every act and inaction counts.

This edited book is a compilation of papers on sustainability and peaceful coexistence for the new geological epoch, the Anthropocene. The contributors to the book take on the challenging task of seeking to outline some of the most central preconditions for a non-violent human existence on this precious planet. The content of the book is presented in four sections. The first part introduces the key concepts, causes and consequences of the Anthropocene. The second part scrutinizes the role of capitalism and neoliberalism in the Anthropocene, suggesting requirements for new economic and legal systems. The third part explores novel ways of thinking about the non-human world and outlines preconditions for thinking in the Anthropocene. The last part of book, discusses the new forms of social organisation needed to respond to the call of the Anthropocene, thus, proposing the preconditions for moving beyond it.

In the first chapter of Part I, Pasi Heikkurinen presents the concept of peaceful coexistence and how it came to complement the notion of sustainability in this book. The chapter deals with the double-edged sword of language and explains the necessity of not limiting the methods of peaceful coexistence and sustainability to human-to-human interaction. It suggests that peaceful coexistence is about radical inclusiveness. Chapter 2 is by Mark Williams, Jan Zalasiewicz and Colin Waters and outlines what the Anthropocene is from a geological perspective. The authors provide a thorough overview of the signs and causes behind the world entering a new geological epoch, and examine the many proposals for defining the boundary of the Anthropocene. In the third chapter, Tarja Ketola outlines the consequences of the Anthropocene with a focus on human displacement. By using qualitative case studies derived from literature and human history, the author builds a model that aims to turn a possibly chaotic search for refuge from climatic shifts into a more predictable, and hence coordinated mobility of humans.

Part II deals with economic structures and legal issues. Chapter 4 explains the absolute contradiction between capitalism and peaceful coexistence. The author, Toni Ruuska, first recapitulates the phenomenon of capitalism, and then contends that capitalism, as a historical socio-economic structure, cannot do other than to continue exploiting its environment. Chapter 5 again focuses on the relation of neoliberalism, law and the Anthropocene. In this chapter, Jessica C. Lawrence notes that the emergence of the Anthropocene discourse coincides with another important contemporary trend, namely the rise of neoliberal governmental rationality. By drawing on examples from the European Union's environmental policy, the chapter addresses the question: how does law deal with the Anthropocene?

Part III offers ways to rethink the axiological, epistemological and ontological assumptions about the world, in particular, the place of non-humans within human thought. In Chapter 6 Todd LeVasseur calls for a new kind of ecological thought. Building on the work of Timothy Morton and empirical illustrations from a radical resistance movement, LeVasseur argues that a truly democratic encounter with the non-human world necessitates that industrial civilisation as we know it be disassembled. Chapter 7, written by J. Mohorčich, again explores the relevance of the 'system of ideas' for the new geological epoch dominated by humans. The chapter revisits the idea of the *noosphere* and suggests a more comprehensive understanding of this concept that is not limited to the sphere of human thought on and around Earth.

Part IV investigates the human organisations and societies for the post-growth era that will follow the destructive industrial modes of production and consumption. Marko Ulvila and Kristoffer Wilén apply a class perspective to the Anthropocene and degrowth discussions. The authors argue that in order to have wider appeal and to become a transformative force for desired change, deliberations on the approaches that imagine and construct alternative futures need to be situated in a context of socio-economic classes. In Chapter 9, Eeva Houtbeckers and Tiina Taipale conceptualize a new, class-aware worker agency to respond to the challenges of the Anthropocene. The authors use empirical case studies from the Global North to demonstrate how 'work' can be used as a site to reflect on the myriad responsibilities present in the Anthropocene. As the final chapter of Part IV, and the concluding contribution of the whole book, Karl Johan Bonnedahl recaps the main problems of the conventional sustainable development discourse and action. To break free from the ongoing exploitation and expansion that characterizes the present epoch, Bonnedahl proposes a strategy of evolutionary coexistence that could enable humans to survive and prosper in a just and peaceful way beyond the Anthropocene.

As the ideas presented in this volume are to work as an early invitation to a transdisciplinary dialogue under the rubric of the Anthropocene, this book does not wish to state a conclusion, but instead to propose a novel direction for the dialogue around the topic of the Anthropocene. Each of the chapters carries a message on the necessity of human cultures, and particularly those highly consuming ones, to change fundamentally in order to reach any mode of coexistence between humans and other beings. The contributors provide important signposts from diverse perspectives on how things can, and should, be transformed. Nevertheless, there remain many perspectives on peaceful coexistence and sustainability in the Anthropocene that the book cannot encompass.

The chapters by Jessica Lawrence, Todd LeVasseur, J. Mohorčich and Toni Ruuska were presented at the first Peaceful Coexistence Colloquium held at the UN-mandated University for Peace, Costa Rica, in April 2015. The chapters by Karl Johan Bonnedahl, Evva Houtbeckers and Tiina Taipale, Pasi Heikkurinen, Tarja Ketola, Marko Ulvila and Kristoffer Wilén, as well as Mark Williams, Jan Zalasiewicz and Colin Waters are invited contributions to complement the content of the book. Thank you all for your involvement! I hope you enjoy the content.

Part I

Concepts, causes and consequences

1 On the emergence of peaceful coexistence

Pasi Heikkurinen

The philosopher George Henrik von Wright noted that the gift of language was the central element in the rise of human cultures. By means of language, humans are able to transfer their experiences and their acquired skills to following generations, and hence create tradition. One of the problems von Wright ([1978] 1981) identified was that language also enabled the transmission or the reproduction of those traditions that were destructive, or violent. And, unfortunately, the transmission of violent human traditions can be witnessed in the contemporary Anthropocene epoch, where brutal force is used to dominate the non-human world, as well as human citizens. To become a part of, as well as to pass on, a non- or less-violent human culture, a central task is to first identify the violent patterns of human existence and then to investigate carefully how to break free from them.

As a linguistic species, humans cannot fully escape the categories that their language creates, even if they would like to. After a commitment to a practice of stillness, one may experience a state of non-thought where all categories become absent, but language cannot be dismissed entirely. That being so, language remains a fundamentally important part of human life due to its power to shape thinking and action. The organization of everyday routines and living with fellow humans would not be feasible without the use of language, but that is not to suggest the use of language is never problematic. Words and numbers are what humans use to separate and form order in the objects of human thought, and the objects are then named to distinguish them from other objects. While sentences can combine words and mathematical formulas bring numbers together in a logical order, the narratives and models formed separate them again from other orders that are often competing sets of narratives and models. And this way, language effectively divides the world into *ones* and *the other ones*, or to *self* and *the other* from its essential whole, where being is one. This splitting, I would describe as the greatest problem of language.

Language can, once the method of addressing things is shared, of course also be thought of as a connector of communities. However, it is important to recall that Martin Heidegger ([1976] 1981) noted with regard to the limits of language that language is never fully shared. Hence, one cannot completely translate a thought or a poem: '[a]t best, one can paraphrase it', [but when] 'one attempts a literal translation, everything is transformed' (Heidegger, [1976] 1981, p. 63). This fluidity bounds the idea of shared communication with language. 'Language is like some kind of infinitely interfertile family of species spreading or mysteriously declining over time, shamelessly and endlessly hybridizing, changing its own rules as it goes', as Gary Snyder (1990, p. 7) remarks. But while the complete, mutual understanding by means of language continually escapes its users, and can hence be considered a cul-de-sac, some degree of shared language is certainly within the reach of humankind.

The so-called bridge language, or *lingua franca,* has appeared to address the practical challenges between people who did not previously share a language or a dialect. In the past, most often the reason for finding a common ground for mutual understanding of the state of affairs has been related to trade, but cultural, religious and diplomatic reasons have also undoubtedly motivated the exchange of words and numbers between communities. Today, a common language of many humans from Western-influenced cultures is English, a dialect first spoken in early medieval England. The reasons for using this West Germanic language as a *lingua franca* are diverse and beyond the scope of this text, but its role today is significant. Albeit the English language has a clear Western bias, the central importance of having an almost globally shared language is arguably the enhanced ability to read and listen to a variety of viewpoints from a variety of backgrounds. Another worthy aspect of a somewhat shared language is the possibility that it provides for people to comment on other people's viewpoints and, hence, to begin creating a dialogue.

Such a language, which many citizens of the Earth can speak in addition to their regional language and dialect, importantly also opens up an opportunity for integrating existing ideas into new, more inclusive narratives and models that are able to capture the complexities and shape the intricacies of life in a *sound* manner. What is meant by the notion of 'sound' in this context calls for a consultation of not only the English dictionary but also the community that attempts to accomplish such an ambitious task of language reconfiguration and use. Let us first turn to the lexicon. According to the *Cambridge Online Dictionary,* 'sound' when used as an adjective refers to a good condition or judgement and to completeness. In other words, when something is sound it is not broken or damaged, but is whole and healthy. The second interpretation of the word relates to showing good judgement and being trusted. For instance, 'she gave me some very sound advice', or, 'the pesticides were not ecologically sound'. And as a third reading of the term, someone can have sound knowledge or understanding of a particular object or phenomenon.

To obtain a more insightful description of the concept, however, it is requisite to also turn to the community that is after a sound language and practice. In 2013, my partner and I moved to Costa Rica for work. Before we left Europe, a few of my dearest colleagues encouraged me to organize a conference under the Latin American sun, which is of course the same sun but it feels quite different there. One of the colleagues, Susan Meriläinen, was interested in gender, another one, Toni Ruuska, in nature, and a third, Niklas Toivakainen, in technology.

Besides their curiosity towards *pura vida*, it was not clear what united these persons in scholarly terms. It was not until later that I realized that some of it had to do with their courage and openness to explore original ideas and their keenness to develop novel perspectives that had societal and political relevance; and by relevance, I do not mean the suitability for any kind of purpose – and definitely not to be apt for the homogenizing mind-sets and practices that lead to exclusion – but research that contributed to the consideration of others. Another important aspect worth mentioning here is their mutual integrity as reflected in academic work. All of them seem to be driven by the cause rather than their career, which is rather exceptional in today's higher education and research industry.

But problematically in pragmatic terms, these beautiful personal qualities of theirs were difficult to translate into a conference theme that could be used in the organization of the desired meeting. As the nominated and self-selected chair of the conference, I had to put out a semi-formal written document to call for research papers, and of course to devise a name for the colloquium. So the search for the lynchpin began. The University for Peace, where I worked at that time, had its mission statement printed on the wall of the foyer. As determined in the charter of the university, the mission of this United Nations mandated organization was, and hopefully still is:

> to provide humanity with an international institution of higher education for peace with the aim of promoting among all human beings the spirit of understanding, tolerance and peaceful coexistence, to stimulate cooperation among peoples and to help lessen obstacles and threats to world peace and progress . . .

On the way to lunch, I often stopped to read this passage, which is quite unique for a university. It captures one of the most important missions of our time, namely putting an end to violence. But, of course, the statement (as it comprises of words) is not perfect. When certain words are used, others are left out. Language is always exclusive. For example, the first thing that may cause a few raised eyebrows is the lack of explicit mention of the non-human world, or the natural (or non-human built) environment. In the midst of the severe climatic catastrophe that the Earth is enduring caused by the long-standing systematic violence towards the non-human world, one might expect that this be addressed boldly in the mission statements of all conscious organizations striving for peace. Another related aspect of the passage might also ring a bell, namely the use of the heavily loaded and bloody word *progress*. Without a doubt, the final nail in the coffin of this precious planet and the majority of its beings is surely the removal of the obstacles and threats to conventional progress, as encouraged by the mission statement.

Or could the word 'progress' signify something else in this context? Does it really refer to increasing the affluence and rights of humans at the expense of non-humans? Is progress here to signify the same kind of quantitative progress that the planet and its inhabitants have witnessed since the Industrial Revolution, that is: the development of more advanced means to transform the non-human-made world for the economic and political gain of the capitalist class? Because, if it truly is so, then the soundness of the statement must be questioned for two weighty reasons.

First, on the more social side, there is a strong empirical case for the rising inequality between humans both globally and locally, as reported by Thomas Piketty (2014). In other words, within the human species, a greater lack of fairness or justice exists. While the people living in poverty might have increased their incomes by a dollar or two, the ultra-rich are creating a class of their own, a global elite that is beyond any standard comprehension of affluence and power (e.g. Vitali, Glattfelder and Battison, 2011). Secondly, and on the more ecological side, there is robust evidence of the increasing rate of habitat destruction (e.g. Wake and Vredenburg, 2008). That being so, a greater lack of fairness or justice exists also between species – not to mention the objects of the vegetal and mineral spheres that seem to be beyond the ethical consideration of even the most 'peaceful' humans.

To return to the mission statement, a peculiar thing about language is that it often allows an alternative interpretation; and at times, words and numbers in sentences even start to take on a life of their own, one independent of their original, intended meaning. So, perhaps the term 'progress' might refer broadly to a 'movement to an improved or more developed state, or to a forward position', as the *Cambridge Online Dictionary* suggests. This could then refer to the kind of qualitative economic development that Herman Daly (1996) calls for, or the moral development that Lawrence Kohlberg (1971) has described. 'Progress' could even be thought of in the sense of the existential evolution that Friedrich Nietzsche ([1883–1891] 1997) spoke of, or viewed as relating to exploring a higher consciousness, as several spiritual teachers, such as Jiddu Krishnamurti ([1969] 2009), have advised. In this context, maybe progress refers to peace among beings? And perhaps the preceding part of the mission statement that leaves the non-humans unmentioned may not have to be so anthropocentric after all. The 'spirit of understanding, tolerance and peaceful coexistence' that is to be promoted among human beings can doubtless also include the consideration of the needs of the non-human world.

At least for now, the two chosen meanings above will be my reinterpretations – generous or otherwise. Nevertheless, it may not be a good idea to deploy the word progress in any desired connotation, as it is still largely favoured amongst the inherently violent cornucopian tradition and other dangerous techno-optimists. Peaceful coexistence, which was also mentioned in the mission statement, seems again to be an attention-grabbing conceptual pairing yet still up for grabs, that is, open to interpretation by different parties.[1] What I mean by this

1 Up for grabs at least in the contemporary world. That is, during the Cold War it was used to refer to the hope that communism and capitalism would coexist in peace.

availability is that it has not been co-opted by the homogenizing techno-industrial machine or hijacked to serve the purposes of any other progressive political or economic ideology, as has happened to some extent to the concept of sustainability. And aptly, for the purpose of finding a name for the conference, a close colleague of mine from Sweden, Karl Johan Bonnedahl, had recently published a book on sustainable development where coexistence was also presented as a central, complimentary concept to sustainability. Subsequently, I became convinced that 'peaceful coexistence' would be a fitting name for this conference. It is simultaneously both broad and informative. It embraces the diversity of perspectives and participants but still magically attracts people from outside the mainstream, somewhat on the fringes of academia, where all the sunniest ideas tend to be. Most importantly, peaceful coexistence can be considered a precondition for not only sustainable but also meaningful life on Earth.

First, the concept of coexistence is vital, as the human species cannot *exist* without other beings. Existence is essentially coexistence (Nancy, [1996] 2000). Existence always comes with the prefix 'co', referring to cooperation or working together. The adjective 'peaceful' is also critical because approaches to coexistence can also become violent. For instance, groups of people and non-humans can be forced to coexist, to live side-by-side, which of course is not desirable due to the involuntary nature of the arrangement and the restriction of their freedoms. Efforts to protect environments may also entail forms of violence towards the human population, as is happening to indigenous communities (see Dalby, 2016). So what is important to note is that the escalation of the ecological and social problems creates a fertile ground for violent approaches. Hence, the exhortations of Mahatma Gandhi ([1961] 2001), Henry David Thoreau ([1845–1949] 2012), and Vandana Shiva (2016) to follow non-violent forms of resistance ought to be explored and taken seriously in order to avoid reproducing the violent traditions of humanity. Finally, when it might be too late for human society to reach global sustainability, instead of resorting to violence and other desperate acts, people can still find meaning by peacefully coexisting until the end of (human) time.

I sat down for lunch. At the table, I was quickly drawn into a rather animated discussion with members of the faculty of the Department of Environment and Development. The debate was over the concept of the Anthropocene. Should scholars use this term to refer to the new geological epoch when arguing for sustainability? On the one hand, the concept of the Anthropocene is critical but is it critical enough? It highlights the imbalance between human and non-humans but it is quiet on the intra-species difference, that is: who *within* the human species is causing the destruction? When acknowledging the complementarity of these two levels of analysis, the Anthropocene debate could take a giant leap forward. With this idea, the concept of the Anthropocene cemented itself during the heated lunch discussion as an important signpost for the conference.

Then there was some extra quality to this concept, as it not only incorporated our rationales but also our emotions in the debate. The logical discussion on the potential and pitfalls of using the term was swiftly seasoned with feelings. And who does not love that feeling! The emotional reactions may have been due to many other factors as well, but I consider that one of the key reasons for it was that the Anthropocene tempts us to revisit and reflect on the ontological, as well as the epistemological and axiological positions. The concept of the Anthropocene extends the ideas of time and space by introducing a broader spatial and deeper temporal understanding of life. Human presence and impacts are now global and viable in the geological time of the Earth. The very word carries the disturbing message that the human species has become the global force in relation to the rest of the world. Then the natural science based narrative accompanied by persuasive empirical data demonstrates that what has come to be known as progress has led life to a time and place where the impact of a single species is significant in planetary terms. In the Anthropocene, a large volume of life-supporting conditions and processes of ecosystems are profoundly altered by human activities; and findings indicate that the sixth mass extinction might be ahead of us on Earth, unless a radical reorientation takes place soon (Barnosky et al., 2011; Ceballos et al., 2015).

With this kind of a message, the Anthropocene touches many nerves among social scientists and humanists. One of them is the realist ontology typical of the practice of the more formal, natural sciences and another is the positivist epistemology and methodology behind discoveries. So, on the one hand, the Anthropocene brings back the old-school Kuhnian paradigm war: the idea that scientific paradigms preceding and succeeding a paradigm shift are incommensurable (Kuhn, 1962), but, on the other hand, it opens up the possibility of burying the hatchet and continuing by peacefully coexisting. In fact, this would surely be needed, as in order to conduct a radical reorientation, experts from all academic disciplines must come together to halt the insanity and put the cause ahead of career. There is a dire need for people from the humanities, social sciences, natural sciences and formal sciences to start thinking about the Anthropocene together, and to develop sounder frames of thought and practice, as well as actually relevant policy measures.

It was from putting all these pieces together that the meeting got its name 'Peaceful Coexistence: Genders, Natures, and Technologies in the Anthropocene'.[2] The conference was held at the University for Peace in Costa Rica over three days at the end of April in 2015. The first two days comprised of presentations and discussions on the breath-taking campus full of diverse life. The colloquium attracted researchers, teachers and students from around the world, bringing together a great diversity of people with different cultural backgrounds and varying scholarly approaches. This mixture resulted in novel, thought-provoking ideas and in-depth discussions ranging from the everyday practices to the politics and philosophies of contemporary humans, inviting everyone to reflect on their assumptions about the world. The good-natured debate continued during the

2 A decision was made to use technology, gender, and nature in the plural to make room for different interpretations of the phenomena. This does not mean that these words could or should not also be used in the singular.

conference dinners at the local restaurants in Ciudad Colón. The final day was reserved for a social programme on Playa Blanca, a beach on the Pacific Ocean, where it was decided the form of the meeting should have continuity. The second Peaceful Coexistence Colloquium was scheduled to take place in Finnish Lapland in the summer of 2017. The theme 'Reimagining Ethics and Politics of Space for the Anthropocene' will continue the dialogue on the Anthropocene started in the first conference.

After this brief history of the emergence of peaceful coexistence, a few concluding remarks on its current content can be made. First and foremost, however, it must be noted that both the concepts and the community have themselves just started unfolding, and, hence, all suggestions made in this text are preliminary. Moreover, this introductory chapter to the book represents only my personal reflections and should be taken as such, not as the voice of the community – everyone in the colloquium. While the present book is able to encompass a broader set of viewpoints on peaceful coexistence and sustainability, they are still partial and do not represent the community at large.[3] Nevertheless, I hope these early interpretations of mine, as well as those of the other contributors of this book, work principally as an invitation to a dialogue under the heading 'peaceful coexistence'. A central aim of the peaceful coexistence community would hence be to bring discussants together to exchange experiences on what peaceful coexistence means and what are the preconditions for it. While it is of crucial importance to seek common understanding by linguistic means, it is also important to acknowledge the limits of language and to complement the experience and knowledge sharing with non-linguistic methods. In attempting to access a truly inclusive dialogue, this openness to alternative pathways of communication is the key. The main novelty of the peaceful coexistence dialogue could hence be seen, not only in the emancipatory aspirations for all life forms, but particularly in the radical inclusiveness of diverse forms of life in the process:

> The dialogue to open next would be among all beings, toward a rhetoric of ecological relationships. This is not to put down the human: the "proper study of mankind" is what it means to be human. It's not enough to be shown in school that we are kin to all the rest: we have to feel it all the way through. Then we can also be uniquely "human" with no sense of special privilege.
>
> (Snyder, 1990, p. 68)

So the dialogue that is opening at this very moment is about sharing a channel of communication between humans and humans, as well as between humans and non-humans in order to address the injustices between humans and humans, as

3 For instance, the content of the book represents the two themes of the first conference quite well, namely technologies and natures, but the gender perspectives are missing. Hopefully, this aspect of peaceful coexistence will be discussed in more detail in the next volume.

well as the inequities between humans and non-humans. As language by its very nature divides the world and constructs borders between things in the world, it would not make sense to attempt to deny the categories of different entities (such as nature and culture), but we should instead embrace all objects as they are: unique and intrinsically valuable (Heikkurinen et al., 2016). Furthermore, to return to the question of soundness, it could be suggested that something is sound if it embraces both sameness and diversity, and hence contributes to the peaceful coexistence of all objects in time and place. This kind of framing calls for far-reaching openness to beings within and in between, as well as outside, the categories of language.

Bibliography

Barnosky, A. D., Matzke, N., Tomiya, S., Wogan, G. O., Swartz, B., Quental, T. B., Marshall, C., McGuire J. L., Lindsey, E. L., Maguire K. C., Mersey, B. & Feffer, E. A. (2011) Has the Earth's Sixth Mass Extinction Already Arrived? *Nature*. 471(7336), 51–57.

Ceballos, G., Ehrlich, P. R., Barnosky, A. D., García, A., Pringle, R. M. & Palmer, T. M. (2015) Accelerated Modern Human-Induced Species Losses: Entering the Sixth Mass Extinction. *Science Advances*. 1(5), e1400253.

Dalby, S. (2016) Peace in the Anthropocene. *Peace Review: A Journal of Social Justice*. 25(4), 561–567.

Daly, H. E. (1996) *Beyond Growth: The Economics of Sustainable Development*. Boston: Beacon Press.

Gandhi, M. K. ([1961] 2001) *Non-Violent Resistance*. New York: Dover Publications.

Heidegger, M. ([1976] 1981) "Only a God Can Save Us": The Spiegel Interview (1966). Trans. Richardson, W. In: Sheehan, T. (ed.) *Heidegger: The Man and the Thinker*. New Brunswick, NJ: Transaction Publishers, pp. 45–67.

Heikkurinen, P., Rinkinen, J., Järvensivu, T., Wilén, K. & Ruuska, T. (2016) Organising in the Anthropocene: An Ontological Outline for Ecocentric Theorising. *Journal of Cleaner Production*. 113, 705–714.

Kohlberg, L. (1971) Stages of Moral Development as a Basis for Moral Education. In: Beck, C. M., Crittenden, B. S. & Sullivan, E. V. (eds) *Moral Education*. Toronto: University of Toronto Press, pp. 24–92.

Krishnamurti, J. ([1969] 2010) *Freedom from the Known*. New York: HarperCollins Publishers.

Kuhn, T. (1962) *The Structure of Scientific Revolutions*. Chicago: The University of Chicago Press.

Nancy, J-L. ([1996] 2000) *Being Singular Plural*. Stanford, CA: Stanford University Press.

Nietzsche, F. ([1883–1891] 1997) *Thus Spake Zarathustra*. Ware: Wordsworth.

Piketty, T. (2014) *Capital in the Twenty-First Century*. Cambridge, MA: Harvard University Press.

Shiva, V. (2016) *The Violence of the Green Revolution: Third World Agriculture, Ecology, and Politics*. Lexington: University Press of Kentucky.

Snyder, G. (1990) *The Practice of the Wild*. San Francisco: North Point Press.

Thoreau, H. D. ([1845–1949] 2012) *Walden and Civil Disobedience*. New York: Barnes & Noble.

Wake, D. B. & Vredenburg, V. T. (2008) Are We in the Midst of the Sixth Mass Extinction? A View from the World of Amphibians. *Proceedings of the National Academy of Sciences*. 105(Supplement 1), 11466–11473.

Vitali, S., Glattfelder, J. B. & Battison, S. (2011) The Network of Global Corporate Control. *PLoS One* 6(10), e25995.

Von Wright, G. H. ([1978] 1981) *Humanismi elämänasenteena*. Trans. Kaila, K. Keuruu, Finland: Otava.

2 The Anthropocene

A geological perspective

Mark Williams, Jan Zalasiewicz and Colin Waters[1]

1 What is the Anthropocene?

At the beginning of the twenty-first century, Nobel-Prize winning atmospheric chemist Paul Crutzen (Crutzen and Stoermer, 2000; Crutzen, 2002) proposed that we were living in the Anthropocene, a time when humans had become agents of geological change, driving significant global chemical, physical and biological modifications to the atmosphere, landscape and oceans. Such ideas had already surfaced in the writings of the Milanese geologist Antonio Stoppani more than a century earlier (Stoppani coined the term 'Anthropozoic era' in 1873), but they took on a new significance in the early twenty-first century, with the recognition that human impacts, whilst geologically brief, were already substantial. The Anthropocene provided a context by which, for example, the increased levels of carbon dioxide in the atmosphere and the concomitant effects on global climate, sea level and icesheet stability could be compared with past changes in the Earth System. And, it could be considered as a means by which human impacts on biodiversity could be assessed. The term entered the geological literature as a potential stratigraphical concept in a paper written by the Stratigraphy Commission of the Geological Society of London (Zalasiewicz et al., 2008; see also Zalasiewicz, Williams and Waters, 2014a).

The Anthropocene has been the focus of studies published by the Royal Society in London (Williams et al., 2011) and the Geological Society of London (Waters et al., 2014), of a major initiative of the International Geosphere-Biosphere Programme (IGBP: www.igbp.net), of major exhibitions at the Haus der Kulturen der Welt in Berlin in 2013–2014, at the Deutsches Museum in 2015, and is due to become a central part of the Smithsonian Institution's new Earth history display. The use of this term to denote the current time interval seems set to continue, and probably to be disseminated yet more widely. Given its widespread

1 Colin Waters publishes with the permission of the Executive Director, British Geological Survey (BGS), Natural Environment Research Council, funded with the support of the BGS's Engineering Geology Science Programme. We are also grateful to Stephanie Bricker (BGS) for commenting on an earlier draft of this manuscript.

use, the Anthropocene is being examined by the Anthropocene Working Group (AWG) of the Subcommission on Quaternary Stratigraphy, being a component of the International Commission on Stratigraphy (ICS).[2] The AWG does not comprise only Earth scientists, but includes a mix of historians, archaeologists, social and environmental scientists and commentators, as well as geologists, geochemists and palaeontologists. The role of the AWG is to examine evidence that the Anthropocene is a discrete unit of the Geological Time scale (www.stratigraphy.org/index.php/ics-chart-timescale) characterized by a stratigraphic record of humans as agents of global change, and most likely considered at the level of epoch. The evidence gathered by the AWG will be presented to the ICS, who can recommend its formalization, a process that also involves ratification by the International Union of Geological Sciences (IUGS). The Anthropocene might therefore join such evocative geological epoch names as the Miocene, Pliocene, Pleistocene and Holocene, it being proposed as the youngest unit of geological time succeeding the Holocene Epoch. The process of formalizing the Anthropocene has involved detailed analysis since 2009, when the AWG was established, but its formalization by the ICS and IUGS is not assured. The term must be shown to be technically valid and also of practical application to geologists (see Waters et al., 2016). Should it not be recognized as a formal stratigraphical unit by the ICS, the term will continue to have widespread use and value across the geological sciences and a multitude of other disciplines.

In this chapter we review the geological impact of humans set against past changes in the Earth system. We describe the problems associated with identifying a geological boundary for the Anthropocene that identifies the magnitude of human influence. And, we discuss at what stratigraphical level in recent geological history such a boundary might be defined and why.

2 A brief history of geological time

Humans have made only a recent appearance on Earth. To decipher their impact it is important to place this in the context of overall Earth time. The Earth is an old planet, a third of the age of the entire cosmos, with a geological record that unfolds over 4.54 billion years (Ga). The rock record on Earth has proved extremely important for subdivision of this geological time. At a large scale geologists can distinguish eons of time (Figure 2.1). The Hadean Eon is assigned to the earliest half billion years of Earth's history, before a preserved rock record, though even from this time mineralogical remnants of an early crust are occasionally preserved (Wilde et al., 2001). An Archean Eon, which lasted from 4 to 2.5 Ga, has its rock record preserved in the cores of ancient continents, for example in the Canadian Shield, Africa and Australia. Archean rocks provide the earliest consistent evidence of a biosphere (Grassineau et al., 2006), though life may

2 Information about the AWG can be found at: [www.quaternary.stratigraphy.org.uk/workinggroups/anthropocene/]

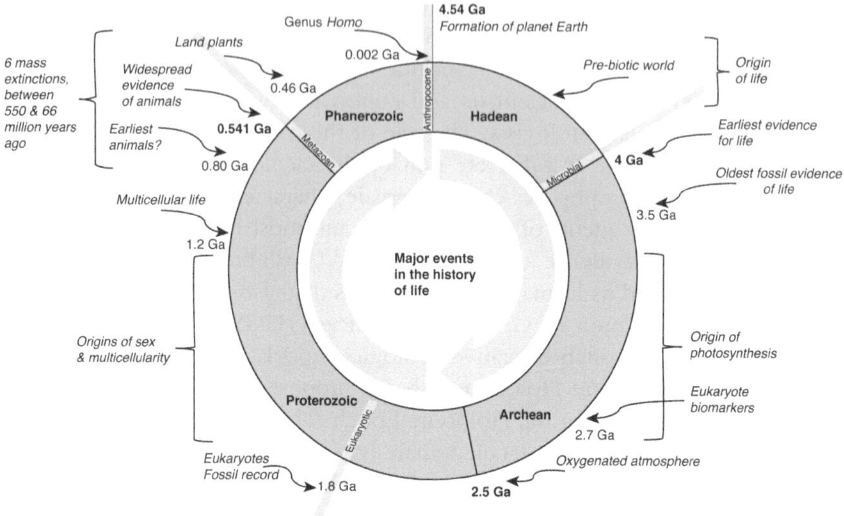

Figure 2.1 Major events in the evolution of life on Earth: time scaling of events is only approximate. Grey bars represent suggested fundamental changes to the biosphere from microbial (prokaryotic), to eukaryotic, animal (metazoan) and Anthropocene. The six major extinction events between 550 and 66 million years ago includes the five events of the Phanerozoic, and the demise of the Ediacaran Biota at the end of the Proterozoic.

have evolved even earlier in the Hadean (Bell et al., 2015). From 2.5 Ga, and helping to demarcate the Proterozoic Eon, there is widespread chemical evidence in rocks for a fundamental change in the Earth's atmosphere, called the Great Oxygenation Event (Pufahl and Hiatt, 2012), likely a response to the evolution of microbes that used oxygenic photosynthesis. In the Phanerozoic Eon (from 0.541 Ga), animals, which first evolved in the late Proterozoic, formed complex marine ecosystems that left a preserved record in such familiar fossil animals as the trilobites (between 0.52 and 0.25 Ga; Figure 2.2). Later, from 0.46 Ga a terrestrial biosphere of plants and animals evolved (for a review of all these changes see Williams et al., 2016). The Phanerozoic Eon is the backdrop to the extraordinary biodiversity of life at present, which includes our species, *Homo sapiens*, evolving some 195,000 years ago in Africa (Figure 2.3).

The physical, chemical and biological changes that have left signals in the stratigraphic record of Earth's evolution over more than 4 Ga are almost always only partially represented, the result of an incomplete rock record. Therefore, geologists use a pragmatic approach to define geological boundaries, looking for the signal that is most distinctive and widely traceable, for example the giant asteroid impact at the Cretaceous-Paleogene (K-Pg) boundary 66 million years ago (Molina et al., 2006), which was essentially instantaneous, and left traces that can be correlated around the planet to define an isochronous surface (a surface of exactly equivalent time everywhere). In reality, recognition of an isochronous

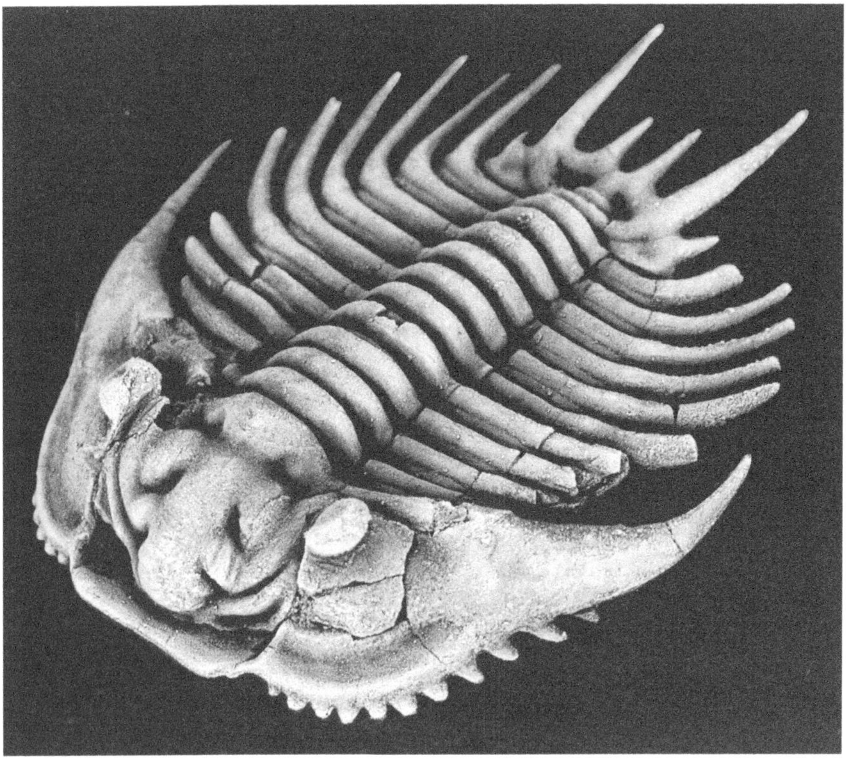

Figure 2.2 Trilobites, a group of fossils found in rocks between 525 and 251 million years ago, and a defining fossil for the Phanerozoic Eon (see Figure 2.1). The specimen is a couple of centimetres in length.

Source: Picture courtesy of Derek Siveter (Oxford University).

boundary is rarely possible, with the K-Pg boundary being a rare exception. In defining a specific event as a boundary, geologists recognize its place as part of an unfolding and connected continuum of events that may extend over millions or tens of millions of years, as is the case with the definition of the base of the Phanerozoic noted above (see Williams et al., 2014). Geologists also recognize different subdivisions of time, dependent on the degree of changes that are associated with them in the rock record. Enormous packets of time are eons (billions or hundreds of millions of years), and then are eras (hundreds or tens of millions of years), periods (tens of millions to millions of years), epochs (tens of millions of years to tens of thousands of years) and ages (typically a few million years or much less).

Against this backdrop of Earth evolution over 4.54 Ga, is the human impact on Earth significant? Is it of sufficient degree that geologists can define a boundary in the stratigraphic record, an isochronous surface above which it is possible to recognize the profound influence of humans across the planet?

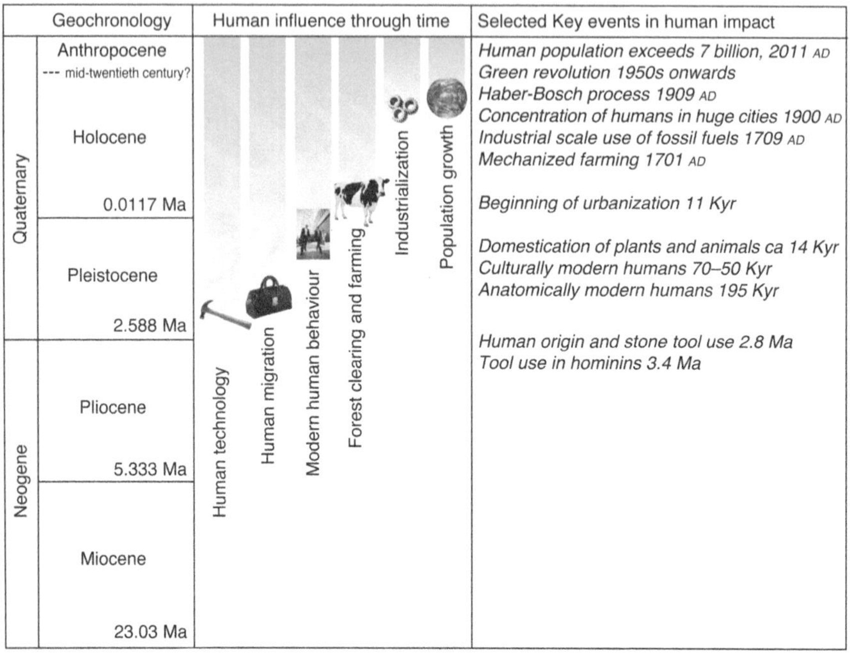

Figure 2.3 The growing impact of humans through the past 4 million years: right-hand column shows selected major advances that have extended human influence.

3 Growing human influence

A stratigraphical signal of human influence is evident from the earliest stone tools, technofossils (in the sense of Zalasiewicz et al., 2014b) manufactured by hominins ca 3.4 million years ago (McPherron et al., 2010). The early record of tool use is sparse and limited to Africa, but becomes progressively more global as species of *Homo* migrated out of Africa. Thus, the development of tools shows a stratigraphical record of increasing complexity reflecting greater human cognitive ability. Anatomically modern humans originating in Africa at ca 195,000 years BP (McDougall and Fleagle, 2005) developed stone blade technologies evident in the fossil record from ca 50,000 years ago (Bar-Yosef, 2002), and extended the use and impact of this technology as they migrated across the world. This may have impacted on the extinctions of many large mammal and bird species (the megafauna) that coincide closely with the appearance of anatomically modern humans in widely different regions (e.g. Roberts et al., 2001; Koch and Barnosky, 2006).

The initial development of agriculture from about 10,000 years ago (Weisdorf, 2005) resulted in subsequent major modification of the landscape and the increasing influence of humans over species and ecosystem evolution (Williams et al., 2015b; Lyons et al., 2016). Agriculture sustained a greater population of people, and provided the environment in which human specialist activities unrelated to food production could evolve (Weisdorf, 2005). Human population grew from perhaps ca 1–10 million at 10,000 years BP, to ca 1 billion people by 1800 AD (see United States Census Bureau figures, accessed July 2015). From the seventeenth to mid-twentieth century continued technological advances in farming facilitated increasing appropriation of primary production (see Williams et al., 2016 for a recent summary) and the Haber-Bosch process of nitrogen fixation developed in the early twentieth century is estimated to sustain some 40 per cent of global human population today (Cornell, 2010). With the addition of the Green Revolution of the mid-twentieth century, with development of new crop varieties, biocides and irrigation techniques, by the early twenty-first century human population had grown to over 7 billion.

The human influence can be measured by its impact on the biosphere. This includes a potential widespread extinction event that may come to match those of the five earlier Phanerozoic mass extinctions (Barnosky et al., 2011), and also some completely unique patterns (Williams et al., 2015a; Lyons et al., 2016). The latter include the widespread translocation of plants, animals and microbes around the globe (see McNeeley, 2001), both in terrestrial and marine settings, beginning in early Paleolithic times with the migration of humans out of Africa. Unique changes also include the way that humans appropriate net primary production (NPP) of potential vegetation in the biosphere, such that *Homo sapiens* now appropriates some 25 per cent of NPP (Krausmann et al., 2013, note that some estimates are higher), likely representing an unprecedented figure for a single species. It also includes human-induced changes to animals and plants, through domestication, breeding and genetic manipulation, such that humans can contemplate transplanting the photosynthetic systems of prokaryotic cells into those of higher plants to improve productivity (Lin et al., 2014). Each of these impacts on the biosphere might realistically leave a fossil record (see Kidwell 2015, for example), for example in the bones and pollen of domesticated, introduced and modified species. The biosphere represents just one component of human-induced change to the Earth System that also includes modifications to patterns of sedimentation (Syvitski and Kettner, 2011; Williams et al., 2015b), ocean chemistry (Tyrrell, 2011) and the atmosphere and climate (Hay, 2014).

Given that the story of human influence has evolved over millions of years, and differs between the continents – for example with only recent impact in the Antarctic, how might geologists decide where a significant boundary is located within the stratigraphic record, and how might they define this?

4 Cities as a model of complex human stratigraphy

An illustration of the problems confronting the geologist in defining an Anthropocene component to the Geological Time scale is illustrated by the process of urbanization, producing human structures that in many cases have evolved over thousands of years, with different regional histories, technofossil assemblages and stratigraphies.

Urban centres are potential fossil structures in the making, recording – likely for geological timescales – the complexity of modern human society. Humans have developed urban areas for about 11,000 years (Edgeworth, 2013), representing a tiny fraction of the time in which Earth's biosphere has evolved. Despite this geologically short time frame, urbanization is a good illustration of human impact, as towns and cities represent major centres of population that act as foci for the increasing influence of humans over biological production, much of that production being consumed in cities. The trace fossils and technofossils generated over millennia in towns and cities show a progression in technological development from early stone, brick and ceramic technologies that culminate in the gigantic complex plastic, glass, metal, silicon and concrete structures of modern cities. As fossils, some city structures are greater in size than anything in pre-human nature, and of much greater complexity. Consider, for example, the scale and complexity of an underground train system beneath a megacity like London or New York (see Williams et al., 2014), compared to the burrowing systems of other animals, which are also preserved in the rock record (Figure 2.4). The human structures signal, from the nineteenth century onwards, changed human behaviour as people transferred from agriculture to industry and services, and massed in great cities.

However, as with the geological record, the stratigraphical signal of towns and cities is patchy and incomplete, with some materials predisposed to fossilize, especially resistant materials such as bone, brick and plastic, whilst labile materials decay quickly, unless encapsulated by exceptional conditions (Figure 2.5). Location is also a significant control on city preservation, with the long-term

Figure 2.4 Non-human and human trace fossil systems. (a) The trace fossil *Beaconites antarcticus*, a putative animal burrow, and here represented in rocks of Devonian age signalling ancient river deposits in South Wales. (b) Colossal human burrow systems under London, the beginning of the London Underground rail system in 1861.

Source: Figure 2.4a courtesy of David Siveter (University of Leicester). Figure 2.4b is a Wikimedia Commons image available at https://en.wikipedia.org/wiki/Metropolitan_line#/media/File:Constructing_the_Metropolitan_Railway.png

Figure 2.5 Houses in a suburb of the town of Shimabara, Nagasaki Prefecture, Kyushu Island, Japan, inundated by volcanic deposits from the eruption of Unzen Dake in 1993 (the volcano can be seen rising in the distance). In this case, encapsulation of the town is likely to preserve it over a geological timescale.

fossilization of city structure biased towards zones of subsidence in low-lying coastal areas, while cities and citadels atop mountains and hills are likely to be reworked through the rock-cycle as sedimentary particles into future strata.

The stratigraphical signal of urban centres and buildings records a regional 'biogeographical' evolution of cultures that evolved independently. Thus, one could identify a characteristic Srivijayan architecture in Indonesia and neighbouring parts of South East Asia (during the late first millennium AD), a contemporaneous Mayan architecture on the Yucatan Peninsula in the Americas and a 'dark ages' Anglo-Saxon architecture on the western fringes of Europe in England (Figure 2.6), each of which has preserved a distinctive stratigraphical signal of its presence. Regional architectural styles persisted into the early twentieth century. Thereafter the 'international style' of architecture (Hitchcock and Johnson, 1997) evolved in large urban areas and this produced a marked convergence of form and structure (and likely of geological signal – in the metal, glass and concrete that were used to make these buildings) that shows a breakdown of regional architectural styles. This echoes other patterns in the globalization of the stratigraphical record of human influence, for example

Figure 2.6 Long-lived regional styles of architecture gave way to the 'International Style' in the mid-twentieth century. (a) The Anglo-Saxon church at Brixworth in the English Midlands. (b) The Borobodur, Java, Indonesia. Both were constructed at about the same time, and both have potential to be preserved in the stratigraphical record of humans (they are made from recalcitrant materials), recording distinctive regional styles. By the mid-twentieth century though, architectural styles had converged across the planet, thus buildings in London, England (c) and Jakarta, Indonesia (d) are similar in style, and likely similar in building materials also.

the translocation of animals and plants around the Earth to form a global neobiota (Williams et al., 2015a). This architectural convergence represents, in its stratigraphical signal, the emergence of humans as a major influence on the Earth System by the mid-twentieth century, especially their ability to move commodities such as concrete and steel around the planet to make buildings.

5 Defining the boundary for the Anthropocene

The first proposals of the Anthropocene by Paul Crutzen and Eugene Stoermer (2000; and Crutzen, 2002) linked its beginning with the Industrial Revolution, around the beginning of the nineteenth century, following the invention of James Watt's steam engine. This coincides approximately with a change from a long period of slow human population growth, expanding agricultural modification of the landscape and energy use primarily from a combination of wind, water, wood-burning and muscle-power, to an interval of rapid population growth, urban growth and industrialization powered by the increasing use of fossil fuels. This is a key shift in global process, but as the Industrial Revolution spread across the world over some two centuries, its accompanying stratigraphic signals are similarly time-transgressive, and so not ideally suited to best represent a geological time boundary.

An alternative suggestion posits an early onset of the Anthropocene, marked by human impacts on the landscape including agriculture and forest clearance (Kaplan et al., 2011; Ellis et al., 2013), terrestrial changes to biota (e.g. Barnosky, 2008) and, partly related to this, the hypothesis that early agriculture changed atmospheric carbon dioxide levels, raising them from 260 to 280 ppm over several thousand years (Ruddiman, 2003, 2013). Yet further back are the Late Pleistocene extinctions of 'megafauna', though as with the spread of agriculture, these extinctions are markedly diachronous (over millennia) between different continents (Koch and Barnosky, 2006).

An alternative suggestion was made by Lewis and Maslin (2015) at 1610 AD, based on a ~10 ppm dip in atmospheric carbon dioxide recognized in ice core records that was linked to the colonization of the Americas. However, this signal is not outside the range of Holocene variability, is not certainly linked to New World colonization, is not recognizable away from ice cores, and associated signals (e.g. the spread of transported species such as maize) are also diachronous over centuries (Zalasiewicz et al., 2015). Hence, this suggestion seems also not to be optimal as regards chronostratigraphical definition.

Examination of more recent environmental history has identified a phase of enhanced population growth, global economic growth and associated environmental change commencing in the mid-twentieth century. This is termed the 'Great Acceleration' by Steffen et al., (2015), and includes, for example, the bulk of the rise in atmospheric carbon dioxide levels since pre-industrial times, an intensification in agriculture (the Green Revolution) and a massive expansion in the use and spread of manufactured goods, including white goods, fast food restaurants, automobiles, etc. that have left a distinctive technofossil signature around the globe (Zalasiewicz et al., 2014b).

However, it is important to try and identify a stratigraphic signal that is effectively isochronous, one similar to the impact of the giant asteroid that hit the Earth at the Cretaceous-Paleogene boundary. One potential boundary that is both widely detectable in sedimentary deposits (e.g. those of lakes) and glaciers and defines an effectively isochronous boundary (± 10 years) is the spread of radionuclides from atmospheric nuclear weapons tests (Hancock et al., 2014; Waters et al., 2015; Zalasiewicz et al., 2015), effectively synchronous with an isotopic signal of fixed nitrogen from fertilizer manufacture (Holtgrieve et al., 2011) and of a marked inflection in a global signal of industrial fly ash (e.g. Rose, 2015), both of which date from ca 1950 AD. This date also broadly coincides with the 'Great Acceleration'.

There is also the question of the stratigraphic magnitude of the Anthropocene, of whether it represents an 'age', 'epoch', 'period' or even an 'era'. Currently it is being considered as an epoch (Waters et al., 2016), equivalent in stratigraphic rank to the Miocene or Pliocene epochs (see Figure 2.3). And yet the greatest changes arising from anthropogenic modifications to the Earth System may yet be to come (Wolff, 2014). Likely there will be considerable changes to the biosphere (Barnosky et al., 2012), with a mass extinction event perhaps marking a period or even era-level change. Therefore, the stratigraphic character of the Anthropocene may appear distinctly different from a far future perspective. There are many other candidates for defining the boundary (see Waters et al., 2016 for a thorough summary), and the pros and cons of each must be considered prior to any decision on formalization of the Anthropocene.

6 Conclusion

Anatomically modern humans, evolving 195,000 years ago in Africa, have had a profound impact on Earth. This impact has unfolded over millennia, for example in the extinctions of megafauna, the spread of agriculture and industry. Early stratigraphic signals of this impact, such as stone tools, are localized and diachronous. By the mid-twentieth century human impact became global and manifested in substantial physical (e.g. sedimentary), chemical (e.g. nitrates) and biological changes (e.g. neobiota) to the Earth System. The sum of these changes leaves a distinctive stratigraphical signal in Earth's sedimentary record, for example in the radionuclides of atomic bomb tests from the 1950s, that may signal a new stage in Earth evolution, one in which humans have become global geological agents. A possible new epoch of geological time characterized by humans is being analysed by the Anthropocene Working Group. If formalized by the International Commission on Stratigraphy, the Anthropocene would be the newest and youngest addition to the Geological Time scale. If it is not formalized the term will nevertheless likely still carry considerable currency across many disciplines as a way of discussing and debating the impact of humans on the Earth System.

Bibliography

Barnosky A. D. (2008) Megafauna biomass trade off as a driver of Quaternary and future extinctions. *PNAS.* 105, 11543–11548.

Barnosky, A. D., Matzke, N., Tomiya, S., Wogan, G. O. U., Swartz, B., Quental, T. B., Marshall, C., McGuire, J. L., Lindsey, E. L., Maguire, K. C., Mersey, B. & Ferrer, E. A. (2011) Has the Earth's sixth mass extinction already arrived? *Nature.* 471, 51–57.

Barnosky, A. D., Hadly, E. A., Bascompte, J., Berlow, E. L., Brown, J. H., Fortelius, M., Getz, W. M., Harte, J., Hastings, A., Marquet, P. A., Martinez, N. D., Mooers, A., Roopnarine, P., Vermeij, G., Williams, J. W., Gillespie, R., Kitzes, J., Marshall, C., Matzke, N., Mindell, D. P., Revilla, E. & Smith, A. B. (2012) Approaching a state-shift in the biosphere. *Nature.* 486, 52–56.

Bar-Yosef, O. (2002) The Upper Paleolithic revolution. *Annual Reviews of Anthropology.* 31, 363–393.

Bell, E. A., Boehnke, P., Harrison, T. M. & Mao, W. L. (2015) Potentially biogenic carbon preserved in a 4.1 billion-year-old zircon. *PNAS.* 112, 14518–14521.

Cornell, J. (2010) Fertilizer. *Encyclopedia of the Earth*. Available from: www.eoearth.org/view/article/152758.

Crutzen, P. J. (2002) Geology of mankind. *Nature*. 415, 23.

Crutzen P. J. & Stoermer E. F. (2000) The 'Anthropocene'. *IGBP Newsletter*. 41, 17–18.

Edgeworth, M. (2013) Scale. In: Graves-Brown, P., Harrison, R. & Piccini, A. (eds) *The Oxford Handbook of the Archaeology of the Contemporary World*. Oxford: Oxford University Press.

Ellis, E. C., Kaplan, J. O., Fuller, D. Q., Vavrus, S., Klein Goldewijk, K. & Verburg, P. H. (2013) Used planet: A global history. *PNAS*. 110, 7978–7985.

Grassineau, N., Abell, P., Appel, P. W. U., Lowry, D. & Nisbet, E. (2006) Early life signatures in sulfur and carbon isotopes from Isua, Barberton, Wabigoon (Steep Rock), and Belingwe Greenstone Belts (3.8 to 2.7 Ga). In: Kesler, S. E. & Ohmoto, H. (eds) *Evolution of Early Earth's Atmosphere, Hydrosphere, and Biosphere—Constraints from Ore Deposits*. London: Geological Society of America 198, 33–52.

Hancock, G. J., Tims, S. G., Fifield, L. K. & Webster, I. T. (2014) The release and persistence of radioactive anthropogenic nuclides. In: Waters, C. N., Zalasiewicz, J., Williams, M., Ellis, M. A. & Snelling, A. (eds) *A Stratigraphical Basis for the Anthropocene*. London: Geological Society Special Publications 395, 265–281.

Hay, W. W. (2014) The accelerating rate of global change. *Rendiconti Lincei. Scienze Fisiche e Naturali*. 25, 29–48.

Hitchcock, H. R. & Johnson, P. (1997) *The International Style*. New York: W.W. Norton & Company.

Holtgrieve, G. W., Schindler, D. E., Hobbs, W. O., Leavitt, P. R., Ward, E. J., Bunting, L., Chen, G., Finney, B. P., Gregory-Eaves, I., Holmgren, S., Lisac, M. J., Lisi, P. J., Nydick, K., Rogers, L. A., Saros, J. E., Selbie, D. T., Shapley, M .D., Walsh, P. B. & Wolfe, A. P. (2011) A coherent signature of anthropogenic nitrogen deposition to remote watersheds of the Northern Hemisphere. *Science*. 334, 1545–1548.

Kaplan, J. O., Krumhardt, K. M., Ellis, E. C., Ruddiman, W. F., Lemmen, C. & Goldewijk, K. K. (2011). Holocene carbon emissions as a result of anthropogenic land cover change. *The Holocene*. 21, 775–791.

Kidwell, S. (2015). Biology in the Anthropocene: Challenges and insights from young fossil records. *PNAS*. 112, 4922–4929.

Koch, P. L. & Barnosky, A. D. (2006) Late Quaternary extinctions: State of the debate. *Annual Review of Ecology, Evolution and Systematics*. 37, 215–250.

Krausmann, F., Erb, K-H., Gingrich, S., Haberl, H., Bondeau, A., Gaube, V., Lauk, C., Plutzar, C. & Searchinger, T. D. (2013) Global human appropriation of net primary production doubled in the 20th century. *PNAS*. 110, 10324–10329.

Lewis, S. L. & Maslin, M. A. (2015) Defining the Anthropocene. *Nature*. 519, 171–180.

Lin, M. T., Occhialini, A., Andralojc, P. J., Parry, M. A. J. & Hanson, M. R. (2014). A faster Rubisco with potential to increase photosynthesis in crops. *Nature*. 513, 547–550.

Lyons, S. K., Amatangelo, K. L., Behrensmeyer, A. K., Bercovici, A., Blois, J. L., Davis, M., DiMichele, W. A., Du, A., Eronen, J. T., Tyler Faith, J., Graves, G. R., Jud, N., Labandeira, C., Looy, C. V., McGill, B., Miller, J. H., Patterson, D., Pineda-Munoz, S., Potts, R., Riddle, B., Terry, R., Tóth, A., Ulrich, W., Villaseñor, A., Wing, S., Anderson, H., Anderson, J., Waller, D. & Gotelli, N. (2016) Holocene shifts in the assembly of plant and animal communities implicate human impacts. *Nature*. 529, 80–83.

McDougall, I. B. F. & Fleagle J. G. (2005) Stratigraphic placement and age of modern humans from Kibish, Ethiopia. *Nature*. 433, 733–736.

McNeely, J. A. (ed.) (2001) *The Great Reshuffling: Human Dimensions of Invasive Alien Species*. Gland/Cambridge: International Union for Conservation of Nature and Natural Resources (IUCN).

McPherron, S., Alemseged, Z., Marean, C. W., Wynn, J. G., Reed, D., Geraads, D., Bobe, R. & Béarat, H. A. (2010) Evidence for stone-tool-assisted consumption of animal tissues before 3.39 million years ago at Dikika, Ethiopia. *Nature*. 466, 857–860.

Molina, E., Alegret, L., Arenillas, I., Arz, J. A., Gallala, N., Hardenbol, J., von Salis, K., Steurbaut, E., Vandenberghe, N. & Zaghbib-Turki, D. (2006) The Global Boundary Stratotype Section for the base of the Danian Stage (Paleocene, Paleogene, "Tertiary", Cenozoic) at El Kef, Tunisia – original definition and revision. *Episodes*. 29, 263–273.

Pufahl, P. K. & Hiatt, E. E. (2012) Oxygenation of the Earth's atmosphere-ocean system: A review of physical and chemical sedimentologic responses. *Marine and Petroleum Geology*. 32, 1–20.

Roberts, R. G., Flannery, T. F., Ayliffe, L. K., Yoshida, H., Olley, J. M., Prideaux, G. J., Laslett, G. M., Baynes, A., Smith, M. A., Jones, R. & Smith, B. L. (2001) New ages for the last Australian megafauna: Continent-wide extinction about 46,000 years ago. *Science*. 292, 1888–1892.

Rose, N. L. (2015) Spheroidal carbonaceous fly ash particles provide a globally synchronous stratigraphic marker for the Anthropocene. *Environmental Science and Technology*. 49, 4155–4162.

Ruddiman, W. F. (2003) The Anthropogenic Greenhouse Era began thousands of years ago. *Climatic Change*. 61, 261–293.

Ruddiman, W. F. (2013) Anthropocene. *Annual Review of Earth and Planetary Sciences*. 41, 45–68.

Steffen, W., Broadgate, W., Deutsch, L., Gaffney, O. & Ludwig, C. (2015) The trajectory of the Anthropocene: The Great Acceleration. *The Anthropocene Review*. 2, 81–98.

Stoppani, A. (1873) *Corsa di Geologia*. Milan: Bernardoni and Brigola.

Syvitski, J. P. M. & Kettner, A. (2011) Sediment flux and the Anthropocene. *Philosophical Transactions of the Royal Society*. A369, 957–975.

Tyrrell, T. (2011) Anthropogenic modification of the oceans. *Philosophical Transactions of the Royal Society*. A369, 887–908.

United States Census Bureau (2015). *Historical Estimates of World Population*. Available from: www.census.gov/population/international/data/worldpop/table_history.php.

Waters, C. N., Syvitski, J. P. M., Gałuszka, A., Hancock, G. J., Zalasiewicz, J., Cearreta, A., Grinevald, J., Jeandel, C., McNeill, J. R., Summerhayes, C. & Barnosky, A. (2015) Can nuclear weapons fallout mark the beginning of the Anthropocene Epoch? *Bulletin of the Atomic Scientists*. 71, 46–57.

Waters, C. N., Zalasiewicz, J., Summerhayes, C., Barnosky, A. D., Poirier, C., Gałuszka, A., Cearreta, A., Edgeworth, M., Ellis, E., Ellis, M., Jeandel, C., Leinfelder, R., McNeill, J. R., Richer, D., Steffen, W., Syvitski, J., Vidas, D., Wagreich, M., Williams, M., An, Z., Grinevald, J., Odada, E., Oreskes, N. & Wolfe, A. P. (2016)

The Anthropocene is functionally and stratigraphically distinct from the Holocene. *Science*. 351, aad2622.

Waters, C. N., Zalasiewicz, J., Williams, M., Ellis, M. A. & Snelling, A. (eds) (2014) *A Stratigraphical Basis for the Anthropocene*. London: Geological Society Special Publications 395.

Weisdorf, J. L. (2005) From foraging to farming: Explaining the Neolithic Revolution. *Journal of Economic Surveys*. 19, 562–586.

Wilde, S. A., Valley, J. W., Peck, W. H. & Graham, C. M. (2001) Evidence from detrital zircons for the existence of continental crust and oceans on the Earth 4.4 Gyr ago. *Nature*. 409, 175–178.

Williams, M., Zalasiewicz, J., Haywood, A. & Ellis M. (eds) (2011) The Anthropocene: A new epoch of geological time? *Philosophical Transactions of the Royal Society*. A369, 833–1112.

Williams, M., Zalasiewicz, J. A., Haff, P. K., Schwägerl, C., Barnosky, A. D. & Ellis, E. (2015a) The Anthropocene biosphere. *The Anthropocene Review*. 2, 196–219.

Williams, M., Zalasiewicz, J. A., Davies, N., Mazzini, I., Goiran, J.-P. & Kane, S. (2015b) Humans as the third evolutionary stage of biosphere engineering of rivers. *Anthropocene*. 7, 57–63.

Williams, M., Zalasiewicz, J. A., Waters, C. N., Landing, E. (2014) Is the fossil record of complex animal behaviour a stratigraphical analogue for the Anthropocene? In: Waters, C. N., Zalasiewicz, J. A., Williams, M., Ellis, M. A. & Snelling, A. (eds) *A Stratigraphical Basis for the Anthropocene*. London: Geological Society Special Publications 395, 143–148.

Williams, M., Zalasiewicz, J., Waters, C. N., Edgeworth, M., Bennett, C., Barnosky, A. D., Ellis, E. C., Ellis, M. A., Cearreta, A., Haff, P. K., Ivar do Sul, J., Leinfelder, R., McNeill, J. R., Odada, E., Oreskes, N., Revkin, A., Richer, D., Steffen, W., Summerhayes, C., Syvitski, J. P., Vidar, D., Wagreich, M., Wing, S. L., Wolfe, A. P. & An, Z. (2016) The Anthropocene: A conspicuous stratigraphical signal of anthropogenic changes in production and consumption across the biosphere. *Earth's Future*. 4, 34–53.

Wolff, E. W. (2014) Ice sheets and the Anthropocene. In: Waters, C. N., Zalasiewicz, J., Williams, M., Ellis, M. A. & Snelling, A. (eds) *A Stratigraphical Basis for the Anthropocene*. London: Geological Society Special Publications 395, 255–263.

Zalasiewicz, J., Williams, M., Smith, A., Barry, T. L., Coe, A. L., Bown, P. R., Brenchley, P., Cantrill, D., Gale, A., Gibbard, P., Gregory, F. J., Hounslow, M. W., Kerr, A. C., Pearson, P., Knox, R., Powell, J., Waters, C., Marshall, J., Oates, M., Rawson, P. & Stone, P. (2008) Are we now living in the Anthropocene? *Geological Society of America Today*. 18, 4–8.

Zalasiewicz, J., Williams, M. & Waters, C. N. (2014a). Can an Anthropocene Series be defined and recognised? In: Waters, C. N., Zalasiewicz, J., Williams, M., Ellis, M. A. & Snelling, A. (eds) *A Stratigraphical Basis for the Anthropocene*. London: Geological Society Special Publications 395, 39–53.

Zalasiewicz, J., Williams, M., Waters, C. N., Barnosky, A. D. & Haff, P. (2014b) The technofossil record of humans. *Anthropocene Review*. 1, 34–43.

Zalasiewicz, J., Waters, C., Williams, M., Barnosky, A., Cearreta, A., Crutzen, P., Ellis, E., Ellis, M.A., Fairchild, I.J., Grinevald, J., Haff, P. K., Hajdas, I., Leinfelder, R., McNeill, J., Odada, E. O., Poirier, C., Richter, D. deB., Steffen, W., Summerhayes, C., Syvitski, J. P. M., Vidas, D., Wagreich, M., Wing, S. L., Wolfe, A. P., An, Z. & Oreskes, N. (2015) When did the Anthropocene begin? A mid-twentieth century boundary level is stratigraphically optimal. *Quaternary International.* 383, 196–203.

Zalasiewicz, J., Waters, C. N., Barnosky, A. D., Cearreta, A., Edgeworth, M., Ellis, E. C., Gałuszka, A., Gibbard, P. L., Grinevald, J., Hajdas, I., Ivar do Sul, J., Jeandel, C., Leinfelder, R., McNeill, J. R., Poirier, C., Revkin, A., Richter, D. deB., Steffen, W., Summerhayes, C., Syvitski, J. P. M., Vidas, D., Wagreich, M., Williams, M. & Wolfe, A.P. (2015) Colonization of the Americas, 'Little Ice Age' climate, and bomb-produced carbon: Their role in defining the Anthropocene. *Anthropocene Review.* 2, 117–127.

3 Immigrants or refugees of the Anthropocene

Adapting to or denying climate change?

Tarja Ketola

1 Introduction

Climate change will have more devastating impacts than wars. 'I offer only hunger, thirst, forced marches, battle, and death', Giuseppe Garibaldi told his Italian Army in 1849 (Guerzoni, 1882). 'I have nothing to offer but blood, toil, tears, and sweat', Winston Churchill told the British in 1940 when he was appointed prime minister during the Second World War. Who will be the truth-telling leader of the twenty-first century to wake up people to fight the lethal consequences of climate change? If climate change refugees fleeing their homelands could be turned into planned migration, there would be toil, sweat and tears, but not necessarily blood, hunger, thirst, forced marches, battle and death.

People have migrated and taken refuge through the ages for a great variety of reasons. These include political, economic, social, cultural and environmental motives, often an entanglement of many. Early humans migrated from Africa to Europe and throughout the Eastern Hemisphere as far as Australia where the Aboriginals settled (Manning, 2013). Later, the Huns from Asia and other tribes invading the declining Roman Empire pushed Europeans into the great migration period 400–800 BC (Heather, 1995). The 'discovery' of America by Christopher Columbus in 1492 started mass migration of Europeans to the 'New World', although people from Asia had already migrated there 13,000–16,000 years previously by crossing over a land bridge existing at the time between Siberia and Alaska, forming tribes of Native Americans (Daniels, 2002; Meltzer, 2009; Reich et al., 2012). Religious persecution initiated another mass migration from the Eastern Hemisphere to America in the seventeenth century. Yet another, more economic mass migration wave from Europe to North and South America took place 1820–1930 (Daniels, 2002; UN, 2004). The Second World War created 60 million refugees (Bade, 2003).

Subsequent wars, political and ethnic conflicts, disasters and erosions of ecological and socio-cultural environments have continued to produce masses of refugees globally. Voluntary migration, on the other hand, has been largely individually motivated permanent resettlement or temporary movement. Nowadays most voluntary immigrants are well-to-do executives, experts and skilled workers employed by multinational corporations or free academic and artistic souls. At the other extreme are the refugees fleeing persecution. Their numbers amount to 45 million of which international refugees account for 15 million (UNHCR, 2013). Many of them have been somewhat cynically labelled economic refugees as their motives are intertwined: they come from war zones or otherwise chaotic societies where their life or freedom is threatened and they wish to build a normal life with a good livelihood in a peaceful, orderly society. The rich–poor polarization may increase or decrease in the future, depending on how countries and the global community respond to new challenges.

Immigration is a part of globalization, just like climate change. The unpleasant future prospect of immigration is climate change immigration, which has taken place through the ages, but not on such a scale as predicted now. The even more unpleasant future prospect of refuge (or asylum) seeking, already present in many areas, is climate change refuge seeking, which may explode into uncontrollable floods, if not organized into controllable flows.

People who seek refuge are called asylum seekers until their claim has been definitely evaluated to warrant a refugee status (UNHCR, 2014). The United Nations Refugee Convention from 1951 says that a refugee is any person who seeks refuge, 'owing to a well founded fear of being persecuted for reasons of race, religion, nationality, membership of a particular social group or political opinion' (UNHCR, 1951, p. 14). Climate change is not yet included in the reasons for gaining a refugee status (Morinière, 2009, p. 22); hence climate refugee and climate refuge seeking are still theoretical concepts.

This chapter aims to build a model that could turn chaotic climate refuge seeking into planned climate migration by learning from history. It uses qualitative case studies derived from literature and compiled into a framework as a research method. The cases used are summarized in the following sections and Figure 3.1.

2 Climigrants and clirefugees

Climigration is the concept Bronen (2009) uses for forced permanent migration of communities due to climate change. I suggest that climigrants may belong to three groups of environmental migrants defined by Renaud et al., (2008): (1) environmental emergency migrants who must flee because of rapid onset events and take refuge to save their lives; (2) environmentally forced migrants who are compelled to leave to avoid gradual environmental deterioration and may not have a choice to return; and (3) environmentally motivated migrants who choose to leave a deteriorating environment in order to avoid further weakening of their livelihoods (see also Morinière, 2009).

El-Hinnawi (1985, p. 4, cited in Lübken, 2012, p. 6) called environmental refugees 'people who have been forced to leave their traditional habitat, temporarily or permanently, because of a marked environmental disruption . . . that jeopardized their existence and/or seriously affected the quality of their life'. This chapter suggests that in synchrony with climigration, the concept of clirefuge could be used of seeking climate change refuge. Whether people who have to move because of climate change should be called climigrants or clirefugees is a topical issue.

In 2013 a family from the sinking South Pacific nation of Kiribati tried to challenge in New Zealand the International Refugee Convention's position that climate change is not a reason to give refugee status, but the fact that the Kiribatians are facing risk to their health and lives as rising ocean levels are contaminating drinking water, killing crops and flooding homes did not convince the High Court (Schwartz, 2013). Kiribati has now bought land in Fiji to grow food and build a resettlement site for its displaced people. Moreover, Kiribati has adopted a 'migration with dignity' approach by teaching its people skills to become more attractive as immigrants (Reklev, 2014). Kiribatians wish to stay as independent and self-sufficient as possible, maintain their cultural identity and live sustainably (Randall, 2013). Other famous low-lying Pacific islands like this are the Maldives, Tuvalu and Vanuatu (Lazrus, 2009; Marino, 2009; Nanda in the Foreword of Westra, 2009; Farbotko and Lazrus, 2012). New Zealand's Immigration and Protection Tribunal granted a Tuvalu family residency in 2014, because their children were considered vulnerable to climate change – but emphasized that climate change was only one of the factors leading to granting residency on 'exceptional humanitarian grounds' (*ABC News*, 2014).

Reluctance by the United Nations High Commissioner for Refugees (UNHCR) to extend its concept of refugee to incorporate clirefugees is due to the special status of refugees, which gives them access to services and resources in their resettlement country unavailable to other migrants (Bronen et al., 2009). The socio-economic burden of countries accepting clirefugees might become unbearable with prospective mass exoduses. Yet in some countries, such as Sweden and Finland, laws allow people fleeing their country because of environmental disaster to qualify for refuge (Sgro, 2009).

3 Sources and directions of climigrants and clirefugees

Bronen (2009, p. 68) segregates the drivers of climigration into three categories: (1) random extreme weather events (e.g. hurricanes and tornadoes); (2) the depletion of ecosystem services (e.g. drought and salt water intrusion); and (3) on-going ecological changes caused by the mix of (1) and (2) that have a severe impact on public infrastructure and the livelihoods of people. The ecological causes of climigration or clirefuge seeking comprise sea level rise, flooding and drought, which are the three major consequences of climate change stated by the Intergovernmental Panel on Climate Change (IPCC, 2007).

About 10.5 per cent of the world's population live in low elevation coastal zones (altitude of less than 10 metres) threatened by rising water levels, higher tides and further-reaching waves; that means some 700 million people, of whom 438 million live in Asia and 246 million in the poorest countries of the world (Piguet, 2008). Migration may be the last resort, but it will be a reality to a great many in the near future.

Glaciers all over the world are melting rapidly as temperatures rise. The melting of the Arctic (and less so of the Antarctic) ice cap and permafrost are warming oceans, releasing massive amounts of methane, and will be altering global ocean currents, thereby impacting global climate further. If the Greenland Glaciers melt altogether, sea levels will rise by 7.2 metres and affect 1 billion people far inland. At present the scenarios exhibit exponential global warming, rather than a new ice age, caused by these ice melts, as the heat of the sun is no more reflected back by ice and snow and the melting waters will warm up and start drying up. And when the Tibetan Plateau Glaciers melt, another billion people will be affected, first by floods, then by droughts.

Flooding in population-rich poor countries like Bangladesh and Vietnam's Mekong River Delta as well as coastal cities such as Manila, Guangzhou, Lagos, Ho Chi Minh City, Kolkata, Shanghai, Mumbai, Tianjin, Yangon and Bangkok (IPCC, 2014) will be catastrophic and result in hundreds of millions of clirefugees, if well-planned precautions are not taken. So far these areas have had periodical flooding, and people have evacuated, but they have mostly returned as soon as the water has retreated, with the exception of Bangladesh (Piguet, 2008) where a large number of evacuees have become forced clirefugees or climigrants. Once flooding becomes frequent and water does not retreat completely, the inhabitants of other populated areas and cities will suffer the same fate. It is the very poorest, most exposed and most vulnerable who cannot leave who will have to stay and eventually perish (cf. IPCC, 2014).

Developed countries are not safe, either. There are large parts of New Orleans that are unpopulated after Hurricane Katrina in 2005 – many of the hundreds of thousands evacuated have not been able to return but have instead become permanent clirefugees (Black et al., 2011). Hurricane Sandy in 2012 was another warning of what to expect in the near future: deaths, hundreds of thousands of clirefugees and massive damage in the Caribbean (Bahamas, Cuba, Dominican Republic, Haiti, Jamaica and Puerto Rico) and all along the eastern coasts of Canada and the USA, including the lowest-lying parts of New Jersey and New York.

Low-lying cities on any coastline or by any major river are vulnerable to sea level rises, storms, waves and floods, leading to millions of clirefugees. The Thames flooded in February 2014 in Greater London, Middlesex and Surrey, waking up the inhabitants and authorities to the future realities. Low-lying Netherlands, Belgium and Germany's Eastern Friesland are better prepared but not secure as the flood effects of climate change increase. As almost two-thirds of the world's population live less than 100 kilometres from the coast and 30 of the 50 largest cities in the world are situated on the coast, sea level rise is a real threat (IOM, 2008).

Drought is another mover of the masses. Climate change accelerates droughts leading to food and water crises (Ketola, 2011). Ever-more frequent and severe, spreading, longer-lasting and permanent droughts cause water shortages and desertification, shrinking arable land all over the world, from Africa to Asia, Australia, the Americas and Europe. Cook et al., (2014) calculate that a warming climate will subject 30 per cent of the Earth to drought. This will turn the major agricultural areas of the Great Plains of the USA and a swathe of southeastern China into aridity, and spread the dry zones in Central America, the Amazon, Southern Africa and Southern Europe farther (Cook et al., 2014).

According to the IPCC (2007), severe droughts will decrease freshwater availability in the large river basins of Central, South, East and Southeast Asia, affecting over a billion people by 2050. Already, over the past five decades mass migrations due to droughts have taken place in Africa (Sahel, Ethiopia), South America (Argentine, Brazil), the Middle East (Syria, Iran), Central Asia and Southern Asia (Piguet, 2008). Every year hundreds of thousands of rural inhabitants have been displaced in the Sahel, with the peak of 1 million in Niger in 1985 (Hammer, 2004, pp. 232–234). Similarly, drought and desertification forced 3.4 million North Eastern Brazilians to migrate between 1960 and 1980 (Leighton, 2006, p. 47).

Traditionally, the Sahel area in Africa suffers from periodical harsh droughts but climate change has made the drought permanent and spread it further north to the Arabic countries and south to Southern Africa (IPCC, 2014). The East and Horn of Africa has already experienced an exile of 5 million climate refugees (Afifi et al., 2012). Moreover, early 2014 witnessed the severest ever droughts in Brazil's coffee belt, California and Australia's New South Wales and Queensland. Grave water shortages are predicted to the Mediterranean, the Middle East, the southern USA and southern China (Schewe et al., 2014).

In many developing countries temporal migration is used by some members of households during drought periods as a strategy to improve food security. Case studies in eight countries – Guatemala, Peru, Ghana, Tanzania, Bangladesh, India, Thailand and Vietnam – show that successful temporal migration of some household members can reduce food insecurity by increasing the available resources to buy food when young, relatively better-educated migrants can send food or cash remittances to other household members (content migration), but unsuccessful migration can exacerbate food insecurity when older, less educated migrants cannot send remittances or food and their absence means a reduced labour supply in the household for food production (erosive migration) (Afifi et al., 2014; Etzold et al., 2014; Milan and Ho, 2014; Milan and Ruano, 2014; Murali and Afifi, 2014; Rademacher-Schulz, Schraven and Mahama, 2014; Sakdapolrak, Promburom and Reif, 2014; Smith, 2014; Warner and Afifi, 2014).

Many countries will be able to resettle their climigrants within the boundaries of their nation. This is what the USA is planning to do with the Inupiat, Malemiut, Yupik and other indigenous peoples in Alaska (Bronen, 2009), but the Inupiat, at least, are frustrated by the government's failure to negotiate with them over making their migration sustainable, by preserving their unique culture and local decision-making (Marino, 2009). The 3,000 inhabitants of the very low-lying Carteret Islands have been gradually been permanently evacuated to other islands of Papua New Guinea since 2005 (Piguet, 2008). For all the Pacific nations, this will be an ever-increasing problem, and will involve relocation of the evacuees as well as the original inhabitants when their resettlement islands start sinking, too, because of sea level rise. This problem will escalate in population rich countries faced by forced migration as poor migrants 'cluster in high-density areas that are often highly exposed to flooding and landslides, with these risks increasing with climate change' (IPCC, 2014, p. 13).

Climigrants are just as vulnerable as clirefugees, if they are not allowed to decide on their own future. While a great majority of climigration will take place internally within nations, many developing (and some developed) countries will be so holistically overwhelmed by climate change that they will not be able to provide even for their own unaffected or less affected inhabitants, not to mention their internal climigrants. International migration, or more probably, desperate international refuge seeking, will be the only option.

At our longitude the direction of climate exile is from Africa to Southern Europe, then to Central Europe and, finally, to Northern Europe, when drought and water shortage drive the masses further north. In Northern Europe summer drought and extreme winter flooding will alternate because of climate change, but areas still remaining arable will become 'the most valuable real estate on the planet, besieged by millions of climate refugees from the south' (Ahmed, 2010, p. 58). In North and South America and Asia the development will be more complicated since all three extreme weather phenomena – drought, rising sea water and flooding – interact there massively and simultaneously.

The same applies to Australia: intolerable heat, massive bush fires, droughts and water shortages are spreading from the centre of the continent towards the coastal areas in which the sea water is rising; simultaneously storm floods make the strip of land in between uninhabitable. Australia illustrates in extreme form the exponentially accelerating climate change impacts the whole world is facing (Diamond, 2005). It is predicted that Australia will be mostly uninhabitable before 2040 (Kirsch, 2010), and the whole population of the Australian continent will have to be evacuated – only the island of Tasmania will be inhabitable in the late 2030s. The current Abbott government's denial of climate change and the abolishment of the earlier Gillard government's climate package – including an emissions trading scheme with the first three years' fixed carbon price, renewable energy target, biodiversity fund, carbon farming futures programme and clean technology programme – make mitigation of climate change impacts and planning of climigration impossible. Moreover, the Abbott government's scrapping of the Tasmanian Forests Agreement signed in 2013 under the Gillard government, adding 170,000 hectares to the Tasmanian Wilderness World Heritage Area (Ketola, 2013), will lead to intensive logging, which will make Tasmania more vulnerable to climate change effects and will shorten the period this island will be able to inhabit climigrants from mainland Australia. In the long run, most Tasmanian forests will be logged to make room for the arrivals and to make money, which will further accelerate the impacts of climate change and ultimately make Tasmania uninhabitable. This will leave Australians without any homeland, at the mercy of the global community, which will already be overwhelmed by clirefugees from Asia and Africa. The current and previous Australian governments' treatment of boat refugees – indefinite detention, human rights violations, physical and mental violence, relocation to poor, unstable countries and the intentional creation of total hopelessness among the refugees – may make other countries reluctant to take Australian climigrants or clirefugees. 'Treat others the way you would like to be treated' is a wise piece of advice in this day and age.

Responsible governments should start looking for more land elsewhere and negotiate on its purchase or lease. The Maldives is already saving all its tourist revenues for the purchase of a new homeland (Ramesh, 2008). Tuvalu, on the other hand, has a bilateral migration agreement on an annual quota of immigrants with New Zealand called the Pacific Access Category (PAC), but this does not refer to climate change or state any responsibility for the displacement of Tuvaluans (Sgro, 2009).

Bigger nations have bigger problems, but any developed country can afford to plan organized climate change immigration, if they do not deny its need. Conversely, most inhabitants of developing countries will be left to their own devices, and these billions of refugees will cause global chaos, if the global community does not acknowledge the situation and start cooperating to adapt to the human consequences of climate change.

4 Climigration types

Bronen (2009, p. 68) maintains that there are three patterns of climate-induced migration: 'the migration of individuals and households where climate change is one of several factors causing migration, mass migration where entire communities are forced to temporarily evacuate, and mass migration where entire communities are forced to permanently relocate'. In reality, the tapestry of climigration is more varied than that. Climate change often interweaves ecological, political, economic and social factors. Moreover, in addition to temporary evacuation and permanent relocation, there is intermediary longer-term climigration taking place. And temporary, longer-term or permanent climigration may sweep away not only individuals and communities, but also the populations of larger entities, such as towns, cities and metropolises as well as whole nations of different sizes.

In Figure 3.1 an outline of climigration types is drafted according to the length of climigration and the number of climigrants, and it organizes the cases mentioned above as examples for the different types. Climigration can be roughly divided into temporary (short-term), longer-term and permanent climigration (horizontal axis), although the borders between these divisions are vague, and the intended kind of climigration can become another because of changing circumstances. Climigration can also be divided on the basis of the numbers of climigrants involved (vertical axis) ranging from individual members of households to hundreds of millions of people. The two divisions make 24 different types of climigration ranging from temporary climigration of some members of households to send money to other household members (1a) to permanent climigration of large nations (8c). The examples embrace both currently on-going climigration and prospective and possible climigration up to the year 2050. For some types there are no examples available.

Number of climigrants	a. Temporary climigration	b. Longer-term climigration	c. Permanent climigration
8. Hundreds of millions	8a. Temporary climigration of large nations	8b. Longer-term climigration of large nations	8c. Permanent climigration of large nations
7. Tens of millions	7a. Temporary climigration of medium-sized nations or metropolises	7b. Longer-term climigration of medium-sized nations or metropolises	7c. Permanent climigration of medium-sized nations or metropolises
6. Millions	6a. Temporary climigration of small nations or cities	6b. Longer-term climigration of small nations or cities	6c. Permanent climigration of small nations or cities
5. Hundreds of thousands	5a. Temporary climigration of tiny nations or towns	5b. Longer-term climigration of tiny nations or towns	5c. Permanent climigration of tiny nations or towns
4. Tens of thousands	4a. Temporary climigration of micro-nations or municipalities	4b. Longer-term climigration of micronations or municipalities	4c. Permanent climigration of micro-nations or municipalities
3. Thousands	3a. Temporary climigration of villages	3b. Longer-term climigration of villages	3c. Permanent climigration of villages
2. Hundreds	2a. Temporary climigration of households	2b. Longer-term climigration of households	2c. Permanent climigration of households
1. Tens	1a. Temporary climigration of some members of households to send money to other household members	1b. Longer-term climigration of some members of households to send money to other household members	1c. Permanent climigration of some members of households to send money to other household members

Length of climigration →

1a. & 1b. & prospected 1c., 2a., 2b. & 2c. Case studies from Guatemala, Peru, Ghana, Tanzania, Bangladesh, India, Thailand, and Vietnam now (Warner and Afifi 2014)
2c. & 3c. Inupiat, Malemiut, Yupik and other indigenous peoples in Alaska now (Bronen 2009, Marino 2009); The Carteret Islanders of Papua New Guinea since 2005 (Egan 2008)
4c. Tuvalu now (Lazrus 2009, Marino 2009, Farbotko and Lazrus 2012, Sgro 2009)
5c. Kiribati and the Maldives now (Ramesh 2008, Randall 2013, Reklev 2014, Schwartz 2013)
5a. & 5b. & prospected 5c. New Orleans, still largely unpopulated after Hurricane Katrina 2005 (Black et al. 2011)
6a. & 6b. & 6c. Sahel area, spreading north and south now; prospect for Brazil's coffee belt, California and Australia's New South Wales & Queensland (IPCC 2014)
6c. East and Horn of Africa now (Afifi et al. 2012)
6a. & 6b. & prospected 6c. Bahamas, Cuba, Dominican Republic, Haiti, Jamaica & Puerto Rico, and eastern coasts of Canada & USA, incl. New Jersey & New York (IPCC 2014)
6a. & 6b. & possible 6c. Prospect for Greater London, Middlesex and Surrey (EA 2011); prospect for the Netherlands, Belgium and German's Eastern Friesland (IPCC 2014)
7c. Prospect for Australia's mainland (Diamond 2005, Kirsch 2010), Vietnam's Mekong River Delta and coastal metropolises Manila, Guangzhou, Lagos, Ho Chi Minh City, Kolkata, Shanghai, Mumbai, Tianjin, Rangoon and Bangkok (IPCC 2014)
8a. & 8b. parts of coastal Bangladesh now; **8c.** Prospect for Bangladesh (IPCC 2014)
8a. & 8b & 8c. Prospect for the Mediterranean, the Middle East, the southern United States and southern China (Schewe et al. 2014), dried-up large river basins of Central, South, East and Southeast Asia (IPCC 2007)

Figure 3.1 Climigration types according to the length of climigration and the number of climigrants, with examples.

The same categorization can be applied to clirefuge seeking, with the exception of level 1, as it constitutes planned migration of individuals to provide for those staying behind. The other levels (2–8) of clirefuge seeking create an exponentially growing emergency for the departure, transit and arrival countries. To avoid panic and chaos, careful advance planning of climigration is needed between the emigration, intervening and immigration countries – and with the global community in order to share the burden as fairly and equally as possible.

5 Predicted climigrant numbers

Christian Aid (2007) has estimated that there will be one billion environmentally driven migrants between now and 2050. However, since climate change, its impacts and resulting migration are accelerating exponentially (Morinière, 2009), these numbers will become manifold and the problem will exacerbate earlier. Soon billions of people on all continents will have to leave their homes because of rising sea levels, persistent droughts and water shortages or unrelenting storms, floods and contaminated water.

A study (Motesharrei, Rivas and Kalnay, 2014) financed by the National Aeronautics and Space Administration (NASA) predicts that our civilization could collapse because of climate change and population problems, which have been caused by the unsustainable exploitation of resources and increasingly unequal distribution of wealth, resulting in water, food and energy shortages that have started to kill the masses (commoners) but have not yet affected the elites who continue business as usual despite the approaching catastrophe until they eventually perish, too. Motesharrei et al., (2014) point out that civilizations have collapsed in a similar way throughout history, mentioning the Roman Empire, Minoan and Mycenaean civilizations, many Mesopotamian (Sumerian, Akkadian, Assyrian, Babylonian, Achaemenid, Seleucid, Parthian, Sassanid, Umayyad and Abbasid) Empires, the Hittite and Harrapan civilizations, the Mauyran and Guta Empires, the Khmer Empire and the Zhou, Han, Tang and Song Empires as some examples.

Once again it is the commoners, and not the elite, who are the clirefugees who desperately try to survive, but their numbers are increasing to such an extent that it is becoming mass clirefuge seeking. The elites fend them off their water, food and energy sources domestically and from their so far unaffected countries internationally – until the elites themselves will have to flee in an attempt to survive.

The report of the IPCC (2007) stating that at existing rates of global warming the Earth will be uninhabitable by the end of the twenty-first century is nowadays considered conservative (Ahmed, 2010; Motesharrei et al., 2014). As carbon emissions and global warming have only increased since 2007, the end will come much earlier, by mid-century. Ahmed (2010) notes that the evidence from front-line scientific research indicates that the rate of global warming is much faster than the IPCC models predict, making the effects of climate change 'occur far sooner, with greater rapidity, and higher intensity, than officially recognized by governments' (Ahmed, 2010, p. 38), thus hastening the end. Like Motesharrei et al., (2014), Ahmed (2010) recognizes this leading to food, energy and water conflicts. The IPCC's (2007) worst-case scenario of a 6°C temperature rise, which means the end of life on Earth in our own lifetimes, will be reached earlier and the temperatures will rise far higher than that. Our society cannot support even the soon to be achieved 3°C-rise conditions, and the 5°C-rise will make all 'humans migrate in search of food and try vainly to live like animals off the land' (Ahmed, 2010, p. 35).

6 Conclusion: climigration model

There is plenty of research on the protection of the rights of indigenous peoples (Westra, 2009), when they have been forced to migrate because big business or governments have destroyed their traditional lands, forests and rivers through logging, mining, dam construction and other damaging activities. Climate change migration naturally erodes the position of indigenous peoples further both as involuntary recipients of climigrants or clirefugees, when their habitats remain unaffected or are favourably affected by climate change, and as climigrants or clirefugees, when their habitats are badly affected by climate change.

Unexpectedly climigration also introduces a new perspective on indigenous rights: the rights of the original, majority inhabitants of the ordinary villages, municipalities, towns, cities and nations of the destinations of the climigrants. So far migrants have constituted a small minority of the population of their host countries, and even the number of refugees, fleeing in millions from countries like Syria have remained small, maximum 0.1–0.5 per cent of the population in most receiving countries – only in the neighbouring country, Lebanon, have refugee numbers totalled up to 25 per cent of the population. When climate change induced migration or refuge seeking starts in earnest, it will turn the tables: the inhabitants of the countries of destination could become minority groups with the massive numbers of climigrants or clirefugees becoming the majority groups.

Every nation wishes to protect its own citizens. Climigration and clirefuge seeking prompt large and medium-sized developed nations with strong armed forces, such as the USA, the UK and Australia, to safeguard their borders to prevent such an invasion:

> Classified studies by the US intelligence community have already red-flagged "regional partners" of the US in key strategic regions in Africa, Central Asia and the Middle East, who are likely to face severe problems, and whose identities remain confidential to avoid diplomatic frictions.
>
> (Ahmed, 2010, p. 58)

Smaller developed nations with weaker armed forces, like the Nordic countries, which cannot defend themselves against a mass invasion, may have to satisfy themselves with passing laws to protect the land, ownership and human rights of their indigenous population, which they hope the new majority will not abolish. Most developing countries do not have the resources to do either – hence those developing countries least affected by climate change will be conquered by climigrants and clirefugees, inducing conflicts with indigenous populations. This problem is emerging already with the world's first clirefugees on Pacific Islands where relocation from sinking islands onto others' lands has been a sensitive issue, but has not yet become a violent conflict (Weir and Virani, 2011). Since most of Australia and the UK and large parts of the USA will eventually also be uninhabitable most of their citizens will migrate to colonialize either those small, developed nations or those developing nations of any size least affected by climate change. Their citizens have the inherited skill to colonialize in their psyche.

The more extreme global warming with weather extremes and sea level rise becomes the more pronounced will human displacement and migration become (IPCC, 2014). The way Ahmed (2010, p. 35) presents the IPCC's scenarios for global warming by Celsius degrees helps us to understand human migration patterns caused by climate change:

> 1°C increase: Ice-free sea absorbs more heat and accelerates global warming; fresh water lost from a third of the world's surface; low-lying coastlines flooded.
> 2°C increase: Europeans dying of heatstroke; forests ravaged by fire; stressed plants beginning to emit carbon rather than absorbing it; a third of all species face extinction.
> 3°C increase: Carbon release from vegetation and soils speeds global warming; death of the Amazon rainforest; super-hurricanes hit coastal cities; starvation in Africa.
> 4°C increase: Runaway thaw of permafrost makes global warming unstoppable; much of Britain made uninhabitable by severe flooding; Mediterranean region abandoned.
> 5°C increase: Methane from ocean floor accelerates global warming; ice gone from both poles; humans migrate in search of food and try vainly to live like animals off the land.
> 6°C increase: Life on Earth ends with apocalyptic storms, flash floods, hydrogen sulphide gas and methane fireballs racing across the globe with the power of atomic bombs; only fungi survive.

At 4°C of warming humans have no choice as to whether to stay or leave; they have to migrate to survive (Gemenne, 2011; IPCC, 2014). At 5°C of warming humans regress to animal-like instinctive migration to meet their basic daily survival needs of food and water.

Piguet (2008) points out that migration research has paid little attention to ecological drivers, and when it has, it has focused on their positive impacts. Historical migration research mentions how the Ice Age made mass migration possible from Siberia to Alaska across the Bering Strait 13,000–16,000 years ago, and how the Medieval Climate Optimum during the period 800–1400 made navigation easy for migration to Polynesia (Perch-Nielsen, 2004, p. 39 in Piguet, 2008, p. 2). Even the desertification of the Sahara and the Arabian Peninsula after

6,000 BC had a positive impact by prompting mass migration to the Nile Valley, thereby contributing to the development of the civilization of ancient Egypt (Hammer, 2004, p. 238 in Piguet, 2008, p. 2).

Crosby (1986) argues that the Europeans colonialized North and South America, Australia and New Zealand and beat the indigenous inhabitants by ecological, rather than military, imperialism: by introducing alien flora and fauna and importing pests and diseases. This may happen again elsewhere. Fagan (2002), on the other hand, reasons that the lesson to be learnt from the Little Ice Age in the period 1300–1850 is that if we have lots of people living on marginal lands at subsistence level, climate change will cause famine. And while the weakest will perish masses will migrate, if they are allowed to. During the Irish Potato Famine 1 million people died and another million emigrated from Ireland, mostly to North America (Fagan, 2002). Between 1875–1903 famines in the tropical world killed an estimated 20–50 million people because of El Niños and colonialism (Fagan, 2002).

Modern-day historical research on migration after industrialization has been mostly devoid of ecological drivers, as political, economic and social drivers have preoccupied researchers. This does not mean that ecological or, especially, climate drivers have not existed; they just have not been paid attention to. Now in the post-modern, post-industrialization era, ecological and, particularly, climate change effects on humans, their environment and their migration have become acute – this time because of their negative impacts.

The upside of the focus of past historical migration studies on the positive climate impacts is that they may help contemporary generations to turn the negative push factors into positive pull factors, and in this way change unorganized, fleeing, clirefuge into organized resettlement, climigration.

There may be something contemporary societies can learn from the traditional nomadic way of life with constant migration (Jónsson, 2010; Singh, 2012), which reduces the adverse environmental impact on humans – and at the same time reduces the adverse human impact on the environment. It might be possible to develop a novel, twenty-first-century nomadic life style, which could help both the climigrants to find new alternatives and the inhabitants of areas of favourable climate change impacts to avoid being overwhelmed by clirefugees.

Well-managed migration could become a useful instrument for adjustment to climate change, but it should not impair the ecological conditions of the host areas or accelerate climate change further. IPCC (2014, p. 5) stresses that 'successful adaptation will depend on our ability to allow and facilitate natural systems to adjust to a changing climate; thus maintaining the ecosystem services upon which all life depends'.

Figure 3.2 builds a climigration model that turns chaotic clirefuge seeking into organized climigration and helpless clirefugees into self-reliant climigrants by learning from history.

As climate change is accelerating exponentially the model uses the future years of climate departures presented by Mora et al., (2013) as prompter decades for mass migration for each geographical area. Figure 3.2 gives examples from Western near

(a) Historical migration events (historical facts).

Learning from history...

1500 Mass migration from Europe to North and South America prompted by colonization 1500–1775

Forced slave trade migration from Africa to North and South America 1500–1850

1600 Religious persecution driven migration from Europe to North America 1620–1640

1700 Migration from Britain to Australia and New Zealand prompted by colonization 1788–1930

1800 Forced indentured labourer migration from India and China to British colonies 1830–1917

Mass migration from all parts of Europe to North and South America, Australia and New Zealand 1820–1930

1900 Post-WWII mass migration from Mexico to the USA, from former colonies to Britain and France, from Turkey to Germany, from Yugoslavia and Italy to Germany and France, from Finland to Sweden, from Britain to Australia 1945/50–1970

Illegal and legal migration from Mexico to the USA 1970–

Mostly illegal migration from North Africa to Europe (mainly Spain, Italy, France, Malta, Greece) 1980–

Legal and illegal migration from Eastern Europe to Western Europe 1990–

(b) Climigration: current (2005–), prospected (2015–), evermore likely (2020–) (concluded from the news and Mora et al. 2013).

...turns chaotic clirefuge seeking into organized climigration

2000 Climigration from small Pacific Islands to large Pacific Islands or...? 2005–

Climigration from coastal Bangladesh to inland or...? 2005–

2010 Climigration from Alaskan coast because of sea level rise to inland or...? 2010–

Climigration from coastal, flooded and desertified South Asia (India, Bangladesh, Pakistan) to...? 2015–

2020 Climigration from large Pacific Islands (e.g. Papua New Guinea, Indonesia), Philippines, Malaysia and Singapore to...? 2020–

Climigration from Arabian Peninsula to...? 2020–

Climigration from coastal, flooded and desertified Western Africa to...? 2020–

Climigration from Alaska because of melted ice to mainland USA or Siberia or...? 2020–

2030 Climigration from Northern, Eastern and Southern Africa to...? 2030–

Climigration from Australia to...? 2030–

Climigration from Southern Europe to...? 2030–

Climigration from Mexico and Central America to...? 2030–

2040 Climigration from coastal, flooded and desertified USA and –Canada to...? 2040–

Climigration from Thailand, Vietnam, North East Asia, coastal, flooded and desertified China to...? 2040–

Climigration from coastal, flooded and desertified South America to...? 2040–

2050 Climigration from Central Asia to...? 2040/50–

Climigration from Central Europe to...? 2040/50–

2060 Climigration from Northern Europe to...? 2060–

Climigration from Northern America to...? 2060–

Climigration from North Asia to...? 2060–

Figure 3.2 Climigration model: from clirefugees to climigrants by learning from history.

history, but all world history migration events from any era can give valuable lessons. Hence the use of this model requires the establishment of a data bank to collect experiences from earlier migrations and refuge seekings for whatever reason, in order to learn about successes and failures to plan organized climigration, and enable climigrants to remain self-sufficient, maintain their cultural identity and live sustainably in their new habitats. It is essential to establish a UN climigration coordination centre in order to prevent people who have to leave their homes because of climate change from becoming helpless, vulnerable clirefugees and helping them to become climigrants with initiative, strength and flexibility instead.

Sgro (2009) claims that the European Union (EU) has a better chance of finding consensus to the climate change refuge/migration problem than others because both the migration/asylum issue and the climate change issue are high on the EU agenda. She suggests that the EU could create a community status of environmental refugees. Another option Sgro (2009) accepts is the proposal by Biermann and Boas (2007, subsequently 2010) that instead of extending the UNHCR (1951) definition of refugees, a protocol for climate refugees or climate forced migrants should be added to the United Nations Framework Convention on Climate Change (UNFCCC). Sgro's (2009) third option is to create a specifically tailored international convention to recognize environmental asylum.

Whatever the global governance decisions are, it is clear that comprehensive international cooperation between all countries in the world is crucial. The global community needs to share the burdens caused by global climate change by preventing and mitigating environmental shocks and stresses as well as by opening migration channels (Piguet, 2008) for the temporarily, longer-term and permanently displaced clirefugees/climigrants.

Bibliography

ABC News (2014) Tuvalu climate family granted New Zealand residency on appeal. *ABC News*. 6 August.

Afifi, T., Govil, R., Sakdapolrak, P. & Warner, K. (2012) *Climate Change, Vulnerability and Human Mobility: Perspectives of Refugees from the East and Horn of Africa*. Geneva: UNHCR.

Afifi, T., Liwenga, E. & Kwezi, L. (2014) Rainfall-induced crop failure, food insecurity and outmigration in Same-Kilimanjaro, Tanzania. *Climate and Development*. 6(1), 53–60.

Ahmed, N. M. (2010) *A User's Guide to the Crisis of Civilization*. London: Pluto Press.

Bade, K. J. (2003) *Migration in European History*. Malden, MA, Oxford and Carlton, VI: Blackwell Publishing.

Biermann, F. & Boas, I. (2007) *Preparing for a Warmer World, Towards a Global Governance System to Protect Climate Refugees*. Amsterdam: Vrije Universiteit.

Biermann, F. & Boas, I. (2010) Preparing for a warmer world: Towards a global governance system to protect climate refugees. *Global Environmental Politics*. 10(1), 60–88.

Black, R., Adger , W. N., Arnell, N. W., Dercon, S., Geddes, A. & Thomas, D. S. G. (2011) The effect of environmental change on human migration. *Global Environmental Change*. 21S, S3–S11.

Bronen, R. (2009) Forced migration of Alaskan indigenous communities due to climate change: Creating a human rights response. *Source*. 12, 68–73.

Bronen, R., Chandrasekhar, D., Conde, D. A., Kavanova, K. Moriniere, L., Schmidt-Verkerk, K. & Witter, R. (2009) Stay in place or migrate: A research perspective on understanding adaptation to a changing environment. *Source*. 12, 12–19.

Christian Aid (2007) *Human Tide: The Real Migration Crisis. A Christian Aid Report*. London: Christian Aid.

Churchill, W. (1940) *Blood, Toil, Tears and Sweat*. First Speech as Prime Minister to House of Commons. May 13. The Churchill Centre, Downers Grove, IL. Available from: www.winstonchurchill.org/learn/speeches/speeches-of-winston-churchill/92-blood-toil-tears-and-sweat (accessed 30 December 2014).

Cook, B., Smerdon, J. E., Seager, R. & Coats, S. (2014) Global warming and 21st century drying. *Climate Dynamics*. 43(9–10), 2607–2627.

Crosby, A. W. (1986) *Ecological Imperialism: The Biological Expansion of Europe, 900–1900*. Cambridge: Cambridge University Press.

Daniels, R. (2002) *Coming to America. A History of Immigration and Ethnicity in American Life*. Second edition. New York: Perennial.

Diamond, J. (2005) *Collapse. How Societies Choose to Fail or Succeed*. New York: Viking Penguin.

EA (2011) *TE2100 Strategic Outline Programme. Thames Estuary 2100*. London: Environment Agency.

Egan, A. (2008) Climate change fuels migration. *MHR Issue Paper* 2. Cambridge, MA: Harvard Kennedy School.

El-Hinnawi, E. (1985) *Environmental Refugees*. Nairobi: United Nations Environmental Programme.

Etzold, B., Ahmed, A. U., Hassan, S. R. & Neelormi, S. (2014) Clouds gather in the sky, but no rain falls. Vulnerability to rainfall variability and food insecurity in Northern Bangladesh and its effects on migration. *Climate and Development*. 6(1), 18–27.

Fagan, B. (2002) *The Little Ice Age: How Climate Made History 1300–1850*. New York: Basic Books.

Farbotko, C. & Lazrus, H. (2012) The first climate refugees? Contesting global narratives of climate change in Tuvalu. *Global Environmental Change*. 22(2), 382–390.

Guerzoni, G. (1882) *Garibaldi*. Florence: G. Barbèra.

Gemenne, F. (2011) Climate-induced population displacements in a 4°C+ world. *Philosophical Transactions*. 369(1934), 182–195.

Hammer, T. (2004) Desertification and migration. In: Unruh, J. D., Krol, M. S. & Kliot, N. (eds) *Environmental Change and Its Implications for Population Migration*. Dordrecht: Kluwer.

Heather, P. (1995) The Huns and the end of the Roman Empire in Western Europe. *The English Historical Review*. CX(435), 4–41.

IOM (2008) *Migration, Development and Environment*. IOM Migration Research Series No 35. Geneva: International Organization for Migration.

IPCC (2007) *Climate Change 2007: Synthesis Report*. Geneva: Intergovernmental Panel on Climate Change.

IPCC (2014) *Climate Change 2014: Impacts, Adaptation, and Vulnerability*. Working Group II. Geneva: Intergovernmental Panel on Climate Change.

Jónsson, G. (2010) The environmental factor in migration dynamics – a review of African case studies. *International Migration Institute Working Paper* 21.

Ketola, T. (2011). Food, energy and water (FEW) security analysis cube: Finland, Bolivia, Bhutan and Botswana as examples. In: Auffermann B. & Kaskinen J. (eds) *Security in Futures – Security in Change*. FFRC eBOOK 5, 280–299. Turku: Finland Futures Research Centre.

Ketola, T. (2013). Sustainable forests' strategy for Tasmanian forest companies. *Australasian Business Ethics Network (ABEN) Conference*, Hobart, Tasmania, Australia, 2–3 December.

Kirsch, S. (2010). How it will end? Available from: www.skirsch.com/politics/globalwarming/Extinction.htm (accessed 31 March 2014).

Lazrus, H. (2009) Perspectives on vulnerability to climate change and migration in Tuvalu. *Source*. 12, 32–39.

Leighton, M. (2006) Desertification and migration. In: Johnson, P. M., Mayrand, K. & Paquin, M. (eds) *Governing Global Desertification*. London: Ashgate.

Lübken, U. (2012) Chasing a ghost? Environmental change and migration in history. *Global Environment: A Journal of History and Natural and Social Sciences*. 9, 5–24.

Manning, P. (2013) *Migration in World History. Themes in World History Series*. Abingdon: Routledge.

Marino, E. (2009) Immanent threats, impossible moves, and unlikely prestige: Understanding the struggle for local control as a means towards sustainability. *Source*. 12, 42–50.

Meltzer, D. J. (2009) *First Peoples in a New World: Colonizing Ice Age America*. Berkeley, CA: University of California Press.

Milan, A. & Ho, R. (2014) Livelihood and migration patterns at different altitudes in the Central Highlands of Peru. *Climate and Development*. 6(1), 69–76.

Milan, A. & Ruano, S. (2014) Rainfall variability, food insecurity and migration in Cabricán, Guatemala. *Climate and Development*. 6(1), 61–68.

Mora, C., Frazier, A. G., Longman, R. J., Dacks, R. S., Walton, M. M., Tong, E. J., Sanchez, J. J., Kaiser, L. R., Stender, Y. O., Anderson, J. M., Ambrosino, C. M., Fernandez-Silva, I., Giuseffi, L.M. & Giambelluca, T. W. (2013) The projected timing of climate departure from recent variability. *Nature*. 502, 183–187.

Morinière, L. C. E. (2009) Tracing the footprint of 'environmental migrants' through 50 years of literature. *Source*. 12, 22–29.

Motesharrei, S., Rivas, J. & Kalnay, E. (2014) Human and nature dynamics (HANDY): Modeling inequality and use of resources in the collapse or sustainability of societies. *Ecological Economics*. 101, 91–102.

Murali, J. & Afifi, T. (2014) Rainfall variability, food security and human mobility in the Janjgir-Champa district of Chhattisgarh state, India. *Climate and Development*. 6(1), 28–37.

Perch-Nielsen, S. (2004) *Understanding the Effect of Climate Change on Human Migration – The Contribution of Mathematical and Conceptual Models*. Diploma Thesis. Zurich: Department of Environmental Sciences, ETH.

Piguet, E. (2008) Climate change and forced migration. *New Issues in Refugee Research*. Research Paper No. 153. Geneva: Policy Development and Evaluation Service, United Nations High Commissioner for Refugees (UNHCR).

Rademacher-Schulz, C., Schraven, B. & Mahama, E. S. (2014) Time matters: Shifting seasonal migration in Northern Ghana in response to rainfall variability and food insecurity. *Climate and Development*. 6(1), 46–52.

Ramesh, R. (2008) Paradise almost lost: Maldives seek to buy a new homeland. *Guardian*. 10 November.

Randall, A. (2013) Climate refugees? Where's the dignity in that? *Guardian*. 17 May.

Reich, D., Patterson, N., Campbell, D., Tandon, A., Mazieres, S., Ray, N., Parra, M. V., Rojas, W., Duque, C., Mesa, N., García, L. F., Triana, O., Blair, S., Maestre, A., Dib, J. C., Bravi, C. M., Bailliet, G., Corach, D., Hünemeier, T., Bortolini, M. C., Salzano, F., M., Petzl-Erler, M. L., Acuña-Alonzo, V., Aguilar-Salinas, C., Canizales-Quinteros, S., Tusié-Luna, T., Riba, L., Rodríguez-Cruz, M., Lopez-Alarcón, M., Coral-Vazquez, R., Canto-Cetina, T., Silva-Zolezzi, I., Fernandez-Lopez, J. C., Contreras, A. V., Jimenez-Sanchez, G., Gómez-Vázquez, M. J., Molina, J., Carracedo, Á., Salas, A., Gallo, C., Poletti, G., Witonsky, D. B., Alkorta-Aranburu, G., Sukernik, R. I., Osipova, L., Fedorova, S. A., Vasquez, R., Villena, M., Moreau, C., Barrantes, R., Pauls, D., Excoffier, L., Bedoya, G., Rothhammer, F., Dugoujon, J-M., Larrouy, G., Klitz, W., Labuda, D., Kidd, J., Kidd, K., Di Rienzo, A., Freimer, N. B., Price, A. L. & Ruiz-Linares, A. (2012) Reconstructing Native American population history. *Nature*. 488(7411), 370–374.

Reklev, S. (2014) Pacific island states pushed aside in race for UN funds: Kiribati. *Canberra Times*. 13 March.

Renaud, F., Dun, O., Warner, K. & Bogardi, J. (2008) Deciphering the importance of environmental factors in human migration. *Environment, Forced Migration and Social Vulnerability Conference*. United Nations University, Institute for Environment and Human Security (UNU-EHS), Bonn, 9–11 October.

Sakdapolrak, P., Promburom, P. & Reif, A. (2014). Why successful in situ adaptation with environmental stress does not prevent people from migrating? Empirical evidence from Northern Thailand. *Climate and Development*. 6(1), 38–45.

Schewe, J., Heinke, J., Gerten, D., Haddeland, I., Arnell, N.W., Clark, D.B., Dankers, R., Eisner, S., Fekete, B., Colón-González, F.J., Gosling, S.,N., Kim, H., Liu, X., Masaki, Y, Portmann, F.T., Satoh, Y., Stacke, T., Tang, Q., Wada, Y., Wisser, D., Albrecht, T., Frieler, K., Piontek, F., Warszawski, L. & Kabat, P. (2014). Multi-model assessment of water scarcity under climate change. *PNAS*, 111(9), 3245–3250.

Schwartz, D. (2013) Kiribatian asks New Zealand to treat him as climate change refugee. *ABC News*. 16 October.

Sgro, A. (2009) Views on, and possible solutions to, the environmental refugees issue within the European Union. *Source*. 12, 74–79.

Singh, V. (2012) Environmental migration as planned livelihood among the rebaris of Western Rajasthan, India. *Global Environment: A Journal of History and Natural and Social Sciences*. 9, 50–73.

Smith, C. S. (2014) Modelling migration futures: Development and testing of the rainfalls agent-based migration model – Tanzania. *Climate and Development*. 6(1), 77–91.

UN (2004) *World Economic and Social Survey 2004: International Migration*. New York: Department of Economic and Social Affairs of the United Nations Secretariat.

UNHCR (United Nations High Commissioner for Refugees) (1951) *United Nations Convention Relating to the Status of Refugees*. Geneva: The UN Refugee Agency.

UNHCR (United Nations High Commissioner for Refugees) (2013) *Facts and Figures about Refugees*. Geneva: The UN Refugee Agency.

UNHCR (United Nations High Commissioner for Refugees) (2014) *Asylum-seekers*. Geneva: The UN Refugee Agency.

Warner, K. & Afifi, T. (2014) Where the rain falls: Evidence from 8 countries on how vulnerable households use migration to manage the risk of rainfall variability and food insecurity. *Climate and Development*. 6(1), 1–17.

Weir, T. & Virani, Z. (2011) Three linked risks for development in the Pacific Islands: Climate change, disasters and conflict. *Climate and Development*. 3(3), 193–208.

Westra, L. (2009) *Environmental Justice and the Rights of Ecological Refugees*. London: Earthscan.

Part II

Capitalism and neoliberal governmentality

4 Capitalism and the absolute contradiction in the Anthropocene

Toni Ruuska

1 Introduction

Environmental degradation as a phenomenon is not a new one, but has occurred throughout recorded history with profoundly negative consequences for numerous past civilizations (see e.g. Diamond, 2005; Tainter, 2015) and, of course, caused widespread harm to the non-human world as well. However, what makes our time distinctive from the times of antiquity, for instance, is the shift to global-scale problems concerning natural environments. One of the most prominent scientific debates highlighting this development is concerned with 'the geology of mankind' (Crutzen, 2002).

At the very beginning of this millennium Paul Crutzen and Eugene Stoermer (2000) proposed that the present geological epoch should be re-termed the Anthropocene due to humanity's vast and all-round impact on the biosphere. Because of this development humanity has become a dominating geological force on Earth.

Unmistakably, humanity's growing power and influence on the Earth's ecosystems, especially since the Industrial Revolution, is a complex and manifold phenomenon. Nonetheless it can be crystallized into three interlinked issues. Magdoff and Foster (2011) point out that on one hand the amount of people on this planet has surged – humans inhabit more land. On the other hand they assert that humans have created technologies that cause far greater damage than ever before. Furthermore, the dominating economic structure, capitalism, Magdoff and Foster argue, neither knows nor accepts limits to its expansion (ibid.).

Notwithstanding capitalism's relatively long roots (see e.g. Wood, 2002; Moore, 2007, 2015; Arrighi, 2010) it has developed to its current industrial form mainly within the past two centuries. In short, capitalism is compelled, as is discussed in this chapter, to expand its scope in order to circulate and accumulate capital, in other words to reproduce itself (Marx, [1867] 1973; Wallerstein, 2003; Althusser, [1995] 2014). Because of this notion there are, indeed, compelling reasons to believe – based on both theoretical and empirical evidence – that there exists an absolute contradiction between capitalism and our precious planet, because the planet Earth is by definition finite (Daly, 1991; Foster, 2009).

The absolute contradiction arises from the fact that capitalism is – to its heart and soul – a grow or die structure. In principle the growth imperative of capitalism is simple. To be able to convert yesterday's profit into capital, the structure depends on an increasing availability and quantity of the means of production, that is, labour-force, energy, food, raw materials (see Harvey, 2014; Moore, 2015). The ever-increasing throughput of raw materials and continuing imperialism and industrialization, on the other hand, suggests that the environmental degradation becomes deeper and more extensive over time because of natural resource depletion and cumulating waste and pollution (Meadows, Meadows and Randers, 2002; Moore, 2015).

In this chapter I concentrate especially on capitalism in the Anthropocene, and outline some of the most prominent insights of the so-called eco-Marxist and neo-Marxist literature on capitalism and its treatment of its environmental surroundings. Meanwhile, as I outline some of the most prominent eco-Marxist critiques, I also touch on some of the overall structural logics of capital(ism). I begin with a brief general definition of capitalism, and then move on to discuss one of the most fundamental characteristics of capitalism, namely the process of capital accumulation. After this, I illustrate the absolute contradiction between capitalism and ecological sustainability in more detail, and complement the argument by criticizing the so-called green or sustainable capitalist doctrine. Finally, in the final section of this chapter, I put forward some complementary remarks on the on-going Anthropocene *or* Capitalocene debate (see e.g. Malm and Hornborg, 2014; Moore, 2015, chapter 7).

2 Characteristics of capitalism and beyond

Edward Said (1993, p. 407) said, 'no one today is purely one thing'. All cultures, socio-economic structures, national and regional contexts are hybrids; none of them are pure or single. Capitalism, especially in the general sense, has been historically remarkably flexible in adopting various forms (see e.g. Boltanski and Chiapello, 2005; Arrighi, 2010; Moore, 2015). Hence, the task of defining capitalism is difficult, and consequently it is no wonder there is a lack of consensus regarding what capitalism is ultimately made of (Graeber, 2014). Yet, in order to understand or to critically analyse capitalism, there arguably needs to be some kind of definition of it.

In any case, and although, there exists and has existed various versions and variations of capitalism around the world, ranging from liberal to authoritarian, I argue, for instance following the analysis of Karl Polanyi ([1944] 2009), that each contextual version of capitalism shares some fundamental similarities. These similarities imply that the basic institutions and practices that characterize capitalism are in place, however intertwined not only with the local relations of production but also with the natural and socio-cultural history.

Capitalism has quite a few identifying characteristics: the first is obviously the production of commodities for an external body (to 'market'). A second one is production of commodities in order to produce, most often private, surplus, which also entails the existence of an institution and abstraction called private property. A third characteristic of capitalism found everywhere around the planet is evidently wage-labour. Yet, these kind of general manifestations are seemingly not enough to really understand or even analyse capitalism. As Wallerstein claims (2013), an exercise seeking merely to identify the different characteristics of capitalism is insufficient if one is trying to understand the basic logics and structures. Wallerstein argues that many scholars focus on a single institution, for example the ones mentioned above, and that many social scientists claim that the most significant aspect of capitalism is the class struggle between capitalists (those who own the means of production) and wage-labourers (those who do not). While these are certainly some of the defining characteristics of historical capitalism (but not necessarily original or exceptional characteristics of a certain socio-economic structure), Wallerstein claims that many scholars seem to miss the most critical characteristic of it, which is the endless accumulation of capital, or in his own words (ibid., p. 11), 'the accumulation of capital in order to accumulate more capital'.

As the name suggests, in capitalism economic actors (such as companies, venture capitalists, investors, states or other economic organizations) organize economic activity through the fluid deployment of wealth – capital – by means of investments in different kinds of surplus-making operations (Harvey, 2014). For these operations, finance, including debt and its associated interest, but also various tradable financial instruments are 'crucial to the liquidity and mobility of capital as well as to expansion and spreading costs over time' (Calhoun, 2013, p. 136). However, as Harvey (2014) argues, capital is not just a *thing* but also a *process* in which capital is constantly circulated or spent in search of more capital by capital accumulators who own the means of production, that is, the capitalists (see also Harvey, 2016, e.g. chapter 2). Harvey (2014, p. 41) explains this in more detail in the following:

> Capitalists . . . take on many different personae. Finance capitalists look to make money by lending to others in return for interest. Merchant capitalists buy cheap and sell dear. Landlords collect rent because the land and properties they own are scarce resources. Rentiers make money from royalties and intellectual property rights. Asset traders swap titles (to stocks and shares for example), debts and contracts (including insurance) for profit. Even the state can act like a capitalist, as, for example, when it uses tax revenues to invest in infrastructures that stimulate growth and generate even more tax revenues.
>
> But the form of capital circulation that has come to dominate from the mid-eighteenth century onwards is that of industrial or production capital. In this case the capitalist starts the day with a certain amount of money. And, having selected a technology and organizational form, goes into the market place and buys the requisite amounts of labour power and means of production (raw material, physical plant, intermediate products, machinery, energy and the like). The labour power is combined with the means of production through an active labour process conducted under the supervision

of the capitalist. The result is a commodity that is sold by its owner, the capitalist, in the market place for a profit.

Following the line of argumentation, and to move beyond mere characteristics, I argue that capitalism is, as Harvey (2014, p. 6-7) puts it, a social formation (socio-economic structure) 'in which processes of capital circulation and accumulation are hegemonic and dominant in providing and shaping the material, social and intellectual bases for social life.' Furthermore, and in this respect, capitalism is a historical formation (a historical socio-economic structure), supported by a set of power networks, such as the ideological, economic, military and political (Wallerstein, 2003; Mann, 2013). In this sense, capitalism as a historical socio-economic structure is a hierarchical and unequally integrated material organization, embedded in nature (Moore, 2015), in which economic actors are crucially dependent on the conditions provided by political power (Calhoun, 2013), that is, to list only a few examples, nation states, various state institutions and transnational organizations (Robinson, 2014; see also Althusser, [1995] 2014).

Thus, to summarize (see Table 4.1 below) and elaborate still further, capitalism is a historical socio-economic structure in constant and endless pursuit of accumulation of capital. A key characteristic of especially twentieth and twenty-first-century capitalism is advanced (material and 'immaterial') commodity production within a competitive capitalist market economy. Another key characteristic of capitalism is, and has been, a class structure in which a group of individuals – capitalists – own the means of production, and appropriate economic surplus value from the use of raw materials and labour-power (conducted by the wage-labouring class and machines), or apply other means to extract surpluses (for example from buying cheap and selling dear, rents, fees, interest or from financial investments). In this structure, the aim of a single capitalist or a single corporation (or other economic actors, such as states) is in principle to accumulate capital from various 'economic' activities and then invest part of the profit back in the production in order to expand production, enhance productivity and increase market share, or find other profitable

Table 4.1 Capitalism summarized.

Characteristics	*Institutions*	*Subjects*	*Objects*
production of commodities	nation states	capitalists	ecosystems
surplus creation	transnational organizations	wage-labourers	human labour
class society	private property	other agents of capital	non-human labour
capital accumulation	limited liability company	self-employers	raw materials
markets and competition	financial apparatus	non-profits	technology

ways to reinvest capital (e.g. infrastructure or education) in order to be able to accumulate more capital in the future and so on and so forth.

Some of the key institutions supporting the reproduction of the capitalist historical socio-economic structure are nation states and their repressive (military, police, judiciary) and ideological (education, church, media) institutions (Althusser, [1995] 2014), and various international organizations (such as Organisation for Economic Co-operation and Development (OECD), World Trade Organization (WTO), European Union (EU), United Nations (UN)) (Robinson, 2014), but also many abstractions and social constructions that are usually protected by law (Poulantzas, 2000), including private property and the joint-stock company (or limited liability company). The history of capitalism has also shown that a particular alliance of class interests has come together to form a so-called hegemonic historic bloc or a dominant class (Thomas, 2009) that seeks to secure and reproduce its dominant position in controlling the means of production and influencing societal conditions in its favour (Robinson, 2014).

To be sure the boundaries of capitalism and 'not capitalism' are seldom as subtle as presented here. This is why it is also important to try to define what is not capitalism in more detail. While it is true that many individuals, organizations or institutions do not partake directly in capitalist accumulation processes, that is, do not directly make efforts to accumulate capital, they do take part in the circulation of capital by buying commodities, paying rents, spending the salaries they have got from working in a university or by donating to a non-profit organization campaigning for human rights. That is to say that from the point of view of capitalism, it does matter where one spends one's euros, dollars or yuans as long as one keeps on spending them and thus keeps capital circulating, for instance through participating in consumption, investment and debt within the capitalist structure. Taking this into consideration, the 'sphere of capitalism' has to be framed accordingly. Thus, I suggest here that all actions, practices and structures beyond the scope of capitalist accumulation processes and circulation of capital can be considered not capitalist. On the other hand, all the actions, practices and structures that do partake in accumulation of capital and circulation of capital one way or another are to be considered capitalist – disregarding their motivations, or whether they take part in capitalist accumulation and circulation processes directly, indirectly, intentionally or unintentionally.

3 The process of capital accumulation

The word capitalism is quite obviously derived from capital. For Marx ([1867] 1973) and many others, capital is the key element in, but also to understanding, capitalism. Capital is accumulated wealth, but when it is analysed in a specific historical context it has more specific definition. Wallerstein (2003, pp. 13–14) explains:

> It is not just the stock of consumable goods, machinery, or authorized claims, or material things in the form of money. . . in this historical system capital

> came to be used (invested) in a very special way. It came to be used with the primary objective or intent of self-expansion. In this system, past accumulations were 'capital' only to the extent they were used to accumulate more of the same . . . it was this relentless and curiously self-regarding goal of the holder of capital, the accumulation of still more capital, and the relations this holder of capital had therefore to establish with other persons in order to achieve this goal, which we denominate as capitalist.

But why does a single capitalist drive towards further accumulation and expansion rather than using the profits for one's personal pleasure? One answer to this question is the so-called 'coercive law of competition' and how it plays a pivotal role in capitalism (Harvey, 2011). If a capitalist (or an economic organization within capitalism) decides for some reason or another not to invest in expansion, or not to come up with new products and services, or not to improve productivity, and one of his rivals does, the one who decided not to, is likely to be driven out of business (ibid.). Thus, capitalists and all the other economic actors (including wage-labourers, but also nation states) within the capitalist socio-economic structure are practically forced to follow suit, that is, to stimulate the economy, to work hard, to maximize profits and market share, if they want to stay and succeed in the competition. This of course means that the requirements of competition and profit-maximization are some of the fundamental rules of life in the capitalist socio-economic structure.

Moreover, what is true of a single capitalist is also true at a more systemic level. Capital accumulation has to continue in an expansive manner or the reproduction of capitalism is in danger. Consequently, as Harvey (2014, p. 222) claims 'capital is always about growth and it necessarily grows at compound rate'. Similarly, Magdoff and Foster (2011, p. 42) state that no-growth capitalism does not exist, or is not desirable, because when capital accumulation ceases, or even slows down, a crisis ensues.

One of the significant reasons for this is a thing called 'return on investment'. David Graeber (2014, p. 332) writes in *Debt: The First 5000 Years* that 'what is "interest"' but the demand that that money never ceases to grow?' The same is true, Graeber continues, for investments, which are in principle capital placed in the continual pursuit of profit. Thus, perhaps it goes without saying that money, finance and banking are and always have been at the heart of the functioning of capitalism, even before the Industrial Revolution (see Graeber, 2014). Credit, interest and growth are deeply intertwined in capitalism. For example, when a finance capitalist lends capital to states, companies or individuals, he or she expects a return for his or her investment to compensate the risk he or she is taking by lending the money capital (Harvey, 2011). This means that someone who has taken the loan in order to build a factory, buy bonds or a wedding ring, for instance, has to pay back more money (interest) than he or she borrowed from the creditor. Systemically this indicates that for most people to be able to pay their debt back and not to default, there has to be growth in the overall economy. Of course, this means that capital has to circulate, practically, endlessly, which on the other hand suggests a never-ending cycle of consumption, new loans, new investments and a constantly expanding requirement for a supply of and demand for goods. On top of all this, transactions, circulation and accumulation need to happen in an accelerating fashion because of interest of interest (or growth of growth) (see Harvey, 2014).

To be sure, it is important to also mention that credit and interest alone do not necessarily bring about economic growth, not to mention capitalism (Herrmann, [2013] 2015). The same goes for money, the market economy and even profit orientation in production. None of these arrangements, historically, have given way to economic growth in the same way that they have done in the era of capitalism. Consequently, it is and was only when credit, interest, money and profit orientation were coupled with other capitalist relationships of production, namely, market competition and profit maximization, that the era of economic growth began, as did the era of capital accumulation through productivity gains and capital investment (ibid.).

To conclude, in capitalism competition of market shares makes sure that economic actors are constantly trying to outdo their competitors and to come up with the means to expand their production. In other words, economic actors are basically forced, whether they like it or not, to submit to the logic of capital and capital accumulation within the capitalist socio-economic structure. This means, in short, taking loans and investing some of their profits to expand production, and improving productivity to produce surpluses in order to accumulate capital to be able to succeed in the market competition but also to be able pay their debts back (the so-called treadmill of accumulation, see Foster, York and Clark, 2010).

4 The absolute contradiction between capitalism and ecological sustainability

Ecological economist Herman Daly is known for emphasizing what he calls the 'impossibility theorem' by which he means the paradox between unlimited economic growth and a finite ecosystem (see e.g. Daly, 1991). Foster (2009, p. 15) has introduced an important extension or variation to Daly's impossibility theorem:

> Capitalism as a world economy, divided into classes and driven by competition, embodies a logic that accepts no boundaries on its expansion and its exploitation of its environment. The earth as a planet, in contrast, is by definition limited. This is an absolute contradiction from which there is no earthly escape.

As already discussed, capitalism is based on its internal logic and compelled to expand its scope in order to be able to circulate and accumulate capital. It is quite obvious that this generates both growth and an imperative to grow the economy, limitlessly and indefinitely, which inevitably will be in conflict with the planet and its limited natural resources (see Foster, 2009; Jackson, 2009; Hornborg,

2014). The authors of *The Limits to Growth* realized this over 40 years ago. Meadows et al., wrote (1972, p. 46) that:

> Much of each year's output is consumable goods, such as textiles, automobiles, and houses, that leave the industrial system. But some fraction of the production is more capital – looms, steel mills, lathes – which is an investment to increase the capital stock. Here we have another feedback loop (in addition to population growth). More capital creates more output, some variable fraction of the output is investment, and more investment means more capital. The new, larger capital stock generates more output, and so on.

After decades of exponential industrial growth, it has been noted that every major ecosystem on the Earth is in decline (Foster, 2009). Jackson (2009) states that it is commonly known that about 60 per cent of the world's ecosystem services have been degraded or over-used since the mid-twentieth century. Furthermore, it is a well known and established fact that global and local ecosystems are undergoing drastic changes in terms of increasing temperatures and decreasing biodiversity because of extensive human activities (Meadows et al., 1972, 2002; IPCC, 2014). Again, a widely acknowledged and accepted scientific consensus states that organized human practices are over-exploiting the Earth's resources and ecosystems pushing them outside safe boundaries with catastrophic consequences (Barnosky et al., 2012; Steffen et al., 2015).

Throughout the history of capitalism, capital accumulation has been achieved through the appropriation of the exploitation of human and non-human labour (Moore, 2015). Such appropriation, as Moore (ibid.) explains, has required the availability of *cheap* resources, but also economically inexpensive ways to dump waste. The availability of cheap resources and cheap waste disposal does not by itself produce capital as 'value', but the conditions that make value creation in capitalism possible through enhancements in labour productivity. Hence, the appropriation of unpaid work that the rising rate of capital accumulation depends upon has been globally derived mainly from the exploitation of labour-power, food production, fossil energy and other raw materials (ibid.).

Furthermore, capitalism depends not only on an ever-increasing amount of raw materials and human labour, but especially on the willingness and compliance of citizens in different societies to take part in the 'externalization of costs of production' processes. In fact, it could be argued that in capitalism profitability depends on externalizing the costs of its activities whether they are human, ecological or financial (Calhoun, 2013). As William Kapp (1971, p. 231) has written:

> Capitalism must be regarded as an economy of unpaid costs, 'unpaid' in so far as a substantial proportion of the actual costs of production remain unaccounted for in entrepreneurial outlays; instead they are shifted to, and ultimately borne by, third persons or by the community as a whole.

Moore (2015) explains that there are good reasons why capitalists do not like to 'pay their bills'. This is because to be able to fully commodify the reproduction of labour-power or commodify the use of 'nature's free gifts' would quite frankly mean that the costs of labour-power and raw materials would skyrocket, and thus capital accumulation – as it is known today – would probably become impossible.

To be sure, the ecological crisis is both grand in its scale and complex to its very core, and cannot be reduced simply to issues like economic growth (Foster, 2009). At the global level the ecological crisis is closely related to the political and power divisions within capitalism, resulting from the fact that the increasingly global world economy is divided into numerous nation states and transnational power blocs (Robinson, 2014). That being the case, the world economy is in practice hierarchically split into different stages and places of centre and periphery, where nations, nation states and various agents of transnational capital hold different positions in the international division of labour, and play different roles of dominance, oppression and dependency (Foster, 2009; Hornborg, 2014).

In addition, addressing the prevailing ecological crisis is made harder, as Calhoun (2013, p. 152) argues, because of the ways in which 'nature' has come to be understood in capitalism or from the perspective of capital:

> It [nature] has long been seen, especially but not only in the West, as the other human society, often an obstacle to be overcome – thus obscuring the extent to which we too are natural beings and live only as a part of nature. More specific to the rise and flourishing of capitalism has been the construction of "nature" as resources. For capitalism, nature has existed to be used, exploited.

Although, for example, mainstream economics tends to portray economy and nature as separate entities (e.g. Hiedenpää, 2012), a more accurate way to describe the connection is to insist that natural history and human history are and always have been inseparable. This realization is backed up by mounting evidence; each and every historical record of each and every economic structure and civilization witnesses that human societies have always been completely dependent on and embedded in their ecological foundation (Multanen, 2001). This is, of course, because humans are part of nature (Foster, 2000). Everything on this planet is interconnected; there are no separate entities (ibid.). Thus, instead of seeing the reality being produced by two separate but interacting entities, society and nature, a more suitable and accurate way of looking at the history of modernity is to see it as being co-produced throughout history. Consequently, the ecological crisis from this perspective is not between capitalism *and* nature, but capitalism-*in*-nature (Moore, 2015). Accordingly, the fundamental problem is that capitalism-*in*-nature operates with paradoxical logic to its ontological reality, that is, in capitalism nature becomes treated as something external to it, and not only as a limitless external entity, but as an object to overcome and as a resource (or a free gift) to be exploited to foster endless accumulation (ibid.).

5 Sustainable capitalism?

Notwithstanding capitalism's antagonistic relations towards its environments, the conventional response to the incompatibility claims of capitalism and planetary ecosystems is to appeal to the 'green economy' or to 'sustainable growth', or, for the sake argument in this chapter, to 'sustainable capitalism'. In this case the idea of 'decoupling' is of the essence. A typical (ecological modernization) argument goes somewhat as follows: as the production processes are reconfigured and goods and services redesigned, economic output becomes less dependent on material throughput (Jackson, 2009). As Jackson (ibid., p. 68) writes, it is vital in this case to distinguish between 'relative' and 'absolute' decoupling:

> Put very simply, relative decoupling is about doing more with less: more economic activity with less environmental damage; more goods and services with fewer resource inputs and fewer emissions. Decoupling is about doing things more efficiently. And since efficiency is one of the things that modern economies are good at, decoupling has a familiar logic and a clear appeal as a solution to the dilemma of growth.

It is important to note that relative decoupling does not mean that there is a decline in the material throughput in absolute terms. Indeed, the proponents of sustainable capitalism seem often to ignore the fact that there is next to no empirical evidence of absolute decoupling so far, especially at the global level – meaning that while economies grow their material throughputs decline (Jackson, 2009). This statement is backed up by an important study by Wiedmann et al., (2015). Authors of this study argue that although some metrics of resource productivity used by governments suggest that a relative decoupling (or even absolute decoupling in some cases) has occurred, their findings based on material footprint (MF) calculations of nations strongly contradict these claims. On the contrary, Wiedmann et al., (ibid.) state that achievements in decoupling, especially in advanced economies, are smaller than reported or even non-existent. Wiedmann et al., (ibid., p. 6271) conclude that:

> By calculating raw material equivalents of international trade, we demonstrate that countries' use of nondomestic resources is, on average, about threefold larger than the physical quantity of traded goods. As wealth grows, countries tend to reduce their domestic portion of materials extraction through international trade, whereas the overall mass of material consumption generally increases. With every 10% increase in gross domestic product, the average national MF increases by 6%.

According to the study, even the claimed relative decoupling has been based – it seems – on 'false accounting'. By measuring only goods that move around, from one nation to another, rather than measuring the total amount of raw materials needed to produce those goods, the previous calculations have greatly underestimated the total use of resources, especially in affluent nations. While an

Organization for Economic Cooperation and Development (OECD) report (2011), for instance, claims that G8 countries halved their resource intensity between 1980 and 2008, Wiedmann et al., (2015, p. 6273) argue based on their metrics that 'the MF has kept pace with increases in GDP and no improvements in resource productivity at all are observed when measured with GDP/MF'.

On the other hand, one is left to wonder, why is it that despite the wide-ranging efforts to tackle environmental problems the ecological crisis is only getting worse? One decisive reason for this is, again, the logic of capital accumulation and circulation, along with all the other imperatives of capitalism. As Foster (2009, p. 15) explains:

> Yet, while it is true that energy and resource-use efficiency have continually risen along with the advance of production, the overall result has not been to reduce the consumption of energy and materials. This is because efficiency gains under a capitalist economy result in further accumulation and economic expansion, with the increase in scale typically overwhelming gains in efficiency (a phenomenon known as the 'Jevons Paradox'). Moreover, what appear to be environmental gains are often the result of simply shifting the problems elsewhere – from rich to poor regions and countries. Ecological modernization has thus not prevented the rapid overall rise in ecological destruction.

Another argument presented in favour of sustainable capitalism is often linked to 'technological progression'. It is often claimed that through technological advancements human societies will reach a stage of development where technology is clean and emission free, thus creating conditions for sustainable growth. However, where technology is concerned, the instruments or technics (see Mumford, 1967, 1970) and the context (industrial capitalism, for instance) where technology is utilized are seldom neutral (see also Hornborg, 2014). On this point, Moore (2015) argues that capitalist *technics* (understood as specific crystallization of tools, nature and power) seek to mobilize and to appropriate the 'forces of nature' to produce surplus value. Calhoun (2013) states that the new (industrial) organization of social life has in fact multiplied demands for energy that have been met primarily by carbon but also by nuclear and other forms of energy. Furthermore the technologies themselves have increased the demand for energy and a range of minerals (ibid.), which ultimately are non-renewable by their very nature.

Likewise, Harvey (2014) argues that the needs of capital accumulation have systematically shortened the turnover time and life cycle of consumer goods by producing commodities that have to be replaced more often than before. In fact it seems that the primary purpose of 'modernizing' technology is not to solve ecological problems but to keep the growth economy rolling (Foster, 2009) or, even more grimly put, to profit from ecological problems. This is not to say that genuine attempts to solve ecological problems by developing technological solutions do not exist, but rather to claim that when new technologies enter the markets they are immediately undermined by competition and accumulation (see Gould, Pellow and Schnaiberg, 2008).

In addition, it is important to note that technological solutions are certainly not created out of thin air, but rely fundamentally on labour and natural resources. Hence, and again given the unlimited and endless accumulation aspiration of capitalism, the new technologies that are supposed to overcome the contradictions between capitalism and ecological sustainability inevitably run up against the challenge of transcending the very laws of physics. What is often neglected in this respect is the notion that in capitalism, savings in one place are used to promote new capital formation and the proliferation of commodities elsewhere, demanding ever greater resources (Foster et al., 2010). In the words of Georgescu-Roegen ([1971] 1999, p. 19):

> Had economics recognized the entropic nature of the economic process, it might have been able to warn its co-workers for the betterment of mankind – the technological sciences – that 'bigger and better' washing machines, automobiles, and superjets must lead to 'bigger' and 'better' pollution.

Apart from transcending the laws of physics, a further bottleneck to unlimited growth is, as Moore (2015) states, the decline of overall ecological surplus over time in capitalism. This means that the mass of accumulated capital tends to rise faster than the appropriation of economic value from labour-force and natural resources. Similarly, ecological surplus declines over time because the reproduction time of capital tends to exceed the reproduction time of the rest of nature (ibid.). The final, and in many ways most pressing, bottleneck of growth is due to the overall industrial production and cumulating waste (ibid.). Overall industrial production has meant historically that the share of unpaid work and energy tends to fall because the accumulation of capital becomes more wasteful over time. In other words, capitalism produces environments that are increasingly hostile to further accumulation and its environment in the long run (ibid.).

It is of course easy to get lost in the general declarations and ideologies of 'sustainable capitalism' or 'sustainable growth'. While it is true that some efficiency gains have been reached locally, it is profoundly problematic to argue that the dilemma of growth can be remedied by producing more (Wiedmann et al., 2015; see also Hornborg, 2013) and by continuing the accumulation of capital in an expansive manner (Foster, 2009; Moore, 2015). As the latest United Nations Environment Programme (UNEP) (2011) report in this regard testifies the growing production of goods and services has led not only to growing atmospheric emissions, but also growing pressure on land and water as they are utilized in the production process. The report (ibid., pp. 17–18) also states that 'during the course of the 20th century, average resource use per capita merely doubled', while 'the global annual material extraction increased . . . by a factor of eight'.

6 Anthropocene and Capitalocene

> Anthropocene . . . means 'New Human'. It represents a new geological epoch in which humanity has become the main driver of rapid changes in the earth system.
>
> (Foster et al., 2010, p. 14)

So far, I have defined capitalism as a historical socio-economic structure in constant and endless pursuit of the accumulation of capital. I have also suggested that there is an absolute contradiction between capitalism and the finite planet and problematized 'sustainable capitalism' from an ecological standpoint. In addition to these statements, there is one final point I wish to make regarding the ongoing *Anthropocene* or *Capitalocene* debate also covered in this book (see also Malm and Hornborg, 2014; Moore, 2015).

From my perspective, the main scientific dispute seems to revolve around the *intra*-species or *inter*-species question. In another words, the question is supposedly whether the human race as 'an undifferentiated whole' (Moore, 2015, p. 170) has produced the Anthropocene, or whether the present geological epoch has been mostly produced by a small group of humans, and thus a more suitable way to characterize it would be, for instance, Capitalocene. Personally, I find both of these arguments plausible. This is primarily because I perceive Capitalocene as a subcategory to Anthropocene. With this argument I do not wish to claim that a hierarchy should exist between natural sciences and social sciences, but rather argue that there exists a hierarchy between humans and the biosphere, for instance. This is because the biosphere does not require humans to prosper, but humans certainly do need a liveable habitat to flourish (for the substitutability and complementarity of human and natural capital see e.g. Daly, 1979, 1996; Heikkurinen et al., 2016).

Moreover, from an *inter*-species perspective (natural science) it is clear that *human beings* as a species have produced the modern ecological crisis and the changes in the Earth system, such as climate change, desertification and acidification of oceans. They have not been caused by insects, birds, fish or other mammals. Thus, the Anthropocene as a term is justifiable, as it casts the blame to one single species in contrast to all others, although it does not examine which humans in particular are culpable for this development. In this sense, it is evident that capitalism, historically, was a small-time operation at first and then expanded gradually to become a structure of global scale (see e.g. Moore, 2015; Malm, 2016). Furthermore, it is also true that even in our day the capitalist structure remains ever polarized between humans in terms of resource consumption (Malm and Hornborg, 2014) and economic equality (Piketty, [2013] 2014; Oxfam, 2016). Hence, from this perspective it is clear that not *all* humans have been responsible for producing the modern ecological crisis, and being so Capitalocene seems justifiable as a term to explain this historical development.

Nonetheless, there is one important aspect regarding this development to be considered. Historically, as the 'sphere of capital' has expanded and become more global especially after the Second World War, more humans have become parts of the capitalist structure and involved in the production process. Consequently, and in spite of drastic inequalities in resource consumption, such as in the use of fossil fuels (Malm and Hornborg, 2014), most human beings in the twenty-first century are arguably part of the capitalist exchange and relations of production. Therefore, in this sense, most humans are indeed culpable of producing the on-going ecological crisis – or at least they have and are participating in it – by being part of the circulation and accumulation of capital processes.

There are two conclusions to be made regarding this notion: first, Anthropocene as a term gains more strength as the capitalist world economy keeps on expanding, because more and more humans are taking part in ecologically unsustainable practices. This is also a perspective that perhaps should be considered in the debate concerned with 'when did the Anthropocene begin?' question. Second, although the Capitalocene argument seems justifiable from an *intra*-species perspective, it generally seems to overlook the *inter*-species level of analysis, and thus the natural scientific perspective on inter-species relations.

7 Conclusion

It seems evident that capitalism, with its compulsion for endless growth and expansion, constitutes the hard core of the current human-caused ecological crisis. The tragedy of capitalism-in-nature, in this respect, in the past and in the present is and has seemingly been the fact that the capitalist economic structure cannot change the way it treats its environment. Therefore, to challenge the logic of capital means in principle that one has to challenge the whole capitalist structure, which is indeed, as David Harvey (2014, p. 252) claims, 'why the environmental movement, when it goes beyond a merely cosmetic or ameliorative politics, must become anti-capital'.

In this respect, while it certainly is important to write PhDs, articles and books about these issues or to teach, give talks and take part in research conferences, ultimately these actions change nothing without organized and planned collective 'anti-capitalist' actions and movements. Accordingly, the issue is to find alternative ways beyond (industrial) capitalism, and to replace it with fundamentally different ways of being that consider both inter- and intra-species questions to peaceful coexistence on planet Earth.

Bibliography

Althusser, L. ([1995] 2014) *On the Reproduction of Capitalism: Ideology and Ideological State Apparatuses.* Trans. Goshgarian, G. M. London: Verso Books.

Arrighi, G. (2010) *The Long Twentieth Century: Money, Power and the Origins of Our Times.* London: Verso.

Barnosky, A. D., Hadly, E. A., Bascompte, J., Berlow, E. L., Brown, J. H., Fortelius, M., Getz, W. M., Harte, J., Hastings, A., Marquet, P. A., Martinez, N. D., Mooers, A., Roopnarine, P., Vermeij, G., Williams, J. W., Gillespie, R., Kitzes, J., Marshall, C., Matzke, N., Mindell, D. P., Revilla, E. & Smith, A. B. (2012) Approaching a state-shift in the biosphere. *Nature.* 486, 52–58.

Boltanski, L. & Chiapello E. (2005) *The New Spirit of Capitalism.* London: Verso.

Calhoun, C. (2013) What threatens capitalism now? In: Wallerstein I., Collins, R., Mann, M., Derluguian, G. & Calhoun C. (eds) *Does Capitalism Have a Future?* New York: Oxford University Press.

Crutzen, P. J. (2002) Geology of mankind. *Nature.* 415, 23.

Crutzen, P. J. & Stoermer, E. F. (2000) The Anthropocene. *Global Change Newsletter.* 41, 17–18.

Daly, H. E. (1979) Entropy, growth and the political economy of scarcity. In: Smith, V. K. (ed.) *Scarcity and Growth Reconsidered*. Baltimore, MA: Johns Hopkins University Press.

Daly, H. E. (1991) *Steady-State Economics*. Second edition. Washington, DC: Island Press.

Daly, H. E. (1996) *Beyond Growth*. Boston: Beacon Press.

Diamond, J. (2005) *Collapse: How Societies Choose to Fail or Succeed*. New York: Viking Press.

Foster, J. B. (2000) *Marx's Ecology: Materialism and Nature*. New York: Monthly Review Press.

Foster, J. B. (2009) *Ecological Revolution – Making Peace with the Planet*. New York: Monthly Review Press.

Foster, J., York, R. & Clark B. (2010) *The Ecological Rift: Capitalism's War on Earth*. New York: Monthly Review Press.

Georgescu-Roegen, N. ([1971] 1999) *The Entropy Law and the Economic Process*. Cambridge, MA: Harvard University Press.

Gould, K. A., Pellow, D. N. & Schnaiberg A. (2008) *Treadmill of Production: Injustice and Unsustainability in the Global Economy*. London and New York: Routledge.

Harvey, D. (2011) *The Enigma of Capital and the Crises of Capitalism*. New York: Oxford University Press.

Harvey, D. (2014) *Seventeen Contradictions and the End of Capitalism*. New York: Oxford University Press.

Harvey, D. (2016) *The Ways of the World*. New York: Oxford University Press.

Heikkurinen, P., Rinkinen, J., Järvensivu, T., Wilén, K. & Ruuska, T. (2016) Organising in the Anthropocene: An ontological outline for ecocentric theorising. *Journal of Cleaner Production*. 113, 705–714.

Herrmann, U. ([2013] 2015) *Pääoman voitto – Kasvun, rahan ja kriisien historia*. Trans. Janatuinen, M. Helsinki: Into Kustannus.

Hiedenpää, J. (2012) Taloustiede. In: Lummaa, K. (ed.) *Monitieteellinen ympäristötutkimus*. Helsinki: Gaudeamus.

Hornborg, A. (2013) *Global Ecology and Unequal Exchange: Fetishism in a Zero-Sum World*. London: Routledge.

Hornborg, A. (2014) Ecological economics, Marxism, and technological progress: Some explorations of the conceptual foundations of theories of ecologically unequal exchange. *Ecological Economics*. 105, 11–18.

IPCC (2014) *5th Assessment Report. Climate change 2014: Impacts, Adaption, and Vulnerability*. Working Group II. Geneva: Intergovernmental Panel on Climate Change.

Jackson, T. (2009) *Properity without Growth: Economics for a Finite Planet*. London: Earthscan.

Kapp, W. (1971) *The Social Costs of Private Enterprise*. Cambridge, MA: Harvard University Press.

Magdoff, F. & Foster J. B. (2011) *What Every Environmentalist Needs to Know about Capitalism*. New York: Monthly Review Press.

Malm, A. (2016) *Fossil Capital: The Rise of Steam Power and the Roots of Global Warming*. New York: Verso.

Malm, A. & Hornborg, A. (2014) The geology of mankind? A critique of the Anthropocene narrative. *The Anthropocene Review*. 20, 1–8.

Mann, M. (2013) The end may be nigh. In: Wallerstein I., Collins, R., Mann, M., Derluguian, G. & Calhoun C. (eds) *Does Capitalism Have a Future?* New York: Oxford University Press.

Marx, K. ([1867] 1973) *Capital: A Critique of Political Economy, Volume 1: The Process of Capitalist Production*. Trans. Moore, S. & Aveling, E. New York: International Publishers.

Meadows, D., Meadows, D., Randers, J. & Behrens, W. (1972) *The Limits to Growth*. New York: New American Library.

Meadows, D., Meadows, D. & Randers, J. (2002) *The Limits to Growth: The 30-Year Update*. White River Junction, VT: Chelsea Green Publishing.

Moore, J. W. (2007) *Ecology and the Rise of Capitalism*. Doctoral Dissertation. Berkeley: University of California.

Moore, J. W. (2015) *Capitalism in the Web of Life. Ecology and the Accumulation of Capital*. New York: Verso.

Multanen, P. (2001) Kehitysmaiden asema osana ekologista kriisiä – Siirtomaakysymys Marxilla ja kehitysmaiden asema nykykapitalismissa. In: Heiskanen, J. (ed.) *Marx ja ekologia*. Helsinki: Kustannusyhtiö TA-Tieto Oy & Demokraattinen sivistysliitto.

Mumford, L. (1967) *The Myth of the Machine: Technics and Human Development*. New York: Harvest/HBJ Publishers.

Mumford, L. (1970) *The Myth of the Machine: The Pentagon of Power*. New York: Harvest/HBJ Publishers.

OECD (Organization for Economic Cooperation and Development) (2011) *Resource Productivity in the G8 and the OECD*. A Report in the Framework of the Kobe 3R Action Plan. Available from: www.oecd.org/env/waste/47944428.pdf (accessed 9 March 2016).

Oxfam (2016) An economy for the 1%. How privilege and power in the economy drive extreme inequality and how this can be stopped. Available from: www.oxfam.org/sites/www.oxfam.org/files/file_attachments/bp210-economy-one-percent-tax-havens-180116-en_0.pdf (accessed 9 March 2016).

Piketty, T. ([2013] 2014) *Capital in the Twenty-first Century*. Trans. Goldhammer, A. Cambridge, MA: The Belknap Press.

Polanyi, K. ([1944] 2009) *Suuri Murros*. Trans. Vilokkinen, N. Tampere, Finland: Vastapaino.

Poulantzas, N. (2000) *State, Power, Socialism*. London: Verso.

Robinson, W. I. (2014) *Global Capitalism and the Crisis of Humanity*. New York: Cambridge University Press.

Said, E. (1993) *Culture and Imperialism*. London: Vintage.

Steffen, W., Richardson, K., Rockström, J., Cornell, S. E., Fetzer, I., Bennett, E. M., Biggs, R., Carpenter, S. R., de Vries, W., de Wit, C. A., Folke, C., Gerten, D., Heinke, J., Mace, G. M., Persson, L. M., Ramanathan, V., Reyers, B. & Sörlin, S. (2015) Planetary boundaries: Guiding human development on a changing planet. *Science*. 347, 1259855.

Tainter, J. A. (2015) *The Collapse of Complex Societies*. Cambridge: Cambridge University Press.

Thomas, P. D. (2009) *The Gramscian Moment: Philosophy, Hegemony and Marxism*. Leiden and Boston: Brill.

UNEP (United Nations Environment Programme) (2011). *Decoupling Natural Resource Use and Environmental Impacts from Economic Growth*. A report of the working group on decoupling to the International Resource Panel. Available from: www.unep.org/resourcepanel/Portals/24102/PDFs/DecouplingENGSummary.pdf (accessed 9 March 2016).

Wallerstein, I. (2003) *Historical Capitalism and Capitalist Civilization*. London: Verso.

Wallerstein, I. (2013) Structural crisis, or why capitalists may no longer find capitalism rewarding. In: Wallerstein I., Collins, R., Mann, M., Derluguian, G. & Calhoun C. (eds) *Does Capitalism Have a Future?* New York: Oxford University Press.

Wiedmann, T., Schandl, H., Lenzen, M., Moran, D., Suh, S., West, J. & Kanemoto, K. (2015) The material footprint of nations. *PNAS*. 112, 6271–6276.

Wood, E. M. (2002) *The Origin of Capitalism. A Longer View*. London: Verso.

5 Managing the environment

Neoliberal governmentality in the Anthropocene

Jessica C. Lawrence

1 Introduction

The notion of the 'Anthropocene' is relatively new, having been coined only 15 years ago by Nobel Laureate Paul Crutzen and Eugene Stoermer (Crutzen and Stoermer, 2000). In the short time since its introduction, however, the Anthropocene has quickly become a recognizable – even trendy – term across the natural and social sciences. Scholars from geography to climatology, from history to sociology have begun to embrace the idea that human intervention has significantly altered Earth systems (in the form of climate change, loss of biodiversity, desertification and so on), to the point that we have entered into a 'human-dominated . . . geological epoch' (Crutzen 2002, p. 23). Though there remains debate about the precise point at which this modern era began, the Anthropocene terminology makes clear that today we live in a world where human activity is the most important factor influencing Earth systems. As such, it also suggests that there is a need for human individuals and societies to shift our understandings of how we relate to, and are responsible for, our collective ecological future.

Part of the Anthropocene's conceptual weight stems from the challenge it poses to the modernist idea that there is a firm conceptual boundary between nature/environment/non-human and culture/constructed/human (see contributions in Hamilton, Bonneuil and Gemenne, 2015). Instead, the Anthropocene suggests that we view the world in terms of 'global systems', which human beings are both part of and the biggest influence on. This alternative understanding of the relationship between the 'human' and 'natural' worlds has brought with it a renewed interest in investigating the ecological impacts of human economic, social and technological systems, as well as in the project of attempting to imagine different systems, outcomes and ecologies, and to encourage human societies to take responsibility for their impact on Earth systems (see e.g. Clark, 2015; Purdy, 2015; Wark, 2015). These new imaginaries are of particular interest to social scientists, who are offered a new paradigm for understanding the relationship between human economic, social, cultural and political institutions and the transformation of the physical environment. Indeed, it is in this way that many of the authors in this volume seek to contribute.

Despite its increasing popularity, however, the notion of the Anthropocene has yet to make its way into the minds of most lawyers, legal bureaucracies and legal scholars. While some initial academic work has begun, 'law and the Anthropocene' remains very much a genre in its infancy, with only a limited number of publications on the subject (for some exceptions, see Fauchald, Hunter and Wang, 2014). Few lawyers or policymakers refer to the Anthropocene, and even fewer mentions can be found in legislative texts or court documents. The language of the Anthropocene has not yet, it seems, become the language of government: the language of law. So what happens when the idea of the Anthropocene does begin to enter the law? This is the discussion that this chapter would like to begin.[1]

The argument that this brief contribution will make is that given current trends in environmental regulation, it is likely that the legal and governmental response to the Anthropocene will be a neoliberal one. That is to say, that as law and government take up the idea that the human/non-human divide has broken down, and that it is therefore necessary to take Earth systems into account in governing, the likely response will be aimed at expanding the efficient and effective management of natural capital, rather than, say, the reconceptualization/limitation of economic growth, or the acceptance of a more holistic, Earth-centric worldview.

Indeed, in some ways the notion of the Anthropocene seems tailor-made for such a neoliberal approach. Thinking about the Anthropocene has arisen at the same time as a revolution in regulatory strategy has been taking place. This revolution consists of a move from a classical governmental rationality based on notions such as 'rights', 'spheres' and 'jurisdiction', to one based on the alternative concepts of 'markets', 'stakeholders' and 'efficiency'. It is a move away from older forms of liberal government, and towards newer neoliberal concepts of how authority does and should function.

A key feature of the neoliberal governmental model, very much as is the case with the Anthropocene, is the rejection of firm boundaries between public and private, between nature and culture, between politics and science that have characterized previous eras. The new model of de-formalized, de-centralized and de-politicized 'governance' accepts that the goal of regulation is efficient, effective, scientifically sound management – irrespective of borders, 'naturalness' or political will. It is the extension of the logic of the economy to the management of all areas of life.

Given the strong shift towards neoliberal governance models that has taken place over the past few decades, and the compatibility of the 'borderless' Anthropocene concept with this managerial impulse, it is easy to imagine that the law of the Anthropocene will be a neoliberal one. In order to flesh out this argument, this

1 To clarify: this chapter deals with the idea of the Anthropocene as a discursive construct. That is, as a word coined for the purpose of trying to make comprehensible the human impact on the human and non-human environment, rather than as the set of physical/ecological impacts themselves. As such, it engages the Anthropocene as a social (specifically a socio-legal) phenomenon, rather than a scientific one.

chapter will proceed as follows. First, Section 2 will further explain the neoliberal governmental model and the regulatory techniques it employs. Section 3 will then illustrate the prevalence and import of the rise of neoliberal governance by demonstrating how it has come to the forefront of environmental policymaking. In order to provide an example of this rise, this section will undertake a brief analysis of environmental policy documents from the European Union (EU), one of the world's most prominent and influential environmental actors.[2] Section 4 will then explore how the notion of the Anthropocene is well suited for assimilation into the neoliberal governmental paradigm, due to its 'borderless' implications. Finally, Section 5 concludes by rehashing the premise of this contribution, and arguing that truly rethinking the human relationship with Earth systems will require much more than simply recognizing our role in shaping it: it will require a fundamental reorganization of our logic of government.

2 Neoliberalism, managerialism and the law

The idea that we are living in a neoliberal era is one that has gained substantial support across the social sciences. Definitions of the term 'neoliberal' differ (Peck, 2010). As Mitchell Dean has written:

> Neoliberalism . . . has been used, usually by a certain kind of critic, to characterize everything from a particular brand of free market political philosophy and a wide variety of innovations in public management to patterns and processes found in and across diverse political spaces and territories around the globe.
>
> (Dean, 2014, p. 150)

Perhaps the most famous definition of neoliberalism is given by Marxist geographer David Harvey, who describes it as:

> A theory of political economic practices that proposes that human well being can best be advanced by liberating individual entrepreneurial freedoms and skills within an institutional framework characterized by strong property rights, free market, and free trade. The role of the state is to create and preserve an institutional framework appropriate to such practices.
>
> (Harvey, 2005, p. 2)

While this Marxist definition is essentially correct, it is important to understand that neoliberalism is not – or at least not only – 'class rule' by another name. Rather, as Foucault's later work began to demonstrate, it is an elaborate set of new

2 In the interest of clarity, this chapter will use the term 'EU' throughout, even if the terms European Economic Community (EEC) or European Community (EC) would sometimes be more appropriate for historical reasons.

governmental rationalities that come to characterize a social and political system (see e.g. Foucault, 1978, 2008). Under neoliberalism, not only the form and focus of government changes, but also the logic by which we (neoliberalism's subjects and objects) understand the means and ends of governing, the likely effects of interventions on human behaviour and the appropriate metric by which to measure the success of its efforts.

Neoliberalism differs from older forms of government in that it makes the market (rather than 'rights' or 'freedom', for example) the regulating principle that guides the actions of the state. Creating and preserving the free market becomes not just the project of government, but also the well from which it draws its legitimacy (Foucault, 2008, p. 131). In this sense, neoliberalism is, as Wendy Brown has written, 'a peculiar form of reason that configures all aspects of existence in economic terms' (Brown, 2015, p. 17). As a corollary of this 'marketization' of the state, neoliberal government de-centres it, leading government to pursue its central task – expanding the field of entrepreneurial activity – by means that are themselves de-formalized and marketized, regulating individuals and organizations by altering the political economy of choice, and distributing governmental tasks to a wider variety of actors, through means such as public-private partnerships, voluntary standard-setting and 'nudging'. In this way, neoliberalism breaks down traditional barriers between 'politics' and 'economics', between 'public' and 'private', and instead seeks to apply economic analysis and market techniques to all areas of life. No longer are individuals regarded as bundles of rights and freedoms, but rather as entrepreneurs who respond to economic incentives and disincentives in the same way as any other market actor (Dean, 2009, pp. 51–52). These 'stakeholders' are continually self-improving in order to increase their human capital, and under neoliberalism the corresponding task of government is to facilitate and guide this interest-maximization through effective and efficient management of the economic and social context in which these stakeholders operate.

To clarify, neoliberalism, from this perspective, is not just deregulation, or any other single set of policies or programmes. In fact, neoliberalism could lead to *more* regulation or *more* social welfare programmes in a particular context, as governments are called on to secure and expand the conditions necessary for the free market to function, and for individuals to maximize their human capital. Rather, what neoliberalism entails is a shift in the operating logic of government. It is a movement towards thinking about and evaluating the activities of governments and individuals on the basis of market criteria. What kind of policy platform emerges from this newly marketized governing rationality will depend very much on the specific context in which it arises. In other words, neoliberalism is much more about the *why* of policymaking than about the *what*. Wendy Brown refers to this definitional difficulty as the 'paradox' of neoliberalism:

> Neoliberalism is a distinctive mode of reason, of the production of subjects, a "conduct of conduct," and a scheme of valuation. It names a historically specific economic and political reaction against Keynesianism and democratic

> socialism, as well as a more generalized practice of "economizing" spheres and activities heretofore governed by other tables of value. Yet in its differential instantiations across countries, regions, and sectors, in its various intersections with extant cultures and political traditions, and above all, in its convergences with and uptakes of other discourses and developments, neoliberalism takes diverse shapes and spawns diverse content and normative details, even different idioms. It is globally ubiquitous, yet disunified and nonidentical with itself in space and over time.
>
> (Brown, 2015, p. 21)

From a legal perspective, the conversion to neoliberal reason has manifested most visibly in terms of a shift in the techniques of government, the mechanisms through which governments accomplish their goals. There has been a movement ***away*** from so-called 'command and control' legislation (that is, regulations that set firm rules regarding what, when and how individuals and businesses can act), formal adjudication, 'spheres' of individual and collective rights and 'government' and ***towards*** 'responsive' and 'flexible' techniques like 'nudging', benchmarking, marketplaces, impact assessments and public-private partnerships. These latter set of techniques do not concern themselves with boundaries between individuals and their rights, between public and private spheres or even between one country and the next. Scholars such as Lemke (2002), Walters (2004), Swyngedouw (2005) and Sokhi-Bulley (2011) have usefully linked the rise of neoliberal management techniques with the notion of 'governance'. Governance – and in particular the notion of 'good governance' – is offered up as a set of neutral, de-politicized, scientific and universally applicable procedural norms that all states and non-state actors should undertake to uphold in order to improve the efficiency and legitimacy of governmental activities. Politics, culture and democratic choice are irrelevant to this governance paradigm: the 'science' of good governance can and should be applied regardless of its context. It can also be linked to what legal scholars like Martti Koskenniemi have termed 'managerialism': an approach 'that suggests that international problems—problems of "globalization"—should be resolved by developing increasingly complicated technical vocabularies for institutional policy-making' (Koskenniemi, 2009, p. 15).

The law of neoliberalism is a law made not by classical jurists concerned with rights and the limits of power, but by experts, technocrats and economists concerned primarily with the efficient and effective management of a 'marketized' social order. The reason why this is an important and even foundational observation is that generally political consciousness, and political debate, seems structured around the distinction between 'the state', which is construed as public, bureaucratic and hopefully democratic, and 'the market', which is imagined as private, fluid and more or less anarchic. From this classical liberal perspective, the function of the state is to constrain 'the market' by means of regulation, representing a rationality that has the 'common good' in mind. Conversely, the market in theory remains uncontrolled, allowing individuals to maximize their self-interests, bringing ultimate benefits to all. What the analytic of 'neoliberalism' makes visible is that this world of firm divides between 'state' and 'market', which still instructs much of our political consciousness, is no longer the governing regime of the day. The market is everywhere, and influences how we perceive and conceive of the state, the social order and ourselves. Likewise, regulation is everywhere. In this way, just as the Anthropocene makes clear that we are much more implicated in the development of Earth systems than previously thought, neoliberalism makes clear that the state and the market are much more implicated in each other than previously thought.

In this pre-neoliberal perspective, 'the market' (which is the sphere of economic activity) is a more or less natural (either in the Hobbesian all-against-all sense, or in the romantic, harmonious sense) phenomenon, and 'government' stands apart from the market, and relates to it in various ways. In the neoliberal perspective, by contrast, 'government' is there to preserve and support 'the market' (which now includes all aspects of family, social and economic life), and 'the market' effectively determines how and why 'government' functions. The two are deeply intertwined, to the point that 'government' is now increasingly little more than the 'manager' of the 'grand marketplace' of all individual activity. The notion of 'management' functions as a conduit between government and society. Management helps to guide how actors function in the market, how corporations function and how entrepreneurs make it big. Management becomes not just how government operates, but also how government assists the market-society to function optimally. Neoliberal government, thus, is the management of individual and collective activity according to market principles, regardless of borders, boundaries or rights.

3 The rise of neoliberal managerialism in EU environmental policy

To provide an example of how this neoliberal style of government has emerged in practice, and thereby set the stage for the conclusions that this chapter will draw regarding the probable path of the law in the Anthropocene, this section will provide a brief analysis of the changes that have taken place in recent years in the field of EU environmental regulation. In particular, it will demonstrate that in EU environmental policy documents there has been a gradual movement away from the language of 'protecting nature' and towards the language of 'sustainable management of resources', which demonstrates a profound shift in the thinking of those who craft the EU's legal approach to environmental management, towards a more neoliberal style of environmental governance.

In order to do so, it will provide examples drawn from the EU's Environmental Action Programmes (EAPs). The EAPs are the central documents that set European legislative priorities in the environmental arena in the medium term. They declare legislative proposals, proclaim the EU's perspectives on various environmental issues and give an indication of the areas in which the EU plans to work. The EAPs do not themselves create binding environmental laws; measures to implement the objectives set out in the EAPs must be passed separately.

However, they provide a 'map' to the landscape of the EU's environmental thinking during a given period of time.

The European Commission began periodically releasing these documents in 1973, following the first United Nations Conference on the Environment in Stockholm in 1972. Thus far, there have been seven EAPs, each of which reflects contemporary thinking about the environment and appropriate responses to the problems of the day. While overall there has been some continuity in terms of the environmental goals and principles that the EU seeks to reach, there have been interesting changes with respect to the discourse and policy tools that it employs (see e.g. Usui, 2003; Hey, 2006; Van der Heijden, 2010).

In particular, by analysing the language and techniques that the EU seeks to use in pursuit of its environmental objectives, one can see in the EU's EAPs a significant change in governmental thinking and technique. In the early days, as will be demonstrated below, the EAPs generally adopted a more traditional governmental approach, expressing a need to pass laws to protect nature and the natural 'sphere', and respect environmental limits to growth. Contemporary EAPs, by contrast, reflect a neoliberal approach to environmental management, adopting a 'green capital accumulation' paradigm in which managing the environment is just one among the many necessary factors for securing 'sustainable' growth (McManus, 1996).

In its first EAP, which covered the period 1973–1976, the EU (then European Community (EC)) set a number of significant goals, using language that focused on protection and preservation of 'the natural environment' (Council Declaration of 22 November 1973). It set as its objectives the prevention and reduction of pollution and nuisances, the protection of the biosphere and the avoidance of damage to 'the ecological balance'. It enshrined the 'polluter pays' principle, and focused on centralized regulatory action as the appropriate technique for enacting environmental protection measures, adopting 'command and control' directives and regulations for resolving specific pollution control problems like acid rain. While not free of the language of management (for example, it notes that 'the natural environment . . . represents an asset which can be used, but not abused, and which should be managed in the best possible way'), it generally approaches its subject from the perspective of limit (limiting pollution, limiting resource exploitation) and protection:

> [The Community environment policy] must help to bring expansion into the service of man by procuring for him an environment providing the best conditions of life, and reconcile this expansion with the increasingly imperative need to preserve the natural environment.

In the language of the first EAP, 'improvement in the quality of life and the protection of the natural environment are among the fundamental tasks of the Community'.

Between the first EAP and today's seventh, however, important changes have taken place with respect to EU environmental policy. Between the 1970s and the 1990s, the EU gradually gained increasing power in the area of the environment, including the authority to act in international environmental negotiations (Hildebrand, 2002). As its competence in this area increased, the EU began to display a desire for leadership in the international environmental arena (Kelemen, 2010). For example, Annex II of the 1990 Presidency Conclusions of the European Council meeting in Dublin, titled 'The Environmental Imperative', states that: 'There is . . . an increasing acceptance of a wider responsibility as one of the foremost regional groupings in the world, to play a leading role in promoting concerted and effective action at global level' (Presidency Conclusions, 1990). Similarly, Romano Prodi (2000) argued that Europe 'must aim to become a global civil power at the service of sustainable global development'.

At the same time as the EU's environmental power and ambition were growing, there was also a shift away from more protective approaches such as that of the 'precautionary principle' to more flexible 'sustainable development'-oriented approaches such as that of the 'regulatory impact assessment' (Löfstedt, 2004). With this shift in focus came a host of new terms and new techniques for environmental management. 'Natural capital' became the discursive hook for applying economic thinking to the stock of (owned and monetized) natural resources (Pearce, 1991). Impact assessments, environmental economics and green growth became hot topics in policymaking circles (Ekins, 2000), as did the notion of 'smart regulation' – a new methodology for European policymaking that involves performing 'fitness checks' to 'evaluate the benefits and costs of existing legislation' and 'ensuring that new legislation is the best possible' by means of impact assessments, audits and consultations (European Commission Communication COM 543, 2010). The new paradigm brought with it the notion that we can have our environmental cake and eat it too: that there is no essential conflict between growth and preservation, so long as we engage in efficient and scientifically sound management techniques (Wanner, 2015).

The results of this shift can be observed in the language of the seventh EAP, which guides EU policy from 2014–2020 (European Parliament and Council Decision 1386/2013/EU, 2013). The seventh EAP contextualizes the EU's environmental goals as being necessary for 'ensuring the Union's long-term prosperity', as helping to 'provide a stable environment for sustainable investment and growth' and as 'a sound investment for the environment and human health, as well as for the economy'. The seventh EAP places much more emphasis on de-centralized governmental techniques, enshrining the EU's commitment to 'smart regulation' in the environmental field and advocating a flexible, market-based approach to environmental policy-making:

> An appropriate mix of policy instruments would enable businesses and consumers to improve their understanding of the impact of their activities on the environment and to manage that impact. Such policy instruments include economic incentives, market-based instruments, information requirements as well as voluntary tools and measures to complement legislative frameworks and to engage stakeholders at different levels.
>
> (European Parliament and Council Decision 1386/2013/EU, 2013)

The seventh EAP, unlike the first, is replete with the language of neoliberalism. The word 'efficiency' appears *80 times* in this 30-page document. It appeared only twice in the first EAP. The phrase 'natural capital' appears 23 times in the seventh EAP; it is entirely absent from the first. The first EAP designated 'protection of the natural environment' as being 'among the fundamental tasks of the Community'; the seventh EAP describes one of the EU's 'priority objectives' as 'to protect, conserve and enhance the Union's natural capital'. The type of discourse prominent in the EU's seventh EAP resonates with the neoliberal view that the role of government is to act efficiently and effectively and, based on sound data, to use market techniques to manage the competitive environment.

This is not to say that the language of limit and protection has disappeared from legal discourse in the environmental arena – it has not. Indeed, there are traces of protectionist, mercantilist, as well as classical liberal rhetoric present throughout the document. But these other rationalities are being supplanted to an increasing degree by neoliberal style 'market' thinking and its associated techniques in the context of EU environmental law, as demonstrated by its EAPs.

In addition to the rise of 'marketized' neoliberal techniques and discourse in EU environmental policy, the EAPs also demonstrate the increasingly porous approach to borders that is characteristic of neoliberal management. Along with its desire to become a leader on the international environmental front, the EU has recognized that in order to be effective, its environmental policy cannot stop at the borders of Europe. The seventh EAP establishes environmental action as an important component of EU external policy, stating: 'Many environmental challenges are global and can only be fully addressed through a comprehensive global approach, while other environmental challenges have a strong regional dimension. This requires cooperation with partner countries, including neighbouring countries and overseas countries and territories (European Parliament and Council Decision 1386/2013/EU, 2013, para. 31).

In addition, the EU has committed to making environmental action a component of its external trade and other policies, leveraging its power in the economic arena to effect changes in environmental behaviour outside its borders (Lawrence, 2015). Concerns about infringing on the sovereignty of third states have not prevented the EU's activities in this area: where its policies have been challenged on such grounds, the EU has responded with an increasingly expansive reading of its own scope of regulatory jurisdiction. For example, Scott (2014) has written of the EU's techniques of 'territorial extension', by which it broadly reads the notion of territory in order to justify what might once have been considered extrajurisdictional regulation. In such practices, one can see the drive towards efficient and effective scientifically based management chafing against the boundaries constructed by older liberal institutions like sovereignty and democracy. A big part of neoliberal globalization has been the breaking down of geopolitical borders that impede the expansion of international commerce and capital (though, of course, for groups like migrants and the poor sovereign borders remain very much intact). Contemporary phenomena like the ever-widening concentric circles of free trade and investment agreements whose dispute settlement mechanisms give multinational business interests the power to directly challenge state regulators and the rise of 'governance by indicators' and the soft law of standards (Davis et al., 2012) have blurred the boundaries between public and private actors, between one jurisdiction and another, and have significantly challenged the old truth that the 'sovereign state' is the alpha and omega of international legal life.

EU environmental law is not, of course, universal, and states have adopted many other approaches to environmental protection. However, the EU is one of the most important actors on the world environmental stage, and prides itself as being a driver of international environmental 'norms', and a trend-setter in the regulatory arena (Manners, 2002; Lightfoot and Burchell, 2005; Vogler, 2005; Zito, 2005; Harris, 2006; Baker, 2007). As such, its governmental practices offer a window onto one potential avenue of development of global environmental law – and far from the least likely one. Indeed, the 'green growth' paradigm has already been taken up in the discourse of institutions like the World Bank, Organization for Economic Cooperation and Development (OECD) and United Nations Environment Programme (UNEP), each of which has issued calls for a move towards a 'green economy' as part of their work (OECD, 2011; UNEP, 2011; World Bank, 2012).

4 Managing the environment: the neoliberal Anthropocene

Thus far, as mentioned in the introduction, even in the environmentally progressive EU, the Anthropocene is still largely in its legal infancy. The word 'Anthropocene' has appeared in exactly zero European court decisions, zero times in EU legislation and almost as few times in EU policy discourse. In fact, the only two instances of an EU official or body using the term that this author could find to date were:

1. in an opinion of the Economic and Social Committee on the importance of science in Europe, in which the Committee mentions that some commentators have coined the term 'Anthropocene' and this should lead to more funding for science (Economic and Social Committee Opinion of 30 May 2001, 2001);
2. in two identical speeches from 2008 and 2009 by then-EU Energy Commissioner Andris Piebalgs, in which the Commissioner describes the Anthropocene as providing a challenge for the EU, which can be solved only by 'develop[ing] a society that uses the earth's resources in a manner that ensures the long-term survival of future generations and [does] so in a manner that provides us increasing health, peace and prosperity' (Piebalgs, 2008, 2009).

How, then, will the concept of the Anthropocene be treated when and if it finally does make its way into the EU's increasingly neoliberal system of environmental governance?

The somewhat pessimistic response is that rather than leading us to curtail growth or limit the human impact on Earth systems, as many critical thinkers and social scientists would wish, it seems probable that our legal/governmental response to the Anthropocene will be a neoliberal one, based on the extension and expansion of market-based managerial techniques in order to encourage more efficient and effective management of natural capital.

The rise of the Anthropocene concept dovetails with the rise of neoliberal governmental techniques. Indeed, in some ways, the Anthropocene seems perfectly designed for neoliberal management. One might even go so far as to suggest that the Anthropocene, as a discursive formation, seems to be (troublingly) open to a neoliberal reading. As with neoliberal governance, the idea of the Anthropocene blurs the boundaries between what were formerly clearly distinguished 'spheres' of governmental influence and control. In the case of neoliberalism, this blurring has removed the hard line between public and private, between government and economy and, increasingly, between local and global and between one sovereign and the next. Neoliberal management utilizes market concepts and techniques as the basis of regulation and policy-making. It shifts traditional responsibilities of government onto the shoulders of private and mixed enterprises. It relies on private individuals and enterprises to self-govern through the use of best practices standards, voluntary regimes and incentives. And it teaches the subjects and objects of government to evaluate its success using criteria formerly reserved for private enterprise: things like efficiency, effectiveness and innovation.

The Anthropocene concept, in parallel, blurs the line between 'nature' and 'culture', between 'human' and 'environment' and between 'local' and 'global'. In the Anthropocene, there is no longer a 'human world' and a 'natural world', each subject to different sets of rules. Instead, the Anthropocene suggests that we view the world in terms of 'global systems', which human beings are both part of and the biggest influence on. That is, it suggests that we should no longer recognize a divide between that which is governed by human social, economic and political systems, and that which is not.

If under the Anthropocene the natural environment is a product of human society, economy and law, then for neoliberally inclined lawyers and policy-makers, it will be governed as such. In other words, the Anthropocene would seem to invite an expansion of efficient, effective management into a zone that was previously seen as a space in need of 'protection' and 'preservation', and within which human effects should be limited. The Anthropocene, from this perspective, is a problem that should be dealt with by means of *more*, rather than *less*, neoliberal regulation.

Neoliberal government is already intervening to help reconstruct capitalist nature/society relationships via the move to a discourse of natural capital, green growth and sustainable development (Brand and Wissen, 2013). The shift that has taken place within the EU's EAPs from 'protecting the natural environment' to 'enhancing natural capital' seems to be highly compatible with a world in which there is no firm nature/culture divide, and human social relations have become a driver of geological change.

Similarly, the increasingly porous borders created by neoliberal capital markets have paved the way for the extension of environmental management across traditional sovereign boundaries. Davor Vidas, Ole Kristian Fauchald, Øystein Jensen and Morten Walløe Tvedt have argued that the effects of the Anthropocene will be profoundly destabilizing for international law. As they write: 'Many aspects of international law rely on an implicit pretext of the familiar conditions of stability. For instance, a defined territory—indeed, *having* a territory—is a basic criterion of statehood under international law' (Vidas et al., 2015, p. 4, italics in original).

The Anthropocene will, indeed, prove a serious challenge to classical liberal conceptions of territorial sovereignty. However, neoliberalism has been posing such a challenge for the past several decades. Talk of the 'end of sovereignty', though certainly prematurely declared, has already become a staple of international legal discourse. While sovereignty is still undoubtedly a central feature of the international legal landscape, it is also true that its pre-eminence has faded since the days when the International Court of Justice (ICJ) declared in the Lotus case that a state 'may not exercise its power in any form in the territory of another State' (*S.S. "Lotus", France v Turkey*, Judgment, 1927, para. 45). When Vidas et al., argue that in the Anthropocene 'the primacy given in international law to the assertion of sovereign rights over territory may have to be reconsidered', therefore, they are only throwing petrol on a fire that was already lit by neoliberal globalization (Vidas et al., 2015, p. 4).

This argument is lent further credence by the fact that thus far, those few legal scholars who have engaged with the idea of the Anthropocene have tended to see it as a reason for greatly expanding the reach of the legal management of Earth systems. Kotzé, for example, argues that 'the Anthropocene presents an urgent call for dramatic regulatory interventions of a kind hitherto unseen' (Kotzé, 2014, p. 252). Robinson calls for robust 'governmentally mandated environmental management systems' (Robinson 2013, p. 498). Somsen argues for a response of 'environmental enhancement' that would involve '[i]ntentional technological interventions to engineer or re-engineer parts of the biosphere, resulting in unprecedented characteristics and capabilities deemed desirable or necessary for the satisfaction of human and ecological imperatives' (Somsen, 2016). And Scott (2012) advocates expanding international agreements and public-private partnerships on geo-engineering as a way of responding to the Anthropocene 'crisis'.

For these legal scholars, and others who advocate enhanced 'Earth systems governance', thinking about the Anthropocene seems to imply a need for more and better governance, expanded regulatory systems, more extensive management of the environment through scientifically grounded applications of human law and technology and the dissolution of sovereign borders that act as impediments to that efficient and effective management.

If this is, indeed, the likely answer to the question 'what will be the law of the Anthropocene?' posed at the outset of this chapter, then one further question still remains: 'so what?' Section 2 described neoliberalism as a *why* of government, not a *what*, and was careful to assert that a whole range of different policy outcomes could be possible under a regime of neoliberal management. Is it possible, then, that efficient, effective, boundary-crossing neoliberal management might be a good way of dealing with the challenges posed by the Anthropocene? That neoliberalism's 'inconstancy and plasticity' means that it might be possible to turn the tide towards a more ecologically sound future even under such conditions (Brown, 2015, p. 21)?

While it does indeed seem possible under neoliberalism to attain a wide variety of policy outcomes, this does not make the neoliberal order an unproblematic one, particularly when dealing with the intersection between the human and non-human. To begin with, it seems inevitable that as neoliberal management exerts expanded control over the previously 'natural' realm, it will bring with it the tools of its trade: monetization, ownership and commodification. Things have value for neoliberal policy only insofar as they can be accounted for – and the process of accounting draws attention to certain values and takes it away from others, while presuming that the values it does see can be compared adequately with one another. Perhaps the most famous example of this neoliberal economic thinking is economist Gary Becker's attempt to propose a 'theory of preference formation' that would account in a scientific way for the 'growth and decay of love and other emotions' in order to adequately take such things as 'love between a mother and her children' into account in calculations regarding individual cost-benefit analysis (Becker, 1996, p. 231).

In addition to the difficulty of 'apples-to-apples' accounting outside of traditional economic marketplaces, neoliberalism faces the problem that the market is not all-seeing. Only those systems, objects and subjects that are visible to the neoliberal gaze can be taken into account in its management calculations. The fantasy of neoliberalism is essentially an omniscient one: truly efficient, effective management of Earth systems would require an impossible amount of information regarding the properties of and interactions between every element of the human and non-human world. Even for less totalitarian and more modest managerial approaches, the problems of anthropocentrism and partiality arise. The neoliberal expert regulator can see only what he or she can cognize. And when dealing with the intersection between the human and non-human worlds, this falls far short of allowing space for the non-human to thrive, not to mention all of those other factors that fall outside the neoliberal imaginary.

Finally, as Wendy Brown warns, neoliberal reason imperils liberal democratic institutions, as well as dreams of radical democracy, by 'converting the distinctly *political* character, meaning, and operation of democracy's constituent elements into *economic* ones' (Brown, 2015, p. 17, italics in original). The marketization of social and governmental life entails a diminishing of political choice. As we move towards a world in which individual and collective behaviour is governed by efficient expert management, older institutions such as popular democracy and equality become obsolete. When the common good is defined in terms of the marketized neoliberal gaze, those things that might not be adequately valued by its particular worldview are cast aside.

Neoliberalism's deep biases towards capitalist valuation systems make it difficult to break free of its problematic accounting and its essentially economic gaze, which imperil both human and non-human values that they cannot adequately recognize. As a platform, then, an expansion of our current trend towards the increasing marketization of all aspects of human society seems a profoundly insufficient basis for the truly revolutionary response to the Anthropocene that many commentators would desire.

This is not intended to imply that there can be no desirable political outcomes even in a neoliberal world. Neoliberalism is far from hegemonic, both with respect to its agnosticism on political ends (though not means) and its coexistence with older rationalities such as classical liberalism. Nor is it to suggest that neoliberalism is the 'final stage' of our historical genealogy, or the only problematic form of reason with respect to the Anthropocene. Indeed, it should be remembered that the rise of neoliberalism has created its own forms of resistance and tools for encouraging accountability (for example, the ubiquity of communications technology and alternative media, the growing power of NGOs and transnational networks) that have arguably made our social order in some ways more responsive to democratic control. Rather, the point is that the resonances between neoliberalism and the Anthropocene create a particular set of concerns that should temper the optimism of contemporary scholars. Though it could be that the Anthropocene concept *does* encourage the development of new social imaginaries and resistance to or from within the neoliberal order, the ease with which it seems capable of cooptation by neoliberal rationality urges care and on-going self-reflexive critique.

5 Conclusion

This chapter has suggested that the Anthropocene as a concept might not have the revolutionary impacts that many scholars have hoped for. This is because the Anthropocene has arisen alongside, is blossoming within the context of, and shares important similarities with neoliberal governance. In particular, this chapter has argued that the Anthropocene's breakdown of conceptual barriers between human and non-human coincides with neoliberalism's breakdown of the barriers between public and private, between market and society and between one jurisdiction and the next. Scholars writing on the subject of the Anthropocene have seemed eager to see it as an opportunity for reimagining human social, economic and political systems in order to build a more harmonious relationship with Earth systems. However, this chapter has suggested that given the increasing neoliberalization of law and governance systems, it seems more likely that our legal/political response to the Anthropocene will come in the form of expanded neoliberal management.

As law and government gradually come to take up the language of the Anthropocene, political systems will have to respond to the new understanding that human beings are part of, and the most important influence on, Earth systems. *How* this political and legal response will happen is emphatically a function of human social organization. As can be seen in this chapter's discussion of EU and international environmental politics, neoliberal management has increasingly become the order of the day for governing the global environment. Given the Anthropocene concept's affinities with neoliberal thinking, and its growing dominance in the political world, there seems little reason to doubt that, if this pattern continues, neoliberal management will be expanded to govern an increasingly boundless set of Earth systems processes.

If there is any hope for truly rethinking the human relationship with the planet, therefore, it will require much more than simple recognition of our role in shaping it: it will require a concerted resistance to and reimagination of our logic of government. The logic of neoliberalism is not one of limits to growth, but rather of extended control. It is not one of expanded consciousness, but rather one of reducing our gaze to what can be recognized and accounted for by expert managers. The Anthropocene may indeed, as some have suggested, offer a platform for imagining a new human social order. However, if it is truly to do so, it will have to break free of and avoid being coopted by a political force that has gained increasing control over our human imagination: neoliberal management.

Bibliography

Baker, S. (2007) Sustainable Development as Symbolic Commitment: Declaratory Politics and the Seductive Appeal of Ecological Modernisation in the European Union. *Environmental Politics.* 16(2), 297–317.

Becker, G. S. (1996) *Accounting for Tastes.* Cambridge, MA: Harvard University Press.

Brand, U. & Wissen, M. (2013) Crisis and Continuity of Capitalist Society-Nature Relationships: The Imperial Mode of Living and the Limits to Environmental Governance. *Review of International Political Economy.* 20(4), 687–711.

Brown, W. (2015) *Undoing the Demos.* New York: Zone Books.

Clark, T. (2015) *Ecocriticism on the Edge: The Anthropocene as a Threshold Concept.* London and New York: Bloomsbury.

Council Declaration of 22 November 1973 on the Programme of Action of the European Communities on the Environment. *Official Journal of the European Union.* C112, 1–53.

Crutzen, P. J. (2002) Geology of Mankind. *Nature.* 415(6867), 23.

Crutzen, P. J. & Stoermer, E. F. (2000) The 'Anthropocene'. *Global Change Newsletter.* 41, 17–18.

Davis, K., Fisher, A., Kingsbury, B. & Merry S. E. (eds) (2012) *Governance by Indicators: Global Power through Classification and Rankings.* Oxford: Oxford University Press.

Dean, J. (2009) *Democracy and Other Neoliberal Fantasies: Communicative Capitalism and Left Politics.* Durham, NC: Duke University Press.

Dean, M. (2014) Rethinking Neoliberalism. *Journal of Sociology.* 50(2), 150–163.

Economic and Social Committee Opinion of 30 May 2001 on the Commission Staff Working Paper SEC (2000) 1973 Science, Society and the Citizen in Europe. *Official Journal of the European Union.* C221, 151–166.

Ekins, P. (2000) *Economic Growth and Environmental Sustainability: The Prospects for Green Growth.* London and New York: Routledge.

European Commission Communication COM (2010) 543 of 8 October 2010 on 'Smart Regulation in the European Union'.
European Parliament and Council Decision 1386/2013/EU of 20 November 2013 on a General Union Environment Action Programme to 2020 'Living Well, within the Limits of Our Planet'. *Official Journal of the European Union.* L354, 171–200.
Fauchald, K., Hunter, D. & Wang, X. (eds) (2014) *Yearbook of International Environmental Law.* 25(1), 3–166.
Foucault, M. (1978) *The History of Sexuality, Vol. 1: The Will to Knowledge.* Trans. Hurley, R. London: Penguin.
Foucault, M. (2008) *The Birth of Biopolitics: Lectures at the College de France, 1978–1979.* Trans. Burchell, G. Basingstoke and New York: Palgrave Macmillan.
Hamilton, C., Bonneuil, C. & Gemenne, F. (eds) (2015) *The Anthropocene and the Global Environmental Crisis: Rethinking Modernity in a New Epoch.* Abingdon and New York: Routledge.
Harris, P. (2006) The European Union and Environmental Change: Sharing the Burdens of Global Warming. *Colorado Journal of International Environmental Law & Policy.* 17(2), 309–355.
Harvey, D. (2005) *A Brief History of Neoliberalism.* Oxford: Oxford University Press.
Hey, C. (2006) EU Environmental Policies: A Short History of the Policy Strategies. In: Scheuer, S. (ed.) *EU Environmental Policy Handbook: A Critical Analysis of EU Environmental Legislation.* Brussels: European Environmental Bureau, pp. 17–31.
Hildebrand, P. M. (2002) The European Community's Environmental Policy, 1957 to 1992: From Incidental Measures to an International Regime? In: Jordan, A. (ed.) *Environmental Policy in the European Union: Actors, Institutions, and Processes.* London: Earthscan, pp. 13–36.
Kelemen, R. D. (2010) Globalizing European Union Environmental Policy. *Journal of European Public Policy.* 17(3), 335–349.
Koskenniemi, M. (2009) The Politics of International Law—20 Years Later. *European Journal of International Law.* 20(1), 7–19.
Kotzé, L. J. (2014) Human Rights and the Environment in the Anthropocene. *The Anthropocene Review.* 1(3), 252–275.
Lawrence, J. C. (2015) *Between Rights and Market: Governmentality in EU Trade and Environment Policy.* Doctoral Dissertation. Amsterdam: Vrije Universiteit.
Lemke, T. (2002) Foucault, Governmentality, and Critique. *Rethinking Marxism: A Journal of Economics, Culture & Society.* 14(3), 49–64.
Lightfoot, S. & Burchell, J. (2005) The European Union and the World Summit on Sustainable Development: Normative Power Europe in Action? *Journal of Common Market Studies.* 43(1), 75–95.
Löfstedt, R. E. (2004) The Swing of the Regulatory Pendulum in Europe: From Precautionary Principle to (Regulatory) Impact Analysis. *Journal of Risk and Uncertainty.* 28(3), 237–260.
Manners, I. (2002) Normative Power Europe: A Contradiction in Terms? *Journal of Common Market Studies.* 40(2), 235–258.
McManus, P. (1996) Contested Terrains: Politics, Stories and Discourses of Sustainability. *Environmental Politics.* 5(1), 48–73.
OECD (2011) *Towards Green Growth.* Paris: Organization for Economic Cooperation and Development.

Pearce, D. (ed.) (1991) *Blueprint 2: Greening the World Economy*. London: Earthscan.
Peck, J. (2010) *Constructions of Neoliberal Reason*. Oxford and New York: Oxford University Press.
Piebalgs, A. (2008) EU Energy Commissioner. Speech 08/578. Paris, 28 October.
Piebalgs, A. (2009) EU Energy Commissioner. Speech 09/18. Brussels, 22 January.
Presidency Conclusions (1990) SN/50/1/90 of the European Council Meeting in Dublin, 25–26 June, Annex II: The Environmental Imperative.
Prodi, R. (2000) 2000–2005: Shaping the New Europe. Speech 00/41 to the European Parliament. Strasbourg, 15 February.
Purdy, J. (2015) *After Nature: A Politics for the Anthropocene*. Cambridge, MA: Harvard University Press.
Robinson, N. A. (2013) Keynote: Sustaining Society in the Anthropocene Epoch. *Denver Journal of International Law & Policy*. 41(4), 467–506.
Scott, J. (2014) Extraterritoriality and Territorial Extension in EU Law. *American Journal of Comparative Law*. 62(1), 87–125.
Scott, K. N. (2012) International Law in the Anthropocene: Responding to the Geoenginerring Crisis. *Michigan Journal of International Law*. 34(2), 309–358.
Sokhi-Bulley, B. (2011) Government(ality) by Experts: Human Rights as Governance. *Law & Critique*. 22(3), 251–271.
Somsen, H. (2016) From Improvement towards Enhancement: A Regenesis of Environmental Law at the Dawn of the Anthropocene. In: Brownsword, R., Young, K. & Scotford, E. (eds) *Oxford Handbook on the Law and Regulation of Technology*. Oxford and New York: Oxford University Press.
S.S. "Lotus", France v Turkey, Judgment (1927) PCIJ Series A no. 10, ICGJ 248 (PCIJ 1927), 7 September 1927, Permanent Court of International Justice (historical) (PCIJ).
Swyngedouw, E. (2005) Governance Innovation and the Citizen: The Janus Face of Governance-beyond-the-State. *Urban Studies*. 42(11), 1991–2006.
UNEP (2011) *Towards a Green Economy: Pathways to Sustainable Development and Poverty Eradication*. Nairobi: United Nations Environment Programme.
Usui, Y. (2003) Evolving Environmental Norms in the European Union. *European Law Journal*. 9(1), 69–87.
Van der Heijden, H-A. (2010) *Social Movements, Public Spheres and the European Politics of the Environment: Green Power Europe?* New York: Palgrave Macmillan.
Vidas, D., Fauchald, O. K., Jensen, Ø. & Tvedt, M. W. (2015) International Law for the Anthropocene? Shifting Perspectives in Regulation of the Oceans, Environment, and Genetic Resources. *Anthropocene*. 9, 1–13.
Vogler, J. (2005) The European Contribution to Global Environmental Governance. *International Affairs*. 81(4), 835–850.
Walters, W. (2004) Some Critical Notes on 'Governance'. *Studies in Political Economy*. 73, 27–46.
Wanner, T. (2015) Economy and Growth Discourse: Maintaining the 'Sustainable Development' of Neoliberal Capitalism. *New Political Economy*. 20(1), 21–41.
Wark, M. (2015) *Molecular Red: Theory for the Anthropocene*. London: Verso Books.
World Bank (2012) *Inclusive Green Growth: The Pathway to Sustainable Development*. Washington, DC: World Bank.
Zito, A. R. (2005) The European Union as an Environmental Leader in a Global Environment. *Globalizations*. 2(3), 363–375.

Part III

Thinking and the non-human world

6 'It's getting better and better, worse and worse, faster and faster'[1]

The human animal in the Anthropocene

Todd LeVasseur

> Future generations are unlikely to condone our lack of prudent concern for the integrity of the natural world that supports all life.
>
> (Rachel Carson, *Silent Spring*)

> Every society honors its live conformists and its dead troublemakers.
>
> (Mignon McLaughlin)

1 Situating the Anthropocene via caloric production

Many scholars and writers have attempted to generate a 'diagnosis' of the current, now almost entirely global, human predicament of ecological collapse and when it began and to summarize events that caused it. Such a diagnosis is typically followed by a prescription: often a set of ideas or policies that, when enacted, may help change the human trajectory from collapse, or at least an impoverished future, towards sustainability and resiliency. These diagnoses range from the invention of written, phonetic script (Abram, 1996); to the formation of totalitarian agriculture (Quinn, 1992); to the domestication of plants and animals, leading to the creation of distant sky gods and concepts of linear time (Shepard, 2004); to the association of female agency, bodies and nature and their combined systematic exploitation via science and technology (Merchant, 1983; Shiva, 1989); to the formation of dualisms that are embedded into our basic ontologies (Bender, 2003); to the specific rise of Western Christianity (White, Jr, 1967). One current running through many of these diagnoses is the association of a certain human technology, the strategic domestication of plants and animals for the purpose of generating human calories, with our current predicament of collapse. Many of these diagnoses contend that with the onset of the Agricultural Revolution approximately 10,000 years ago there was a concomitant increase in population

1 Michael Dowd shared with me this paraphrase of a colleague of his during a private discussion before one of his public presentations in 2008 in Gainesville, Florida.

density, hierarchy, war, patriarchy and exploitation of the natural world, which continues to today (Quinn, 1996).

The bioregionalist Kirkpatrick Sale (2006) falls within this trajectory of writers offering a diagnosis and prescription. However, his work is unique compared to those above in that he traces the roots of human domination of the natural world, now reaching its full flourishing in the Anthropocene, to a series of interrelated events, triggered first by global weather patterns, that then influenced human society and cultural and technological production. According to Sale (2006), the Last Glacial Maximum, begun by a volcanic eruption, resulted in almost all humans on the planet living in severe, harsh, almost permanent winter-like weather. Importantly, beginning 37,000 years ago, nearly all humans, according to Sale (2006, p. 72), were congregated almost entirely in two areas:

> the river valleys of the Russian plain and southern France and Cantabrian Spain, but even there the climate was harsh . . . year after relentless year people were forced from all over Europe into these refuge areas as the cold made vast regions uninhabitable.

In Sale's (2006) reading of the archaeological data, the dense packing of most all humans into these areas led to competition for scarce resources. One impact of this competition was that larger mammals were hunted to local extinction, after which humans at that time moved to smaller game. Such pressures meant that 'the twin necessities of killing enough game and avoiding tribal conflict demanded novel, or at least augmented, approaches' (ibid., p. 74), generating tribal diversity coupled with the invention of new weapons. These new weapons included the spear thrower, the bow and arrow, harpoons, the boomerang, woven nets, new types of fishhooks and portable fencing. Such inventions appear in the archaeological record about 18,000 years ago, as 'An explosion of weaponry, then, to respond to the crisis of the cold, a challenge to the human role of domination that drew forth an ingenuity and inventiveness not seen before' (ibid., pp. 78–79). Such weapons helped spawn new hunting strategies and allowed humans to hunt at a further distance, the results of which include more efficient predation and, importantly, a physical and psychological distancing from the subject of the hunt. For Sale, this transition is key – in sum, his argument is that increa-sed technological capabilities influenced subsequent cultural values, leading to an eventual domination/superiority complex of all humans living in these areas. Such a techno-cultural trajectory directly led to the overexploitation of other organisms. At the same time, human-human violence gained ascendency, as well as the ability to store calories, which led to hierarchy and stratification in human society and war between bands of humans. From there, it has been an 18,000-year trajectory to modern concepts of private property, nation-state ideology and the sobering environmental metrics of the Anthropocene. Philosopher and animal abolitionist Jim Mason (2006, p. 180) has coined the results of this trajectory 'misothery', or 'hatred and contempt for animals and, by extension, the natural world as a whole'.

What is important to recognize in this summary of Sale's reading of human history is that all the events of the above paragraph occurred before the typical prescription of humanity's 'fall' from sustainability and an assumed eco-golden age. This date is typically placed at the onset of the Agricultural Revolution, most commonly dated to 10,000 years ago. For Sale, the roots of human domination over the natural world extends further back into a 10,000-year window which ranges from 22,000 years ago, when humans were largely living in the aforementioned two parts of modern Europe and central Asia, to 12,000 years ago, with the onset of the Holocene. According to Sale, by the time the planet's weather began to warm and humans could migrate out of these two areas the concept of human superiority to the natural world was in place. It is at this point that he joins the common narrative of blaming the Agricultural Revolution, which for Sale includes the domestication of first plants, and then of 14 animal species. Thus, over a period from 12,000 to 6,000 years ago, agriculture became 'a superb demonstration that humans could control nature (or believed they could), could literally domesticate it and place it under regular and systematic human will and design' (Sale, 2006, p. 97).

If Sale is correct, then we must pause as scholars (and as citizens of a beleaguered Earth) to think about such a diagnosis. Sale's reading suggests that humans alive today have a deep antipathy towards the natural world, what Mason terms 'misothery'. Such antipathy is not evidence of an innate human urge to dominate and control the natural world, but it is one that is now approximately 22,000 years deep, and has spread throughout the world with the spread of Agricultural Revolution technologies and lifestyles. Furthermore, it suggests that almost all worldviews, past and present, that are not tribal-based (which is not the same as saying all tribal religions and all forms of traditional ecological knowledge are benign), are post facto this formation of 'an environmental assault on the earth' (Sale, 2006, p. 103).

Importantly, the above diagnoses and prescriptions suggest that it is likely that the values embedded by people in religions, and worldviews broadly, whether these values are economic, political and/or ethical, will be those of superiority over the natural world. According to the above scholars, such superiority justifies the continued exploitation of the natural world. This suggests that at best, humans living within these worldviews will most likely not advocate for a more ecocentric understanding of the human animal, where it is hoped that cultural values around teaching restraint in our use of technology and in our fecundity will develop to help ameliorate the Anthropocene. In other words, at possibly the most critical moment of our species' existence, we might have the wrong cultural narratives and worldviews in place to deal with the enormity of the Anthropocene, given our lifestyles based on old forms of carbon have largely triggered this new epoch.

My own scholarly journey, combined with witnessing the inertia (and outright denial) in dealing with emerging environmental metrics that suggest an impoverished future, leads me to believe that Sale's thesis has very strong exploratory power. Specifically, Sale's analysis can help us to understand our use of various technologies and how these have systematically led to further and further exploitation of the natural world. Importantly, it gives a theoretical background to the larger reality that we must face if we wish to understand what preconditions are needed to have a more peaceful coexistence in the Anthropocene. This peaceful coexistence must not just be human-human, but also include human-animal/organismic others. This peaceful coexistence must also address possibly deep-seated misothery and the manifest cultural institutions and technologies that have been scaffolded upon such misothery, with this scaffolding stretching back thousands of years.

If our current existence is built upon systems of domination, and a logic of domination that is especially tethered to how most humans today get their calories, then unpacking an agriculturally based domination of our planet seems to be an important strategy (Warren, 1990; Patel, 2012; Northcott, 2015). Furthermore, such exploitation has significantly gained steam with the onset of the Industrial Revolution and the use of coal, oil and gas (and nuclear) to power our industrial and post-industrial lifestyles, leading to an atmosphere that is now above 400 parts per million (ppm) of CO2, and a planet of almost 7.5 billion humans. Overall, I think the diagnosis of the series of interrelated events after the domestication of key plant and animal crops, and how these created the context of the Industrial and Green Revolutions, respectively, and which taken together have led to the Anthropocene, is apropos. If our agriculture for 10,000 years has never been sustainable, relying as it does on the drawdown of nonrenewable forms of soil and leading to an overshoot of carrying capacity for human numbers, how much more our lifestyles of today? Lifestyles that are dependent upon the Agricultural Revolution, but that now include dependency on rare precious metals and finite resources, and that will most likely face severe shortages in the coming years (Haberl, 2006; Meadows, Meadows and Randers, 2004; Barnosky et al., 2012; Steffen et al., 2015).

2 Discussing the Anthropocene, or cultivating 'ecological thought'

Coming to terms with the implications – moral, religious, political, economic, social, aesthetic, ecological, geological and biological – of the Anthropocene is daunting, sobering and challenging. Maintaining a conviction that there is still hope, or that life has meaning, and escaping the slippery slope of ecoapocalyptic despair and paralysis is a very real ecopsychological challenge (Albrecht, 2005; Cleveland, 2014; Macy and Johnstone, 2012; Schneiderman, 2012). Even discussing the term 'Anthropocene' itself is no easy task (Crist, 2013; Ivakhiv, 2014)! Nonetheless, how are we to make sense of, study, and understand the future of the human animal and our relationship to the technologies and worldviews that have led to the Anthropocene?

One possible lens is provided by the Rita Shea Guffey Chair in English at Rice University, Timothy 'Tim' Morton (2007, 2010, 2013) from where he writes broadly about philosophy, ecocriticism, modernity/postmodernity, and epistemologies of nature. His deft work with analysing meta-narratives and our understandings of the natural world provide key insights into understanding the enormity of the Anthropocene – an epoch triggered in large part by how we get our calories and the worldviews embedded therein.

With regard to the passing of autopoeitic tipping points of planetary boundaries, Morton argues that we need to emplace such realities into the category of 'hyperobjects'. For Morton (2013, p. 1), hyperobjects are 'things that are massively distributed in time and space relative to humans'. He outlines their characteristics as including: viscosity ('they "stick" to beings that are involved with them'); nonolocality ('any "local manifestation" of a hyperobject is not directly the hyperobject'); temporal undulation ('[t]hey involved profoundly different temporalities than the human-scale ones we are used to'); phasing (they are 'invisible to humans for stretches of time'); and interobjectivity ('they can be detected in a space that consists of interrelationships between aesthetic properties of objects') (Morton, 2013, p. 1). Since hyperobjects exist independently of humans, and more so, since humans are embedded within hyperobjects, including especially climate destabilization and the Anthropocene, 'hyperobjects end the possibility of transcendental leaps "outside" physical reality. Hyperobjects force us to acknowledge the immanence of thinking to the physical' (ibid., p. 2). And the key thing to think about the physical through the interrelated hyperobjects of the Anthropocene and global warming is that 'What we desperately need is an appropriate level of shock and anxiety concerning a specific ecological trauma—indeed, *the* ecological trauma of our age' (ibid., pp. 8–9, italics in original), which for this book is the Anthropocene, including anthropogenic climate destabalization. What the hyperobjects of global warming and the Anthropocene confront us with is the chance to question what it is to be human; to question the fidelity to narratives of technological optimism, of capitalist (and/ or communist and socialist) utopias; and to unpack embedded assumptions of anthropocentrism, where some of these forces according to Sale stretch back 20,000 years. As Morton (2015) says on his blog, 'If you were going to reduce my ontology with one sentence, it would be this one: Things shimmer without mechanical input'.

Hyperobjects also confront us with a chance to take geological timespans seriously, as well as the agency of non-human others (whether organisms, or larger natural processes). They also present us with the chance to internalize what dominant worldviews have externalized ('the immanence of thinking to the physical'): we are utterly dependent upon hyperobjects for survival. For example, the formation of soil is a hyperobject, without which we could not grow crops. Therefore, if the prescription of Sale and others that the Anthropocene is a product of post-Agricultural Revolution relations with soil is legitimate, then we might need to rethink our technologies of food production and how these interact with the hyperobjects of soil and climate change.

What is key in Morton's insights, though, is that our effort to produce a peaceful coexistence in the Anthropocene will be marked by failures, in the sense that we cannot assume an autonomous human subject that is exempt from the vicissitudes of hyperobjects. As the anthropologist Tim Ingold (2009, p. 345) explains, our artefacts and tools, including those that we make and use to buttress human domination, are used in 'creative engagements' that co-create our biosocial realities. However, in this co-creation, our survival is not guaranteed. Morton (2010, p. 17) himself writes that, 'Things will get worse before they get better, if at all. We must create frameworks for coping with a catastrophe that, from the evidence of the hysterical announcements of its imminent arrival, *has already occurred*' (my italics). Morton's ecological thought recognizes human embeddedness in natural systems. At our core, we are enmeshed in hyperobjects from which we cannot escape, and upon which we depend, which is all the more reason to be cautious and to change our 10,000-year+ trajectory of domination. If the laudable (but possibly unobtainable) goal is to create a peaceful coexistence in the Anthropocene, then finding the key causes (of many possible) of the Anthropocene, and trying as best as we can to halt these processes, seems an appropriate strategy. For this chapter, certain human actions and worldviews bear more responsibility than others for creating the Anthropocene: modes of tool production and worldviews that stretch back 20,000 years. In other words, if we were to remove this, and remained as gatherer/hunters in the vein of the 180,000 or so years prior, then we most likely would not currently be enmeshed within the hyperobjects of climate change and the Anthropocene.

A further note of caution here is warranted that also explains my privileging of understanding the Anthropocene from the interlinked lenses of caloric production and ecological thought, respectively. Morton is not arguing a pure relativism of multiple cultural trajectories and narratives. Despite the attributes of hyperobjects, and the difficulty with fully understanding their complexity and agency, there are certain hyperobjects that are more relevant to the Anthropocene than others. It might be important to focus on addressing certain human technologies and worldviews that have over-determined the Anthropocene, given timescales and basic laws of thermodynamics. This is why this chapter begins with the largest context I am aware of that gives explanatory power to the Anthropocene: how humans get calories, and the worldviews embedded therein. From there (hyperobject of soil), it is a continual trajectory to the Industrial Revolution, and tapping into hyperobjects of old sunlight stored as oil and/or natural gas. The latter of course have solidified the human entry into the Anthropocene: they allow for industrial agriculture and a human population of over 7 billion; and they allow us to generate forms of electricity that have led to 400 ppm CO_2 in our atmosphere (another hyperobject). Given our hyperobject-emplaced and layered biosocial reality as technocultural beings that operate within worldviews that can be maladaptive, then what new stories and technologies might we need to create to navigate the Anthropocene?

As Morton (2010, p. 5) explains: 'Our continued survival, and therefore the survival of the planet we're now dominating beyond all doubt, depends on our thinking past Nature'. Here Morton is suggesting that environmental/sustainability thinkers and leaders need to move beyond Romantic-tinged views of a reified, pristine 'Nature', and rather adopt what Morton calls 'ecological thought'. This is 'the thinking of interconnectedness . . . It's a practice and a process of becoming fully aware of how human beings are connected with other beings – animal, vegetable, or mineral. Ultimately, this includes thinking about democracy. What would a truly democratic encounter between truly equal beings look like, what would it be – can we even imagine it?' (Morton, 2010, p. 7). This is in part Morton's answer to the new stories and modes of living we need to create in order to cultivate ecological thought: one that recognizes equal value in all beings, and that all beings are derivative of uncontrollable hyperobjects.

It is my argument in this chapter, given the reality of hyperobjects and the Anthropocene, that a truly democratic encounter with non-human nature requires humans to actively dismantle industrial civilization. Such is the precondition for peaceful coexistence in the Anthropocene. This requirement is both normative, and also political/tactical: normative, in the sense that ethically we need to abide by the precautionary principle for ourselves and our progeny, instrumentally; and from an ecocentric point of view, we must stop the destruction of nonhuman lifeforms (O'Brien, 2010; Callicott, 2013). Politically, it means we need clear strategies to change democracy, getting rid of lobbying power in the United States, and corruption everywhere, while putting all our resources from taxes (including a carbon tax) towards generating adaptive resiliency. These moves require challenging capitalism (Daly and Cobb, 1994; Korten, 2001; Patel, 2009; New Economics Foundation, 2015), and also anthropocentrism.

For the remainder of this chapter, I will highlight one of the leading North American-based radical environmental groups that are working on both of these fronts, Deep Green Resistance (DGR). This group has internalized the shock and concern of realizing the hyperobject of global warming and has taken seriously the reality of interconnectedness while arguing for their conception of a democratic global commons. Overall, DGR advocate for decisive ecological warfare (DEW) to help generate industrial collapse, as they claim this is the only viable path towards a resilient future for all lifeforms.

Before proceeding, I must make it clear that while DGR's end-game vision for peaceful coexistence with non-human and human others is similar to mine and others in this book, my summary of their strategies and tactics should not be interpreted as my being a member of DGR, or offering support for all of their tactics. Rather, I am interested as a scholar in how their tactics suggest that if humanity is to navigate to a peaceful coexistence in the hyperobject of the Anthropocene, this navigation may require some groups of humans to act in ways that are at odds with to-date legitimate democratic principles and accepted tactics. The larger implications of our embeddedness in hyperobjects may require new forms of political protest and tactical strategies, of which DGR presents one possible model. Whether this model is valid and worth supporting is for readers to decide on their own, but as scholars, we are remiss to not investigate and analyse the various attempts some humans are making to secure a hoped-for peaceful future.

3 Deep Green Resistance

Deep Green Resistance is a group created by US activists Derrick Jensen, Lierre Keith, and Aric McBay (who has since left the group over disagreements with the other two about DGR's views on transgender issues), who stand firm with the conviction that 'biotic collapse' (McBay, Keith and Jensen, 2011, p. 225) threatens the entirety of all extant lifeforms.[2] DGR interpret various scientific data about species extinctions, global warming, ocean acidification, soil loss (note: all of these are forms of human-induced hyperobjects) and political/cultural issues of power (race, class, gender, Global North/Global South relations, environmental justice), and views these trajectories through a lens of subversive militant tactics. DGR's reading of this data, and their analysis of issues of power, convince them that:

> Mainstream environmentalism has . . . largely ignor[ed] the deeply entrenched nature of ecocidal activities in the capitalist economy, in industry, in daily life, and in the psychology of the civilized. Furthermore, mainstream environmentalists—who often do not come out of a long tradition of resistance—utterly ignore the force that those in power will bring to bear on any threat to that power.
>
> (ibid., pp. 374–375)

For DGR, there is no 'green' techno-fix to the hyperobjects of global warming and species extinction. There is also no permaculture/ecovillage/Transition Town-induced alternative, where people can walk away from industrial capitalism and reside instead in such ecocommunities. For one, DGR argue that such communities will still be vulnerable to hyperobjects (my framing, not theirs); for another, they argue such communities are defenceless against entrenched regimes of power, who DGR maintain will take by violent force what little resources remain in an area in order to stay in power. This would include violently appropriating ecovillages and the like, especially as resource scarcity is encountered in currently protected/sheltered parts of the Global North. For DGR, such protection is currently propped up by importing resources and exporting waste, and access to needed resources is maintained through unequal trade regimes or outright by violent military interventions. Furthermore, while DGR might tactically support groups who recognize that 'action toward sustainability requires criticism and transformation of state structure and policy' (Barry, 2006, p. 33), they maintain that such transformation is based on wishful thinking. While DGR support what they call 'aboveground' political tactics, they nonetheless maintain

2 For a list of frequently asked questions, and DGR's answers, ranging from 'Who speaks on behalf of DGR?' to 'Why does civilization need to be dismantled?', see Deep Green Resistance (2015a). For an interview with Derrick Jensen that summarizes McBay et al., 2011 see Challenging Civilisation Blog (2015).

that these tactics will take way too long to accomplish even if nation-states were willing to move away from ecocidal laws and policies.

Rather, DGR's political analysis is that there is no democratic way to stop industrial capitalism's assault on the planet's resources and its remaining indigenous/women/developing countries. Thus for DGR the only way to hope to stop runaway collapse is to actively work on dismantling industrial capitalism. Their strategy to do so, what they call 'decisive ecological warfare', is justified and outlined in their operating manual, *Deep Green Resistance* (McBay et al., 2011).

DEW calls for the formation of aboveground campaigning, using forms of boycotting, protesting and public community organizing to pressure for political change. Yet, and strategically, what this aboveground presence is intended to do is to grant legitimacy and offer public support for the clandestine subversive warfare-tactics of underground coteries and cells that are engaged in attacking industrial infrastructure. These attacks can be cyber, on for example the computers that help run the stock market; or infrastructural, on for example the power grid that powers the computers that run the stock market. DGR advocate for attacks on remote infrastructure that is poorly guarded, such as dams, or supply trains for coal power plants, or ports, where attacks on such infrastructure are aimed at crippling the ability of the extractive, industrial economy to function. These attacks are in essence strategic targeting of property for destruction by using various types of explosives and other methods of subversive militant warfare. Underground actions are strategically and ethically justified because every action that helps halt the ecocide of the planet, in DGR's opinion, creates operating room for all other lifeforms to continue to thrive. DGR's hope is that enough underground groups emerge in the coming decades to generate sustained attacks on vulnerable industrial infrastructure so that eventually it becomes too cost-prohibitive to keep rebuilding and policing this infrastructure. This creates an active slippery slope such that industrial infrastructure collapses, and with it, industrial civilization.

DGR maintain that elected leaders will not take hyperobjects of the Anthropocene seriously, and that, 'one of the primary functions of government is to protect the rich sociopaths from the outrage of the rest of us' (McBay et al., 2011, p. 388). They further caution that, 'any effective action against those in power will trigger a forceful, and likely violent, response' (ibid., p. 244).

Given the above militant tactics, with an expected violent response from those in power, what motivates those in DGR? The answer, given below, is helpfully analysed by Tim Morton's call for a truly democratic encounter with non-human others within the context of hyperobjects. DGR's answer is also a rebuttal to 10,000+ years of misothery that is embedded in our agriculture, which itself has contributed to the Anthropocene. For DGR, the answer is the protection of life itself, for 'Life wants to live: our communion and battle cry' (ibid., p. 496).

Such religious terminology ('communion') is not haphazardly applied here by DGR. Indeed, they are clear in claiming that what motivates them directly is their love for all life forms, and their mantra for planning both aboveground and underground tactics is 'repair, restore, rejoin' (ibid., p. 509). 'Rejoin' here is similar in connotation to one of the possible meanings of the word 'religion': to rebind, bind back together. For DGR, this binding back together is of humans with the rest of life. To do so for DGR means humans have to repair and restore damaged and desecrated Earth and to rejoin the community of life in a truly democratic encounter. For DGR, such rejoining is ontological – it is a spiritual realization that we are animals, that we are part of life unfolding and that our true human identity is coterminous with the flourishing of all other life forms, which we should treat with reverent care. It is the antidote of human superiority that is embedded in misothery, and it is that antidote that DGR would claim needs to be a precondition for a peaceful coexistence with other lifeforms in the Anthropocene.

With their almost pantheistic view of nature, and of the human place in the natural world, DGR are very clear in their literature (both print and online) that they are motivated by ecocentric concerns. As their guiding statement of principles #1 and #2 proclaim (Deep Green Resistance, 2015b):

> The soil, the air, the water, the climate, and the food we eat are created by complex communities of living creatures. The needs of those living communities are primary; individual and social morality must emerge from a humble relationship with the web of life. Civilization, especially industrial civilization, is fundamentally destructive to life on Earth. Our task is to create a life-centered resistance movement that will dismantle industrial civilization by any means necessary. Organized political resistance is the only hope for our planet.

Here is a value system deduced from hyperobjects – biodiversity in its full flourishing; the soil food web; a stable climate – as well as a political strategy: strategic warfare, to protect sacred life and the future of life from a mode of living that according to Kirkpatrick Sale stretches back 22,000 years.

4 Citizenship in the Anthropocene

What does it mean to be an organism, let alone a social mammal, in a home that is being irreparably altered by our own actions, where some are much more complicit and guilty than others in driving such seemingly pathological alteration? How do we grapple with the imbalances of power, of access and of culpability that are at play in this altering, while recognizing that, as Michael Klare explains, violence is being driven by both greed and grievance, and will only exacerbate in this century of resource shortages?[3] As the Zen-trained poet, neo-animist and bioregional activist Gary Snyder (1990, p. 176) noted,

3 From a public talk, and then classroom visit, to the College of Charleston, SC in October 2014.

> The extinction of a species, each one a pilgrim of four billion years of evolution, is an irreversible loss. The ending of the lines of so many creatures with whom we have traveled this far is an occasion of profound sorrow and grief . . . the loss of lineages and all their future young is not something to accept. It must be rigorously and intelligently resisted.

What does this resistance look like? What does it require? Who is obligated to undertake it? What forces are arrayed to thwart counter-hegemonic narratives and lifestyles? Are the structural dynamics of neoliberal capitalism and representative democracy, either together or separately, capable of promoting the public good? This last question is apropos for this volume, for as the political scientist and sustainability expert Leslie Paul Thiele (2011, p. 201) explains, 'Politics concerns the pursuit of public goods. Sustainability is such a good . . . Without an equitable distribution of power, the equitable distribution of other goods [can]not be achieved or sustained'.

Earlier in this chapter I used Tim Morton's frame of a hyperobject as one lens through which we can better understand the enormity of the Anthropocene, and shared the following quote in so doing: 'What we desperately need is an appropriate level of shock and anxiety concerning a specific ecological trauma—indeed, *the* ecological trauma of our age' (Morton, 2013, pp. 8–9, italics in original). In my analysis, DGR fully recognize – politically, ethically, biologically and, importantly, religiously – the reality of this ecological trauma. Such shock and anxiety motivates DGR's resistance tactics, which include above and belowground insurrection. Aboveground, DEW calls for boycotts, dissemination of propaganda and creating a culture of resistance. The goal of these actions is to create space for underground eco-guerilla fighters to act in clandestine cells, undertaking reconnaissance of vulnerable industrial infrastructure, followed by strategic strikes against said infrastructure. DGR justify this strategy, as it is driven by the pain, sorrow, grief, and yes, trauma, they feel for the systematic destruction of the Earth's ecosystems, indigenous peoples, women and marginalized communities of colour. Theirs is a strategy based on insights from North American radical environmentalism, radical feminism, and armed guerilla movements of the past 150 years going back to North American slave insurrections.

Members of DGR who advocate DEW take ecocentric kinship as their starting point, maintaining that allegiance to the flourishing of life on our home trumps any allegiance to arbitrary and fictitious systems of identity based on class, race or nationality. In so doing, they are acting on Thiele's insight that for sustainability to occur, power must be dispersed and multiple stakeholders must be considered. DGR begin from the position of non-human life and millions of points of view embedded in the organismic plenty of our planetary commons. These voices are silenced in most modern politics, and are equally silenced in the orthodoxy of neoliberal economics. Given this, from the point of view of Christian 'Just War Theory', DGR might argue that the two key litmus tests of Just War – legitimacy and proportionality – are met. From this view, while they recognize that innocent human lives will be lost if DEW is undertaken as they hope, this loss pales into insignificance in comparison to the larger loss of almost all terrestrial and aquatic life if industrial civilization is not halted by active, and even armed resistance.

So although things are getting worse and worse – the Anthropocene, as constituted by a variety of hyperobjects, is going to lead to very different human futures – there are those who are actively responding. These responses, whether militant like DGR, theatrical like the All Species Parade in Olympia, Washington (United States), ethical and/or religious, as with the Pope's encyclical of 2015, signal that things may possibly also improve. One of the emerging hopes of 'globalization from below', or what Paul Hawken (2008) calls 'blessed unrest', is the call that we redefine our citizenship. This is exactly what DGR are asking of their audience, in ways that challenge hegemonic conceptions of technology, civilization, industrial lifeways, neoliberal economics, politics, legitimate tactics of resistance, contemporary religion and anthropocentric ethics.

If emerging forms of Anthropocene citizenship are built upon ecological thought, and take seriously issues of justice, equality and equity, then our entry into the Anthropocene carries with it not only tragedy, but also hope. Such a hope is dependent on us realizing our interconnectedness with all of life, forged by dwelling in the numinous presence of Life. As the hyperobject of the Anthropocene continues, it is plausible that our fragility as a species will become readily apparent, and our dependency upon the Earth will become unavoidable. In effect, the last 22,000 years of power-over life, of psychological distancing and structural violence that is manifested in our technologies and social institutions, is going to be confronted. This confrontation is precisely what DGR are calling for: a militant confrontation with the powers that destroy life. Again, the reader need not agree with their call – rather, their call presents evidence of an emergent ecocentric hope for peaceful coexistence with the rest of life. Their call for biocentric religiosities means that their militant confrontation is couched in seeing life, in its evolutionary diversity, as sacred. The fragility of our tenuous grasp on maintaining a viable habitat – seen already for example in California and Brazil, with their record droughts triggered by climate change, and Syrian refugee crises caused by the same – may very well awaken us to the beauty of the natural world. With luck, there might be enough time yet, for more and more Earth citizens to be inspired to realize that dwelling in 'the presence of the present' (F4GlobalHumanity, 2015) is our human birthright, and we must fight, in our own ways, for a viable future that is just, peaceful and sustainable for all lifeforms.

Bibliography

Abram, D. (1996) *The Spell of the Sensuous: Perception and Language in a More-Than-Human-World*. New York: Pantheon Books.

Albrecht, G. (2005) "Solastalgia". A New Concept in Health and Identity. *PAN: Philosophy Activism Nature*. 3, 41–55.

Barnosky, A. D., Hadly, E. A., Bascompte, J., Berlow, E. L., Brown, J. H., Fortelius, M., Getz, W. M., Harte, J., Hastings, A., Marquet, P. A., Martinez, N. D., Mooers,

A., Roopnarine, P., Vermeij, G., Williams, J. W., Gillespie, R., Kitzes, J., Marshall, C., Matzke, N., Mindell, D. P., Revilla, E. & Smith, A. B. (2012) Approaching a State-shift in the Biosphere. *Nature*. 486, 52–58.

Barry, J. (2006) Resistance is Fertile: From Environmental to Sustainability Citizenship. In: Dobson, A. & Bell, D. (eds) *Environmental Citizenship*. Cambridge, MA: The MIT Press, pp. 21–48.

Bender, J. (2003) *The Culture of Extinction: Towards a Philosophy of Deep Ecology*. New York: Humanity Books.

Callicott, J. B. (2013) *Thinking Like a Planet: The Land Ethic and the Earth Ethic*. New York: Oxford University Press.

Carson, R. (1962) *Silent Spring*. Boston: Houghton Mifflin Company.

Challenging Civilisation Blog (2015) Derrick Jensen Interview Part 1 – Deep Green Resistance. Available from: www.youtube.com/watch?v=avIFnWzY1ZI (accessed 24 April 2015).

Cleveland, D. (2014) Resilience: Antidote for the Anthropocene. *Resilience: A Journal for the Environmental Humanities*. 1, n/a.

Crist, E. (2013) On the Poverty of Our Nomenclature. *Environmental Humanities*. 3, 129–147.

Daly, H. & Cobb, J. (1994) *For the Common Good: Redirecting the Economy toward Community, the Environment, and a Sustainable Future*. Boston: Beacon Press.

Deep Green Resistance (2015a) Frequently Asked Question of Deep Green Resistance. Available from: deepgreenresistance.org/en/who-we-are/faqs/deep-green-resistance-faqs (accessed 15 March 2015).

Deep Green Resistance (2015b) Guiding Principles of Deep Green Resistance. Available from: http://deepgreenresistance.org/en/who-we-are/guiding-principles-of-deep-green-resistance (accessed 15 March 2015).

F4GlobalHumanity (2015) David Adram at the SEED Language of Spirit Conference. Available from: https://www.youtube.com/watch?v=xrLxEKgTGZ4 (accessed 24 April 2015).

Haberl, H. (2006) The Global Socioeconomic Energetic Metabolism as a Sustainability Problem. *Energy*. 31, 87–99.

Hawken, P. (2008) *Blessed Unrest: How the Largest Social Movement in History is Restoring Grace, Justice, and Beauty to the World*. New York: Penguin.

Ingold, T. (2009) On Weaving a Basket. In: Candlin, F. & Guins, R. (eds) *The Object Reader*. New York: Routledge, pp. 339–348.

Ivakhiv, A. J. (2014) Against the Anthropocene. *Immanence: Ecoculture, Geophilosophy, Mediapolitics*. Available from: http://blog.uvm.edu/aivakhiv/2014/07/07/against-the-anthropocene (accessed 4 March 2015).

Korten, D. (2001) *When Corporations Rule the World*. Oakland, CA: Berrett-Koehler Publishers.

Macy, J. & Johnstone, C. (2012) *Active Hope: How to Face the Mess We're in Without Going Crazy*. Novato, CA: New World Library.

Mason, J. (2006) The Animal Question: Uncovering the Roots of Our Domination of Nature and Each Other. In: Best, S. & Nocella, A. II (eds) *Igniting a Revolution: Voices in Defense of the Earth*. Oakland, CA: AK Press, pp. 178–185.

McBay, A., Keith, L. & Jensen, D. (2011) *Deep Green Resistance: Strategy to Save the Planet*. New York: Seven Stories Press.

Meadows, D., Meadows, D. & Randers, J. (2004) *Limits to Growth: The 30-Year Update, a Synopsis*. White River Junction, VT: Chelsea Green.

Merchant, C. (1983) *The Death of Nature: Women, Ecology and the Scientific Revolution*. San Francisco: HarperSanFrancisco.
Morton, T. (2007) *Ecology Without Nature: Rethinking Environmental Aesthetics*. Cambridge, MA: Harvard University Press.
Morton, T. (2010) *The Ecological Thought*. Cambridge, MA: Harvard University Press.
Morton, T. (2013) *Hyperobjects: Philosophy and Ecology After the End of the World*. Minneapolis: University of Minnesota Press.
Morton, T. (2015) Postcolonialists Tweaked Out by OOO, Take Note. Weblog. Available from: http://ecologywithoutnature.blogspot.com/2015/03/postcolonialists-tweaked-out-by-ooo.html (accessed 6 March 2015).
New Economics Foundation (2015). *Economics as if People and the Planet Mattered*. Available from: www.neweconomics.org (accessed 18 March 2015).
Northcott, M. (2015) *Place, Ecology and the Sacred: The Moral Geography of Sustainable Communities*. London: Bloomsbury.
O'Brien, K. (2010) *An Ethics of Biodiversity: Christianity, Ecology, and the Variety of Life*. Washington, DC: Georgetown University Press.
Patel, R. (2009) *The Value of Nothing: How to Reshape Market Society and Redefine Democracy*. New York: Picador.
Patel, R. (2012) *Stuffed and Starved: The Hidden Battle for the World Food System*. New York: Melville House.
Quinn, D. (1992) *Ishmael: An Adventure of the Mind and Spirit*. New York: Bantam.
Quinn, D. (1996) *The Story of B: An Adventure of the Mind and Spirit*. New York: Bantam.
Sale, K. (2006) *After Eden: The Evolution of Human Domination*. Durham, NC: Duke University Press.
Schneiderman, J. (2012) Awake in the Anthropocene. *Contemporary Buddhism*. 13(1), 83–97.
Shepard, P. (2004) *Coming Home to the Pleistocene*. Washington, DC: Island Press.
Shiva, V. (1989) *Staying Alive: Women, Ecology, and Development*. London: Zed Books.
Snyder, G. (1990) *The Practice of the Wild*. New York: North Point Press.
Steffen, W., Richardson, K., Rockström, J., Cornell, S. E., Fetzer, I., Bennett, E. M., Biggs, R., Carpenter, S. R., de Vries, W., de Wit, C. A., Folke, C., Gerten, D., Heinke, J., Mace, G. M., Persson, L. M., Ramanathan, V., Reyers, B. & Sörlin, S. (2015) Planetary Boundaries: Guiding Human Development on a Changing Planet. *Science*. 347, 1259855.
Thiele, L. P. (2011) *Indra's Net and the Midas Touch: Living Sustainably in a Connected World*. Cambridge, MA: The MIT Press.
Warren, K. (1990) The Power and Promise of Ecological Feminism. *Environmental Ethics*. 12(2), 125–146.
White, L. Jr. (1967) The Historical Roots of our Ecologic Crisis. *Science*. 155, 1203–1207.

7 Scale, noosphere two, and the Anthropocene

J. Mohorčich

1 Introduction

Is it productive to think systematically and globally about thought the way it is productive to think globally about life or water? Terms like biosphere or hydrosphere connote a spherical, holistic understanding of the interrelation of ecosystems and hydrological systems. They coordinate ways of thinking about organisms and water at different scales. Though these spheres of understanding – lithosphere, magnetosphere, pedosphere, cryosphere and atmosphere – are familiar intellectual artefacts, the question of what sort of knowledge can be organized under the -sphere rubric remains open. The same question haunts another suffix, -cene, lately in vogue. Debates over whether 'we' are in the Anthropocene, the Capitalocene, the Gynocene, Plantationocene or still just the Holocene will always be in part about how a given set of arguments can be reorganized by a specific metaphoric framework. This recalls arguments in the second half of the twentieth century over what you could rightly append the prefix 'post-' to. In the case of the cenes, as with the posts before them, the question that makes the debate possible has to do with what there is to be gained by reconstituting a set of existing arguments within a new temporal metaphor. The spheres have not caught on in the same way as the cenes or the posts,[1] but they could have just as easily, if the right group of scholars had broken towards spatial metaphors rather than temporal ones, if someone had been reading back issues of the *Journal of Earth System Science* at the right time.

This chapter, then, is going to explore a backroad suffix, -sphere, through an old term, the noosphere, not only to see how workable 'noosphere' itself is, but to offer an avowedly spatial metaphor as a counterpoint to the abundance of temporal metaphors on offer in contemporary planetary thinking. Discussing the noosphere is worthwhile for at least two additional reasons that I can see. Just as a revived geopolitics reminds us that politics occurs on uneven geophysical terrain (Deudney, 2000), and that the contours of this terrain matter a great deal, political

1 As of April 2016, an internet search for 'capitalosphere' returns just three results, all of which are WordPress or Tumblr posts.

and social life also take place on an uneven terrain of thought. Like the lithosphere, cognition is unevenly distributed across populations, space and time. The contours of this distribution bear on the lives of societies, humans and the other animals, and the noosphere offers a rubric for beginning to think about the thicknesses, depths and uneven sedimentation of thought on and around Earth. Second, an analysis of the noosphere begins to backfill one of the persistent gaps that arises in theoretical debates over the competing roles played by material and ideational factors in 'constructing' reality (Putnam and Mumby, 2014). These debates often arrive at a ceasefire brokered by the claim that material and ideational elements mutually co-constitute one another. A fully fleshed-out noosphere story (more detailed than the one I offer here) offers one conceptual route towards filling in the *how* that is so often missing from claims that this or that object of analysis is socially constructed and also physical or that 'materiality and discourse mutually constitute each other' (Putnam and Mumby, 2014, p. 283).

Noosphere seems to collect definitions. Pierre Teilhard de Chardin understands it as a universal synthesis 'in which spirit and its understanding embrace the whole and are blended into a kind of living organism' (Ratzinger, 2000, p. 29). Vladimir Ivanovich Vernadsky writes that it is 'the last of many stages in the evolution of the biosphere in geological history' (Vernadsky, 1945, p. 10). I depart from these views. I make four main arguments about how noosphere can be productively understood. First, I argue that the noosphere scales up with human populations and new systems for the production of knowledge. Second, I argue for a 'material metabolism' between the noosphere and its environment (between, e.g., the noosphere and the biosphere). Third, I emphasize that the noosphere is not wholly determined by material conditions. Exchanges among ideas can drive growth. This point is also linked, through Joseph Tainter, Larry Page and Sergey Brin, with problems of scale and increasing complexity. Finally, I consider the noosphere's non-human inputs.

These arguments involve re-sketching 'the sphere of human thought' (Levit, 2000, p. 161) without resorting to folk psychology, theology, utopianism or mysticism. I am offering a rehabilitation of the term noosphere that de-emphasizes the notion of a unified sphere and emphasizes instead the 'loops that slowly draw' thought on planet Earth (Latour, 2013, p. 95). Here is a list of traits for 'noosphere two':

- the noosphere is made up of the thoughts, ideas, theories and knowledge generated on and around Earth;
- for an idea to be counted as part of the noosphere, it must interact with other items in the noosphere (intentionally recursive, following work by Luhmann, Page and Brin);
- the noosphere continually makes and is made by thought, as autopoietic systems make and are made by their components (Luhmann, 1996);
- no idea is permanent, but must be made and remade – the noosphere's capacity to forget is therefore its capacity to avoid reproducing a set of components;

- the noosphere supervenes on material conditions: brains, nutrients, machine intelligence, ink, data centres – it shares a material metabolism with its physical environment;
- and, as Bruno Latour writes, 'the concept of a loop' takes precedence 'over that of the sphere' (Latour, 2013, p. 95).[2]

Note that this noosphere stakes nothing on being or not being 'secular': this chapter is not a disenchantment project. If it is secular, it is only so in the way Latour might use the term, as the header of a column that reshuffles terms of belief.

2 Scale

Discussing the noosphere means discussing actual complexes of knowledge production: the physical locations, incentives, material conditions, economic arrangements and social formations that make possible the knowledge, theory, observation, description and ideas that constitute the noosphere. This chapter is concerned with human knowledge considered as a global network of interacting constituents in self-replicating loops and nested systems. That is, knowledge considered on the model of the biosphere, and as part of the biosphere.

To make sense of what follows, it is helpful to divide inputs external to the noosphere from those internal to it. Some inputs operate mostly outside the noosphere – material shifts, say, rather than exchanges between ideas. Population growth is an example of an external input.[3] Internal factors take place mostly on the level of ideas – the cycles of intellectual disagreement, anastomosis, synthesis, fracture and so forth that lead to flourishing in certain intellectual areas and reliction in others. Ideas supervene on material conditions, but interact with other ideas and feed back into the material world, reshaping it.

The Toba extinction event (ca 70,000 BC) left alive fewer than 5,000 human breeding pairs (Ambrose, 1998). By 200 BC, while Eratosthenes was writing the *Geographika* and calculating the circumference of the Earth, the human population had hit 231 million (Biraben, 1979). The number of live human brains on planet Earth now numbers 7.17 billion (United States Census Bureau, 2014). By now everyone is familiar with this graph (Figure 7.1).

One conjectured side effect of human population growth, pointed out by both Simon Kuznets (1960) and Pope Benedict XVI (Tenner, 2010), is that the production of knowledge is at least partly a numbers game. Kuznets and the Pope emeritus both suggest that human beings are due for an intellectual windfall in

2 Latour later writes that he does not mean loops in the 'cybernetic sense', but as 'networks of equipment that render the consequences of action visible to all the various agencies that do the acting – not only, for instance, the actions of the former humans, but also those of nitrogen releasing algae or that of rock weathering roots and nodules'. Thankfully, the two usages are not mutually exclusive. I intend both.

3 Although it retains ideational aspects: 'I'm ready to have a child this year', 'I don't believe in contraception', etc.

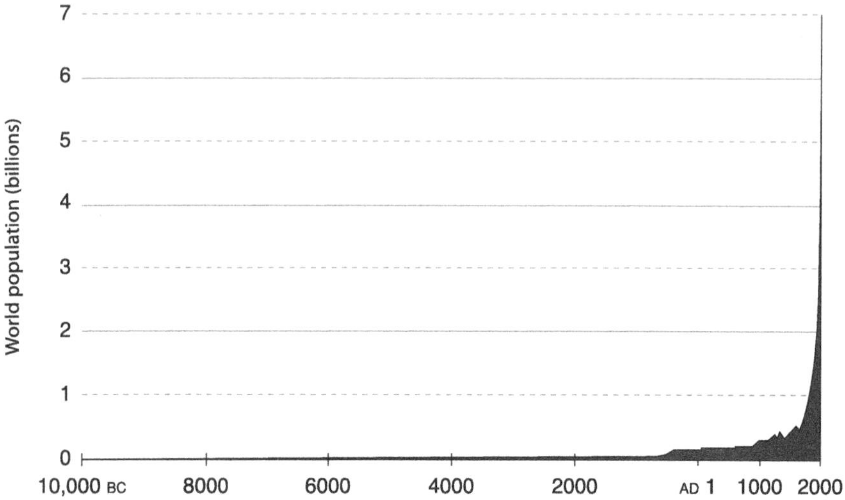

Figure 7.1 World population.

Source: Data from the United States Census Bureau, 2013; for criticism on the scale used see Gallagher, 1993.

proportion to their increasing numbers. We need not accept the idea of a population-driven 'genius machine'[4] to admit that the sheer number of thinking organisms creates the conditions for rapid changes in the noosphere, if for no other reason than the activity of thinking beings is what makes up the noosphere.

The health of human brains and bodies is a major material condition for the growth and complexity of the noosphere. As recently as the 1740s, three-quarters of children born in London died before the age of five (Buer, 1926). Today, London's childhood mortality rate is less than 1 per cent (Merton, 2015). Not only are human numbers larger in an absolute sense, more brains are positioned to exchange ideas with other brains, and to contribute to reproducing and growing the noosphere. Additionally, the growth and professionalization of academe represents a new type of input to the noosphere, a brute-force attack that takes

4 This argument is sometimes made by inviting the reader to imagine a previous genius from history (disproportionately Mozart), pointing out how few people lived at the time of this genius's flourishing, and wondering how many more Shakespeares, Aristotles, Lovelaces, and Eratostheneses are surely alive in a world of 7 billion. Of course, another way of construing this thought experiment is to point out that genius is not a function of how many times humanity plays the genetic lottery per reproduction cycle (otherwise we'd be inundated by Aristotles and Shakespeares) but rather that what ends up recognized as 'genius' has to do with a host of historical, social, nutritional, cultural, scientific, meteorological, technological, and genetic factors, and that we *are* surrounded by Curies and Carvers, but they are unexceptional. In the twenty-first century, genius is simply good dentistry.

advantage of material wealth in the West to finance a system in which the generation and dissemination of ideas (publish or perish) is its own goal. This state of affairs has led to rapid increases in the complexity and quantity of scholarship, and in the way ideas are handled. Derek J. de Solla Price, one of the first academics to quantify the growth of scholarship in the sciences, finds that:

> all crude measures, however arrived at, show to a first approximation that science increases exponentially, at a compound interest of about 7% per annum, thus doubling in size every 10–15 years, growing by a factor of 10 every half century, and by something like a factor of a million in the 300 years which separate us from the seventeenth-century invention of the scientific paper when the process began.
>
> (de Solla Price, 1965, p. 234). For one attempt to plot this growth in the twentieth century, see Figure 7.2.

In their study, Larsen and von Ins (2010, p. 583) note the impact of material conditions on scholarship production as follows:

> The curves for Chemical Abstracts reveal some interesting features. The negative effect of the two world wars and the extremely fast growth after the wars is clearly visible. Also the stagnation in the 1930s caused by the economic crisis from 1929 is clearly visible. This demonstrates that differences

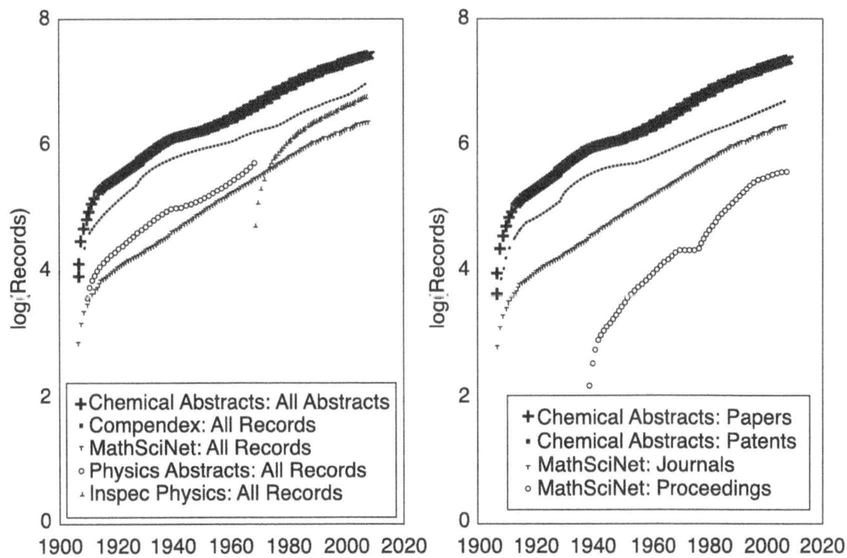

Figure 7.2 Semi-log plot of the total number of records of nine scientific paper databases, 1907–2007.

Source: Larsen and von Ins, 2010, p. 583.

> in growth rates can be explained and comprehended. In the period from 1974 to 1990 there is also a clear decline in the growth rate. This is followed by an increase in the period from 1990 to 2007 but the high values from before 1974 have not been reached again. Six different growth periods, 1907–1914, 1920–1930, 1930–1939, 1945–1974, 1974–1990, and 1990–2007, can be observed.

I return to this question in Section 3, where I suggest that the academy faces an intensifying problem of scale, and that this intensification maps a trend internal to the noosphere. Exponential increases in knowledge production shifts at least some portion of the burden of intellectual labor from generating more ideas toward holistically linking and understanding existing knowledge. The primary challenge, as many academics note, is reading even a tenth of what is relevant to one's field of study. (A similar problem arose during the explosion of the internet in the mid-nineties.)

In the next section, I consider metabolism and the material conditions for the noosphere.

3 Metabolism

The noosphere and biosphere[5] cannot be separated. A 'material metabolism' operates between the two (Urry, 2011, p. 50). Consider John Urry's (2011, p. 50) claim (following Marx) that 'humans are part of nature but, in working on that nature, transform themselves and the material world. In these metabolic relations, new socio-natural forms are constantly being produced'. The major inputs to the noosphere, human brains, draw on a wide array of material processes and resources in order to continue functioning. The production, maintenance and dissemination of knowledge represent key sites of metabolism between the atmosphere, lithosphere, biosphere and noosphere. These metabolic sites can be perfectly literal: modern data centres now account for 1.3 per cent of worldwide electricity usage (Gigaom, 2012). A server rack in one of these data centres, which includes elements such as silicon and lithium drawn from the Earth's crust and is powered by coal and natural gas plants that increase the atmospheric concentrations of carbon dioxide, which changes the acidity and temperature of the world's oceans, which leads to phenomena like coral bleaching. These cycles of organization, consumption and deformation are driven by what are normally thought of as immaterial: emails, log-in pages, forum posts, streaming videos. It is not enough to declare that what passes through the data centres of the world is 'embedded in a material context'. True enough, but understanding these expressions, messages and digital exchanges as part of a sphere of thought with its own varied distributions and flows helps give a fuller account of the way that emails pass through not

5 All living things on and around Earth taken collectively.

just fibre optic cables, but silica sand deposits, the lungs of coal miners, coral reefs and the minds of those who write and read them. Leaving out thought as its own semi-independent sphere makes it difficult to explain the provenance of what actually passes through and makes necessary the infrastructure of information systems. Changes in material conditions affect the noosphere, and changes in the noosphere affect the material world.

Consider, too, Urry's description of 'a new metabolism beginning within the US' (Urry, 2011, pp. 51–53). He argues that 'a dramatically novel cluster of powerful high carbon systems was unleashed in the early to middle years of that century. These interdependent systems produced a powerful metabolism.' Urry shows how new power grids, cars, detached houses, consumer electronics and 'specialized leisure sites' constitute 'high carbon systems' that change the metabolic relationship between human society and the planet. It is easy to see how the noosphere is involved in the development of suburbs, cars and motorist-centred cities: conceiving of the automobile, planning it, constructing roads, imagining traffic patterns and so forth involve ideas and insights about what a car is, what it ought it be and how to do things with and for it. Urry (2011, p. 52) describes a 'path-dependent clustering' that contributes to the perpetuation of carbon-intensive systems. This path dependency can be traced to interactions within the noosphere: of the ascendancy or dissolution of certain ideas about how to move, to eat, to live.

The space of ideas is affected by straightforward material changes, of course: it is obvious that a Torino-10 impact event[6] would alter the noosphere as surely as it would the biosphere. The noosphere and biosphere are interlinked because they share metabolic pathways. They remain, however, partially independent from one another. Can the noosphere alter itself and its material effects through internal processes?

4 Intra-noological changes

In Section 1, I suggested that questions of scale play an increasingly important role in the ways that knowledge circulates and reproduces itself. Recall that the graphs in Figure 7.2 represent only the total number of published entries in certain scientific databases. This data offers a way of estimating the growth of the volume of papers, but says nothing about the quantity, quality and complexity of the ideas in those papers. The material changes I have outlined above (increased population, shifts in nutrition and resource availability) have contributed to easily quantifiable growth described by broad metrics like the total number of scientific papers accessible in a given database, but this skims over which specific ideas or patterns of thought are active within the noosphere.

6 A devastating collision between Earth and a near-Earth object. For more, see Morrison et al., (2004).

One intra-noological phenomenon worth discussing has to do with how increases in conceptual complexity can drive further increases in complexity. As Joseph Tainter argues (2006, p. 96), problem-solving systems tend to generate solutions to problems that are more complex than the original problem.[7] These more-complex solutions beget a second generation of problems. Solving this new, more-complex set of problems involves solutions that are more complex still, breeding a series of increasingly complex problems, and so on. 'Efforts at problem solving', Tainter writes, 'commonly evolve along a path of increasing complexity, higher costs, and declining marginal returns.' This feedback loop is acute in the academy. Because academics are pushed to produce work that generates and solves problems, and because they are compared to each other in a competitive framework, complexity arms races are constantly igniting in various disciplines and sub-disciplines. Consider, as an example, the multi-decade popularity of the practice of showing this or that thing to be 'problematic'. This is not to pass judgement on the validity of any specific theoretical technique – indeed many things *are* problematic, and the hypertrophy of criticism aimed at problematization has helped us see this – but to locate one feedback loop driving the proliferation of scholarship that aims at the further complication of the already complicated work that came before it. The ideas themselves, therefore, are growing more intricate as a reaction to increasingly more complex problems and as a way of competing in an intellectual ecosystem where complexity is one means of survival. Growing complexity, therefore, can be driven by interactions and loops within the noosphere.

Complexity, however, is expensive:

> In 4 million years of hominid existence, complexity is recent and rare. This is because every increase in complexity has a cost. The cost of complexity is the energy, labor, money, or time that is needed to create, maintain, and replace systems that grow to have more and more parts, more specialists, more regulation of behavior, and more information.
>
> (Tainter, 2006, p. 93)

This invites two questions: what are the external costs of the noological complexity – that is, what does an increasingly complex noosphere do to systems with which it shares material metabolism, like the biosphere – and what are the costs of complexity within the noosphere? Answering the first question is a few books beyond the scope of this chapter, but, as I have suggested, one approach to it begins by considering shared metabolic pathways. I consider the second question now.

My answer involves a return to a theme I have mentioned before: exponential increases in the complexity and quantity of knowledge produce a situation wherein

7 This thesis is not universally true, of course: when parsimonious frameworks appear and where they are convincing they can supplant more complicated alternatives.

the primary motivating problem for knowledge producer-consumers (e.g. academics, scientists, writers, citizens) is not the creation of 'new' or 'better' ideas, but rather involves developing a way of making what already exists (and what is constantly being produced) scalable. One instance of this problem arose midway through the first decade of the global expansion of TCP/IP, the internet protocol suite that makes the worldwide web possible – a time period that coincides with an increase of internet users from 3 million in the early 1990s to 350 million by the year 2000 (Internet World Stats, 2014). During this explosion, the internet (the story goes) suffered no lack of content, but became increasingly difficult to navigate and impossible to organize. In Palo Alto, a third-year Ph.D. student named Larry Page began working on a dissertation that involved thinking about the growing amount of knowledge on the internet as a constellation of documents best understood by examining the links between its constituents. Page, joined by Sergey Brin, argued that scale posed the primary challenge for internet search engines:

> Search engine technology has had to scale dramatically to keep up with the growth of the web. In 1994, one of the first web search engines, the World Wide Web Worm (WWWW) had an index of 110,000 web pages and web accessible documents. As of November, 1997, the top search engines claim to index from 2 million (WebCrawler) to 100 million web documents (from Search Engine Watch). It is foreseeable that by the year 2000, a comprehensive index of the Web will contain over a billion documents.
>
> (Page and Brin, 1998, p. 108)

(Modern search engines index between 20 and 45 billion documents.)[8] Page and Brin (1998, pp. 109–110) approach the problem of scale by emphasizing the links between documents, arguing that:

> counting citations or backlinks to a given page . . . gives some approximation of a page's importance or quality. PageRank extends this idea by not counting links from all pages equally, and by normalizing by the number of links on a page . . . a page can have a high PageRank if there are many pages that point to it, or if there are some pages that point to it and have a high PageRank. Intuitively, pages that are well cited from many places around the web are worth looking at . . . PageRank handles both these cases and everything in between by recursively propagating weights through the link structure of the web.

8 Methods for estimating the 'size' of the internet are notoriously unreliable. The best attempts at estimation – even of something as apparently straightforward as 'how many active pages exist?' invariably turn into explanations about why no one really knows (see e.g. WorldWideWebSize, 2014).

The linked structure of knowledge is crucial. There are no noological isolates. In other words, every idea is embedded, connected with others. Page and Brin's method of handling rapidly expanding systems of knowledge represents an influential model for approaching problems of scale in the academy and in the noosphere more broadly. However, it is an imperfect framework rather than an airtight solution, and certain problems of scale remain. I describe two here.

The first problem might be called citation inflation. A system like PageRank that emphasizes connections is only as good as the connections it draws on. If links between documents do not reflect the quality of what they connect, the system reflects only connections, not quality. If links are determined, for example, by mutualistic relationships (a cite for a cite), a system that keys on them may overemphasize the importance of information produced by close-knit groups, whatever their quality. Citation cabals like those that arise in academic disciplines, therefore, present uneven bibliometric terrain.

The second problem is the growth of relevance. Page and Brin (1998, pp. 108–109) write that one of the primary issues created by scale is junk:

> In 1994, some people believed that a complete search index would make it possible to find anything easily . . . However, the Web of 1997 is quite different. Anyone who has used a search engine recently can readily testify that the completeness of the index is not the only factor in the quality of search results. 'Junk results' often wash out any results that a user is interested in. In fact, as of November 1997, only one of the top four commercial search engines finds itself (returns its own search page in response to its name in the top ten results). One of the main causes of this problem is that the number of documents in the indices has been increasing by many orders of magnitude, but the user's ability to look at documents has not.

Irrelevant results choke out relevant ones, and human attention is limited. Page and Brin propose as a solution a more precise, interlinked system for locating and ordering results called PageRank. However, this does not solve the problem of there being many truly relevant results – orders of magnitude more than any person could read and understand. The reader's ability to know is being outstripped by his or her species' capability to produce knowledge. I have previously argued that this state of affairs has been made possible by the loosening – or, rather, unequal global distribution – of material constraints on knowledge production and also by a multibillion-dollar system that rewards the production (but not necessarily the use) of increasingly complex published knowledge.

Material inputs alone do not drive the growth and complexity of the noosphere. Internal developments such as increasingly complex conceptual frameworks and problem-solving methods also contribute. The complexity feedback loop, at least in academe, is accelerated by factors like tenure requirements and competition between academics. Page and Brin's PageRank approach offers one method of dealing with noological growth that has seen relative success on what will soon be regarded as a modest scale (~40 billion items) but fails to resolve all the issues of scale, including the disjuncture between citations and quality and the fact that under conditions of rapid noological expansion, even a search engine that returns only relevant results may still overwhelm the user.

5 Is the noosphere just 'the sphere of human thought'?

If human brains are the noosphere's primary input, can non-human entities contribute to the noosphere? In this section, I consider machine intelligence and non-human animals.

Recall that the primary criterion for recognizing something as an element of the noosphere is relational. If an idea interacts with other ideas – that is, if it modifies, alters, is modified by, mixes with other ideas – then it can be considered an element of the noosphere. Note that, lightly following Niklas Luhmann (1996) and other systems theorists, this interaction must take place on the level of ideas. That is: if you say that water is liquid at room temperature and I add the caveat 'at a pressure >1 kPa and <1 GPa', this is a noological interaction linked to and now part of structures of thought about phase changes, meteorology, epistemology, etc. thousands of years deep. If you say that water is liquid at room temperature and a boulder crushes you to death, the boulder has not joined the noosphere because it has not interacted with your idea on the level of ideas. In Luhmannese, the boulder has only 'irritated' the noosphere, not joined it (Luhmann, 1996, pp. 38–39). The task, then, is to decide if machine intelligence produces knowledge that interacts with other knowledge and therefore partially constitutes the noosphere.

It does. The chess engine Deep Blue's 1997 moves against Kasparov, for example, contribute to a chess match now learned by human grandmasters and new chess programs alike, which themselves combine and recombine to generate new variations, new brilliancies. Machines can contribute to the noosphere, at a minimum, by serving as sites and mechanisms for recombining and generating knowledge. Consider, also, the orbiting network of ~26 active GPS satellites and the thousands of ground computers to which they return data. The information made available by this constellation contributes to the noosphere. Note that it is unnecessary to pick apart the question of whether computers 'have ideas' in the way humans do. They do not seem to, but that does not preclude their contributing to the noosphere, because the decisive criterion is interaction and interrelation, not an analysis of mental states.

Non-human animals are looped into the noosphere too, although their contributions are likely rarer than those of humans. Recall that the criteria for an idea to be recognized as a constituent of the noosphere is that it be able to interact with other ideas. Take Vladimir Nabokov's account of what inspired him to write *Lolita*. He says:

> As far as I can recall the initial shiver of inspiration was somehow prompted by a newspaper story about an ape in the Jardin des Plantes, who, after months of coaxing by a scientist, produced the first drawing ever charcoaled by an animal: this sketch showed the bars of the poor creature's cage.
>
> (Nabokov, 1959, p. 73)

Interaction on the level of meaning is evident. Someone at pains to defend narrow humanism might object that the relevant exchange is Nabokov's inspiration stemming from an idea he himself had *about* the ape, not from an idea the animal had. Recall, however, that Nabokov cites the ape's painting of his own situation. The ape's idea and the ideas that feed into *Lolita* have interacted, which necessitates recognizing the ape's idea as part of the noosphere.

Recall, too, animals that live with humans and learn to communicate with them. Alex the African grey parrot and Koko the gorilla are two famous examples, and even a cursory scan of the literature indicates non-human ideas interacting with those of humans (Matevia, Patterson and Hillix, 2002, Pepperburg, 2012). Consider, finally, suggestions to include whales in a 'global brain' via a cetacean-friendly graphical user interface running on 'solar powered internet stations floating on the ocean with (Iridium) satellite hook-up and (LCD) screens with video/microphone interface. With such an interface a common language is available that could be used for joint global tasks' (Mayer-Kress, 1994, p. 229). I remain chary about the prospect of a unified brain that solves global tasks, but the grounds for barring cetacean, simian, avian and machine thought from the noosphere grow weaker by the day.

6 Conclusion

The noosphere has meant different things to different writers. Which is my noosphere, and whose noospheres do I wish to avoid? I am disinclined to take up Pierre Teilhard de Chardin's (2008; Turner, 2005) vision of a grand progression from lithosphere to biosphere to noosphere to a spiritual 'omega point'. Nor is there any reason to believe that the growth of the noosphere heralds 'the end of war, equality among humans and equitable distribution of wealth', as Vernadsky did (Turner, 2005, p. 506). These accounts and others like them are inadequate to the degree they see the noosphere as a higher stage in a progression, a system of conscious control or a seamless, unified globe. The noosphere is a name for the circulation of ideas, and the loops and networks they create as they attempt to understand themselves, each other and the conditions of their circulation. The noosphere is not a 'mind' in the way we use the term about ourselves, any more than an economic market is touched by a literal invisible hand, any more than Maxwell's demon was a conjecture about theology (Maxwell, 1872). It might be simpler to replace every instance of noosphere in this chapter with 'system of ideas' or 'shifting totality of knowledge' or 'all thoughts considered in their interrelation and the whole formed by that interrelation', but the noosphere has made itself an obligatory point of passage towards these ideas.

Noosphere two acknowledges the material metabolism that sustains and alters it. It allows us to consider what a 'steady-state noosphere' might look like. It reconciles the strange dualism implicit in folk-psychology images of the noosphere as a 'huge mind'. Noosphere two is more cautious of its drive to complexity and the attendant problems of scale, but it is also more capacious, more open to inputs from machine and animal intelligence and uses a more generalizable definition of what counts as part of itself, rather than simply human thought (Levit, 2000). To consider the new noosphere is also to see it as a made object that subsists on physical conditions, not a mind floating frictionlessly above the world. This allows us to argue about what we want this made object to look like, how we want it to function, whose contributions we emphasize. The noosphere's growth is not, as in certain technologist-utopian accounts of a 'coming singularity', an inevitable and self-propelled drive to the exit of want (Kurzweil, 2005). It is partly self-propelled, yes, but its growth is implicated with consumption, strife, scale, pollution, identity, metabolism, peace, conflict, exploitation, communication, innovation and regression. To understand this is 'to shift from the Globe to the loops that slowly draw it', and to see these self-drawing ribbons at scale, unreeling in all directions (Latour, 2013, p. 94).

Bibliography

Ambrose, S. H. (1998) Late Pleistocene human population bottlenecks, volcanic winter, and differentiation of modern humans. *Journal of Human Evolution.* 34(6), 623–651.

Biraben, J-N. (1979). Essai sur l'évolution du nombre des hommes. *Population.* 34(1), 13–25.

Buer, M. C. (1926) *Health, Wealth and Population in the Early Days of the Industrial Revolution.* London: George Routledge & Sons.

de Solla Price, D. J. (1965). The scientific foundation of science policy. *Nature*, 206, 233–238.

Deudney, D. (2000) Geopolitics as theory: Historical security materialism. *European Journal of International Relations.* 6(1), 77–107.

Gallagher, P. (1993) Population growth is caused by renaissances. *Fidelio.* 2(4), 12–7.

Gigaom (2012) *The Era of the 100 MW Data Center.* Available from: http://gigaom.com/2012/01/31/the-era-of-the-100-mw-data-center (accessed 31 January 2012).

Internet World Stats. *Internet Growth Statistics.* Available from: www.internetworldstats.com/emarketing.htm (accessed 24 March 2014).

Kurzweil, R. (2005) *The Singularity is Near.* New York: Viking.

Kuznets, S. (1960) Population change and aggregate output. In: Universities-National Bureau (ed.) *Demographic and Economic Change in Developed Countries.* New York: Columbia University Press, pp. 324–351.

Larsen, P. O. & von Ins, M. (2010) The rate of growth in scientific publication and the decline in coverage provided by Science Citation Index. *Scientometrics*. 84(3), 575–603.

Latour, B. (2013) Facing Gaia. *Gifford Lectures*. Available from: www.bruno-latour.fr/sites/default/files/downloads/GIFFORD-SIX-LECTURES_1.pdf (accessed 4 April 2016).

Levit, Georgy S. (2000) The biosphere and the noosphere theories of V. I. Vernadsky and P. Teilhard de Chardin: A methodological essay. *International Archives on the History of Science/Archives Internationales d'Histoire des Sciences*. 50(144), 160–176.

Luhmann, N. (1996) *Social Systems*. Trans. Bednarz, J. Stanford, CA: Stanford University Press.

Matevia, M. L., Patterson, F. G. P. & Hillix, W. A. (2002) Pretend play in a signing gorilla. In: Mitchell, R. (ed.) *Pretending and Imagination in Animals and Children*. New York: Cambridge University Press, pp. 285–306.

Maxwell, J. C. (1872). *Theory of Heat*. London: Longmans, Green, and Co.

Mayer-Kress, G. (1994) *Messy Futures and Global Brains*. Center for Complex Systems Research. Beckman Institute and Department of Physics. University of Illinois at Urbana-Champaign. Available from: www.ccsr.illinois.edu/web/Techreports/1990-94/CCSR-94-26.pdf (accessed 4 April 2016).

Merton (2015). Child and infant mortality. Available from: www.jsna.suttonandmerton.nhs.uk/ec/update/readnew.asp?id=45 (accessed 4 April 2016).

Morrison, D., Chapman, C. R., Steel, D. & Binzel, R. P. (2004) Impacts and the public: communicating the nature of the impact hazard. In: Belton, M. J. S., Morgan, T. H., Samarasinha, N. H. & Yeomans, D. K. (eds) *Mitigation of Hazardous Comets and Asteroids*. New York: Cambridge University Press, pp. 252–390.

Nabokov, V. V. (1959) On a book entitled 'Lolita'. *Encounter*. 12(4), 73–76.

Page, L. & Brin, S. (1998) The anatomy of a large-scale hypertextual Web search engine. *Computer Networks and ISDN Systems*. 30, 107–117.

Pepperburg, I. M. (2012) Further evidence for addition and numerical competence by a grey parrot (*Psittacus erithacus*). *Animal Cognition*. 15(4), 711–717.

Putnam, L. & Mumby, D. (2014) Discourse and materiality as mutually constituted. In: Putnam, L. & Mumby, D. (eds) *The SAGE Handbook of Organization Communication: Advances in Theory, Research, and Methods*. Third edition. Los Angeles: Sage.

Ratzinger, J. (2000) *The Spirit of the Liturgy*. San Francisco: Ignatius Press.

Tainter, J. (2006) Social complexity and sustainability. *Ecological Complexity*. 3, 91–103.

Teilhard de Chardin, P. (2008) *The Phenomenon of Man*. New York: Harper Perennial.

Tenner, E. (2010) Population growth: A genius machine? *The Atlantic*. 24 November.

Turner, D. P. (2005) Thinking at the global scale. *Global Ecology and Biogeography*. 14, 506.

United States Census Bureau (2013) *Data on World Population*. Available from: www.census.gov/population/international/data/worldpop/table_history.php (accessed 30 December 2013).

United States Census Bureau (2014) *U.S. and World Population Clock*. Available from: www.census.gov/popclock (accessed 2 June 2014).

Urry, J. (2011) *Climate Change and Society*. Malden, MA: Polity Press.

Vernadsky, V. I. (1945) The biosphere and the noosphere. *Scientific American*. 33(1), 1–12.

WorldWideWebSize (2014). *The Size of the World Wide Web (The Internet)*. Available at: www.worldwidewebsize.com (accessed 27 May 2014).

Part IV

Post-growth societies and organizations

8 Engaging with the Plutocene

Moving towards degrowth and post-capitalist futures

Marko Ulvila and Kristoffer Wilén

1 Introduction

Since its introduction by atmospheric chemist Paul Crutzen and biologist Eugene Stoermer (2000), the 'Anthropocene' concept and narrative has become immensely popular, a buzzword of sorts. Indeed, it is becoming a hegemonic worldview (Castree, 2014; Malm and Hornborg, 2014; Hornborg, 2015), and a totalizing discourse in its own right (Di Chiro, 2016). According to the narrative, the Anthropocene is the 'geology of mankind'. It is the geological epoch during which humankind's activities are said to have exerted a significant impact on the environment. The preceding epoch, the Holocene, provided humanity with a 10,000-(or so)-year-long, remarkably stable geo-climatic period, during which human civilization was able to develop agriculture and build its cities (Hamilton, 2013; Swyngedouw, 2015). It was a human-friendly period compared to the previous 100,000 years of climatic chaos (Hamilton, 2013). The shift from the Holocene to the Anthropocene suggests that humans have become a geological force. Hence, the changes (e.g. climate change and loss of biodiversity) taking place in the Anthropocene are no longer naturally occurring, but are in fact anthropogenic, that is, human-induced. All of this is, of course, already well known – and few would dispute these natural scientific facts.

However, while the Anthropocene narrative is becoming ever more popular, criticism of it is likewise becoming ever more frequent, especially that levelled by critical social scientists during the last few years. Their criticism stems from a number of different perspectives, but the common feature and concern seems to be how those scientists who are proponents of the Anthropocene narrative have conceptualized the *anthropos*, human beings, the ones who are causing and have caused the changes to the biosphere and the environmental harm. Who are these humans? The answer given in the Anthropocene narrative is: humankind, humanity, the entire human species. In this chapter we will problematize this notion for being too shallow and inadequate. In so doing, and at the outset, we wish to raise three main concerns. First, historically speaking, the positive and negative effects resulting from industrialization are very unequally 'distributed among social categories within the human species' (Hornborg, 2015, p. 62). More specifically, and to this day, there exists a disconnect between the places of consumption and the places where the environmental consequences are most heavily felt; a temporal and spatial displacement of environmental loads (similar to David Harvey's 'time-space compression'). Second, there is nothing 'natural' or inevitable about the historical development that led to the Anthropocene or about the 'institutions and forms of social organisation' (Hornborg, 2015, p. 62) that made this development possible. And third, does the Anthropocene narrative and conceptualization foster the political action needed for tackling the environmental destruction taking place in the Anthropocene era?

For the purposes of our discussion, we have chosen the perspective of degrowth and post-growth (see e.g. D'Alisa, Demaria and Kallis, 2015) for engaging with and tackling some of the central issues posed by the Anthropocene, namely ecological sustainability and global environmental justice. Degrowth challenges the economic growth imperative and tries to offer alternatives to the growth economy and society. Since we consider the growth imperative to be a central driver of anthropogenic changes to the biosphere, the degrowth perspective is of central importance. Likewise, for our global class analysis:

> degrowth should be pursued in the North, not in order to allow the South to follow the same path, but first and foremost in order to liberate conceptual space for countries there to find their own trajectories to what they define as the good life.
>
> (D'Alisa et al., 2015, p. 5)

It should go without saying that the debate concerning the Anthropocene and the concept is not a debate about nomenclature – what to call it. The name as such is not that important. Instead, what is important, and what the discussion and criticism is about, is that the Anthropocene discourse most often seems to be based upon a particular view of the world – and offering a particular normative guide to action. This matters because depending on the underlying worldview different answers to questions such as these will be given: what and who have caused the global environmental changes, what can and should be done about them and how? So the Anthropocene can in many ways be seen as an attempt to put forward a specific worldview, and is therefore more of a paradigm than 'simply' a new geological epoch or a scientific concept (Baskin, 2015).

Even if one, for a second, does not focus on the social issues involved, the Anthropocene debate matters from an ecological, philosophical (or 'ecosophy') perspective as well, as Vandana Shiva (2016) has pointed out. It can be argued that Anthropocene thinking to a certain degree relies on and also reinforces colonialist assumptions (Shiva and Turhan, 2016). For example, Baskin (2015) has stated that, within the Anthropocene narrative, 'man' (a particular 'humanity') is re-inserted into 'nature' only to simultaneously 're-elevate "him" within it and above it to become a force of nature' (Baskin, 2015, p. 23). We therefore wish to ask: to what extent can the analyses that are based upon the Anthropocene's specific conceptualization of the relations between humans and non- or more-than-human nature assist us in understanding global environmental change and its causes, and help us do something about them?

Hence, to criticize the Anthropocene narrative is not to criticize the natural scientific facts and discoveries that have shown that global environmental changes are in fact anthropogenic, but rather to say that these analyses are inadequate. Analyses focusing on power structures, institutions, social relations and forms of social organizing are still necessary in order to improve our understanding of this new epoch. A large part of the ensuing discussion in this chapter will focus on climate change due to the substantial amount of data available.

We begin this chapter with a brief overview of the criticism of the Anthropocene narrative, especially its 'human species' narrative. After that, we take a closer look at the relationships between income, consumption, material resource usage and emissions. Following this, we apply a consumption class perspective to the Anthropocene debate. We then suggest some future transition and transformation scenarios for the identified classes, which would be some of the first steps in moving towards degrowth and post-growth futures, thereby reducing some of the negative impacts exerted by the Anthropocene. Finally, we draw some conclusions on why a class perspective could re-politicize the sustainability debate within this new epoch.

2 Anthropogenic is sociogenic

When did the Anthropocene begin? This has been the subject of a debate that has been ongoing as long as the concept itself has been around. The debate divides proponents of the Anthropocene effectively into two camps: the 'good' and the 'bad' Anthropocene. According to advocates of the 'good' Anthropocene, the epoch started as early as 8,000 years ago when humans started clearing forests and farming (Ruddiman, 2003). However, the more influential interpretation, and the position adopted by the 'bad' Anthropocene proponents, states that the epoch began with industrialization in the late eighteenth century. For example, Paul Crutzen and Will Steffen, both leading natural scientists in the field, belong to this camp. According to them, at that point in history, the human impact on the global environment was becoming noticeable. The 'good' Anthropocene contains a large dose of techno-optimism, one might even say hubris, suggesting that humans can and should control the natural world (Hamilton, 2013; Baskin, 2015).

The birth date of the Anthropocene is significant for another reason as well. At this juncture, it is worth quoting Clive Hamilton (2013, pp. 202–203) at length:

> if humans have been a planetary force since civilization emerged . . ., then there is nothing fundamentally new about the last couple of centuries of industrialism. It is in the nature of civilized humans to transform the Earth, including by the use of geoengineering, and what is in the nature of the species cannot be resisted. By focusing attention on 'humankind' in general rather than forms of social organization that emerged more recently, the Anthropocene becomes in some sense natural. It is not the product of industrial rapaciousness, an unregulated market, human alienation from

> nature or excessive faith in technological power; it is merely the result of humans doing what humans are meant to do . . .

Andreas Malm and Alf Hornborg (2014, p. 65) highlight this as the 'main paradox of the narrative, if not of the concept as such', since changes in the global environment are at one moment denaturalized – 'relocated from the sphere of natural causes to that of human activities – only to be renaturalized in the next, when derived from an innate human trait, such as the ability to control fire'. Hence, 'not nature, but human nature'. This is one of the reasons why Malm and Hornborg (2014), both social scientists, are not very fond of this particular concept. Among others, Hamilton (2013), also a social scientist, continues to actively use and promote the Anthropocene concept, even though he clearly shares the understanding of the problems involved.

We support the idea that the new epoch began with the dawn of industrialization, which is also becoming the consensus within the scientific community. This, however, still leaves the narrative with a sizeable internal contradiction, since by affirming that the shift towards this new epoch occurred in the late eighteenth century with industrialization and James Watt's invention of the steam engine – all of which required specific forms of social organization – it implicitly (and sometimes even explicitly, as in the case of Hamilton (2013)) admits that the species narrative is too wide, shallow and inadequate, and that the human species as a whole has never been an agent of history. Nonetheless, the whole species-mankind-humanity narrative continues to be widely used by the proponents of the Anthropocene.

'The mastery of fire by our ancestors provided humankind with a powerful monopolistic tool unavailable to other species, that put us firmly on the long path towards the Anthropocene' (Steffen et al., 2007, p. 614, quoted in Malm and Hornborg, 2014, p. 63) is a sentiment characteristic of the attempt by some of the most influential proponents of the Anthropocene to try to understand the development towards industrialization and the fossil fuel economy. This development is thus understood and presented as natural and inevitable, a common journey taken by the entire human species. Yet humanity as a collective did not decide upon this specific development. Only a tiny fraction of humanity, even in the richest parts of the world such as Great Britain, could install steam engines in their factories (Malm, 2013). The fossil fuel economy, the main reason behind the Anthropocene, was from the very start based on highly inequitable processes and unequal distribution among the social classes in the world-system, which was, in fact, an actual requirement for the existence of modern fossil fuel economies and technologies. Industrialization happened in Britain because a tiny wealthy minority realized the possibilities of investing in fossil fuel technologies (Malm and Hornborg, 2014). Further, what made it an economic opportunity was the assemblage of such processes through the displacement of resource extraction and environmental degradation to other parts of the world (e.g. American soil, Australian pastures, Swedish forests), Afro-American slavery and the exploitation of British mine and factory workers (Hornborg, 2001).

Anthropogenic changes to the biosphere are thus largely sociogenic inasmuch as the driver of change is not the human species per se, but specific social relations, orders and structures and forms of organization (Castree, 2014; Malm and Hornborg, 2014; Lövbrand et al., 2015; Moore, 2015; Di Chiro, 2016). Pointing to more specific drivers of change, Hornborg (2015, also Malm and Hornborg, 2014) has, for example, proposed that the new epoch could be called the 'Technocene' instead, with technology as the main driver. Jason W. Moore (2014a, 2014b, 2015) has argued for the 'Capitalocene' (originally coined by Andreas Malm), with its emphasis on the current new epoch as the 'age of capital'. Richard B. Norgaard (2013, 2014, 2015) suggests the 'Econocene', due to the almost religious status of the economy and 'economism' in contemporary society, and because global market activity 'increased 50-fold, or more than 16-fold per capita' during the twentieth century (2014, p. 44). Norgaard's view is consistent with the idea of the 'Great Acceleration', the 'hockey stick charts', prominent in Anthropocene discussions, where most resource usage and emissions indicators and global gross domestic product (GDP) point steeply upwards from the year 1945 onwards.

In the case of climate change, the benefits and disadvantages derived from industrialization and the fossil fuel economy can be seen in the distribution of carbon emissions over time. The Global North, in this case not accounting for per capita intra-country differences, was responsible for 72.7 per cent of the carbon dioxide emitted between the years 1850 and 2008, while only comprising 18.8 per cent of the global population (Malm and Hornborg, 2014; see also Heede, 2014). And in 2015 the richest 10 per cent of the global population were responsible for approximately 45 per cent of CO2e (carbon dioxide equivalent) emissions, while the poorest 50 per cent were responsible for 13 per cent (Chancel and Piketty, 2015). Keeping these figures in mind, the Anthropocene could just as well be called the Plutocene, referring to the plutocratic distribution of emissions (from Greek πλοῦτος, ploutos, meaning wealth). For these reasons, Satterthwaite (2009, p. 550) has argued that 'perhaps up to one-sixth of the world's population has incomes and consumption levels that are so low that they are best not included in allocations of responsibility for GHG [greenhouse gas] emissions'. Acknowledging these interventions, we will move on to discuss the connection between income levels and environmental harm from a consumption class perspective, which will show some possibilities for moving towards a degrowth and post-growth era.

3 A class perspective on sustainability

Much of the discussion about environmental sustainability and social equity is trapped within a nation-state framework or in the idea of all of humanity, the *anthropos*. We argue that a class perspective would provide a much more useful basis for the discussion on how to move towards ecologically sustainable and socially equitable post-growth societies. Income is strongly related to both the fulfilment of basic needs and the scale of environmental harm, and can thus be used as a helpful proxy for creating a clearer, class-based understanding of the issue. Further, such a perspective is also better suited to engaging with solutions.

Building on earlier conceptualizations by Alan Durning (1992) and Brian Czech (2000), as well as calculations by Matthew Bentley (2003) and Chancel and Piketty (2015), we present a class perspective on environmental sustainability and well-being. The basis of the discussion concerns an observation that income and environmental harm go hand in hand. For example, in Finland the correlation between income used for consumption and greenhouse gas emissions (for 1 euro consumed r=0.89) and natural resource usage (r=0.91) is so strong and clear that this can be taken as a sound basis (Nurmela and Mäenpää, 2014; Jousenvirta et al., 2016).

In addition to making use of relevant literature, over the years we have also benefited from dialogues with various actors in three continents for direct inputs from the ground and the balanced representation of different realities. For the study, 11 dialogues on sustainable futures were conducted in six countries: Finland, India, Kenya, Nepal, Sweden and Tanzania. Their purpose was to gain inputs from the rich oral system of communication and knowledge that exists in the Global South in particular (Ulvila and Pasanen, 2009).

3.1 Income ≈ environmental harm

We argue that monetary income and environmental harm are so strongly related that income serves as a very useful indicator for environmental sustainability and unsustainability. Income is almost equal to consumption and consumption is almost equal to environmental harm.

One way of assessing the relationship between the formal economy and environmental impact is to look at the ecological footprint and GDP. When they are presented in a scatter plot for 126 countries, a strong relation between the two emerges. A per capita income of US$10,000 per year at purchasing power parity seems to be an important threshold. With a higher national income, no country manages to stay within the annual 1.8 gha (global hectares) per capita sustainability threshold based on biocapacity (Abdallah et al., 2012). The result of the scatter plot of per capita ecological footprint in relation to per capita GDP is presented in Figure 8.1. The same kind of outcome can be seen when looking at the per capita levels of the material footprint (Wiedmann et al., 2013)

A similar pattern emerges when households and greenhouse gas emissions or material footprints are studied. For example, in the case of Finland, on a per capita basis both have a strong relationship with the incomes of the households. The richer the people, the more they pollute and consume natural resources. In Figure 8.2, data is presented from a household consumption survey conducted in 2012.

In this case from Finland, the members of the richest decile (10 per cent of the population) generate 2.4 times more CO2 emissions and 2.8 times more material flows than the poorest (Nurmela and Mäenpää, 2014; Jousenvirta et al., 2016). And arguably, in countries with larger income inequalities, the difference would be higher.

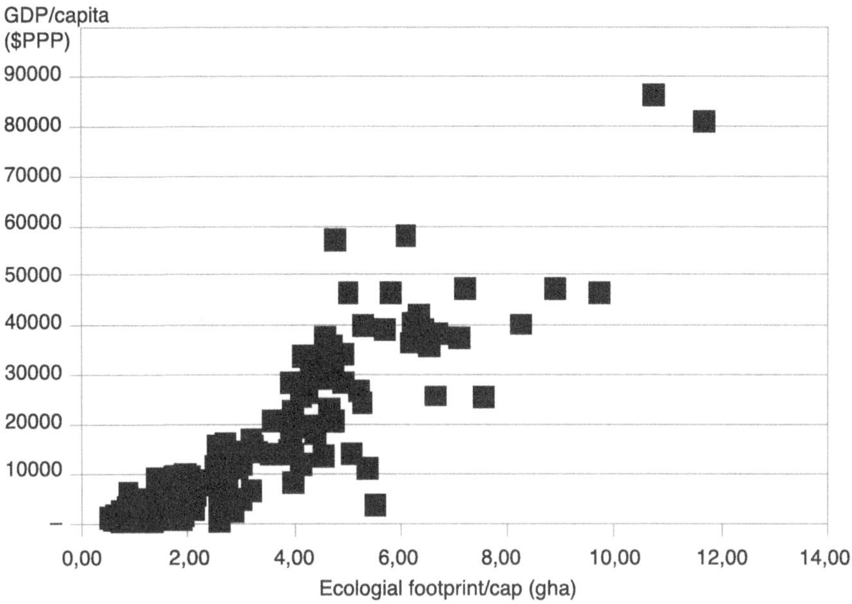

Figure 8.1 Ecological footprint and GDP per capita of 151 countries.

Source: Based on data from Abdallah et al., 2012.

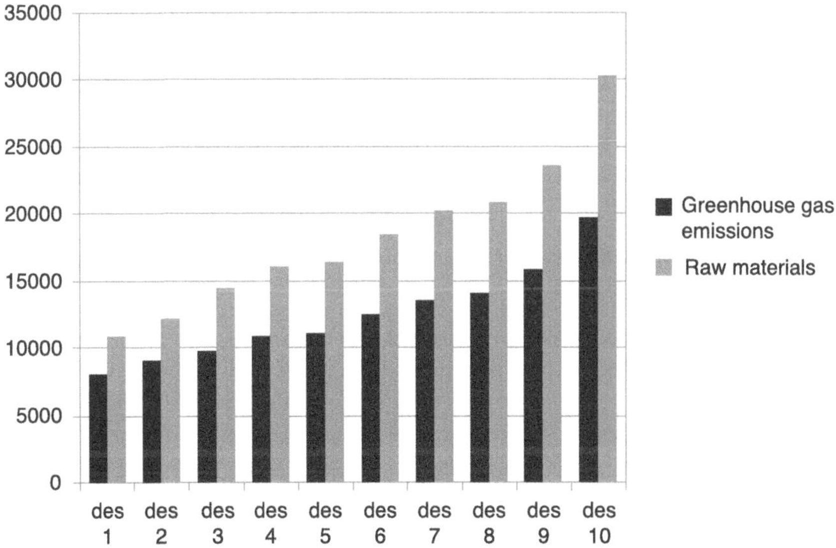

Figure 8.2 Greenhouse gas emissions and material inputs (kg) of households by income deciles in Finland, 2012.

Source: Based on data from Nurmela and Mäenpää, 2014.

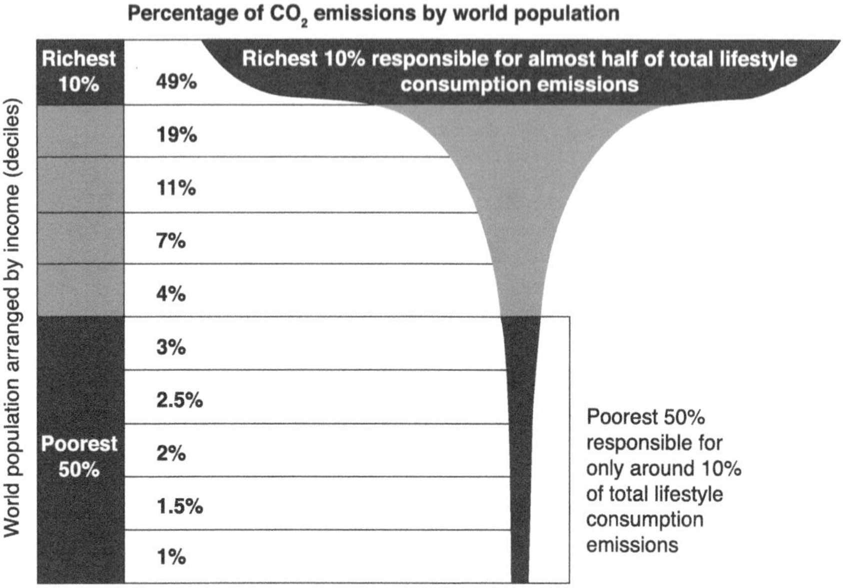

Figure 8.3 Global income deciles and associated lifestyle consumption emissions.

Source: Oxfam, 2015, p. 4.

Given the vast income differences at the global level, the environmental impacts of the different income groups vary tremendously. According to the report *Extreme Carbon Inequality* by Oxfam (2015), the world's richest 10 per cent currently produce half of the global carbon emissions, while the poorest 3.5 billion are responsible for only a tenth. The distribution is presented in a graphical form in Figure 8.3.

3.2 Four income-based classes: over-consuming, consuming, sustainable and struggling

There have been several previous studies on environmental impact with an income-based class perspective. The first such case, to our knowledge, was presented by Alan Durning in his book *How Much is Enough?* in 1992. He described three ecological classes and called them consumers (1.1 billion people), middle (3.3 billion) and poor (1.1 billion). He used the per capita share of gross national product (GNP) at purchasing power parity as the measurement. The threshold for consumers was set at US$7,500 per capita annually, and at US$700 for the poor (Durning, 1992, pp. 26–28).

David C. Korten subsequently used Durning's figures but renamed the categories social-ecological classes, and called them overconsumers, sustainers and marginals. He found Durning's figures where roughly 60 per cent of the world's population are members of the sustainer class encouraging as their basic needs are being met in more or less sustainable ways. In that context, he commented that the problem with the dominant development paradigm is that it 'has pursued a development vision that defines prosperity in terms of bringing both sustainers and marginals into the overconsuming class. In a finite world this is a physical impossibility' (Korten, 1994, p. 1).

Some years later, Brian Czech also divided humanity into three classes. He designated them the liquidating class consisting of the richest 1 per cent of humanity, the amorphic class comprising the next 19 per cent and the steady-state class embracing the bottom 80 per cent (Czech, 2000, pp. 118–122). While Czech's focus on the richest 1 per cent makes good sense, we find that the way he has grouped together those people struggling with hunger and mere survival with the low-income world majority to be wholly disproportionate.

A useful calculation of the world consumer class was made by Matthew Bentley in 2003 in which he defined a member of the consumer class as a person who has an annual share of the GDP exceeding US$7,000 in terms of purchasing power parity. His finding about the consumer class in selected major countries from the year 2002 indicates, for example, that in both the USA and China there were some 240 million members in the consuming class. On the global scale, nearly an equal number of consumers are located in the developed and developing groups (Bentley 2003; Worldwatch 2004).

Building on the earlier work described above, we have developed a somewhat more informed income-based classification applying two criteria. The first is the fulfilment of basic needs. The idea here is that the fulfilment of basic needs is a fundamental human right, also enshrined in international treaties. The dividing line can be roughly established by incomes. With very low incomes, needs for safe and sufficient food, water, shelter and other essentials are not met, but after a certain threshold they are. The second criterion is environmental impact. This rests on the empirical finding that income is strongly associated with environmental damage (see above). Environmental damage increases in proportion with increase in income. We have applied the three elements to form four classes that we call struggling, sustainable, consuming and over-consuming. The result is presented in Table 8.1.

For the purposes of this study, we have estimated the numbers for the four classes in current world population terms of more than 7 billion people. The 2015

Table 8.1 The conceptual basis for the four income-based classes.

Income level	*Basic needs*	*Scale of environmental damage*	*Name of the class*
Low	Not met	Small	**Struggling**
Moderate	Met	Moderate	**Sustainable**
High	Met	Significant	**Consuming**
Very high	Met	Very high	**Over-consuming**

report by French economists Lucas Chancel and Thomas Piketty provides the most recent and comprehensive income-based figures, produced in the context of climate protection and CO2 emissions. Their report builds on two large datasets by Lakner-Milanovic and Anand-Segal, and combines their national income distributions into a global presentation. In their report, the number of people belonging to the high income and high emission groups in geographical regions and the world as a whole are given for the top decile as well as for the top 28 per cent of the surveyed population (Chancel and Piketty, 2015). In terms of our nomenclature, the top 10 per cent belong to the over-consuming class and the next 18 per cent to the consuming class. The figures along with their income thresholds for the two groups are presented in Table 8.2. Due to different infrastructures among regions, the thresholds also differ. A certain income results in more or less emissions, depending on the region's/country's infrastructure.

The second dataset is for the group that we call the struggling class. It is drawn from the same source, by including all the people in the poorest category and two-thirds of those in the second poorest. They form about one-third of humanity and are mainly found in Sub-Saharan Africa, India and other developing countries in Asia. For the industrialized regions, we have included an additional 5 per cent of their population in the struggling class because homelessness, unemployment and inadequate access to healthcare deny at least this many people a dignified life in the high-income societies as well. This adds up to some 1.9 billion people.

The remaining number between these two groups, we have named the sustainable class. The members of the sustainable class have their basic needs met by livelihoods that do not cause excessive industrial greenhouse gas emissions, and

Table 8.2 Number of people belonging to the consuming and over-consuming classes in regions or large countries around the year 2013 (millions) with related rounded income thresholds.

	Consuming Class		*Over-consuming class*	
	income threshold (€)	*number of people (m)*	*income threshold (€)*	*number of people (m)*
North America	5 850	105	14 280	211
EU	6 160	268	13 780	141
China	2 730	370	6 660	59
Russia and Central Asia	5 900	80	14 610	44
Other rich countries	7 080	64	17 280	51
Mid.East and N.Africa	6 510	78	16 660	31
Latin America	10 330	47	23 980	36
India	5 600	25	14 400	13
Sub-Saharan Africa	5 520	22	11 050	9
Other developing Asian countries	5 600	68	14 400	34
World		1127		629

Source: Data from Chancel and Piketty, 2015.

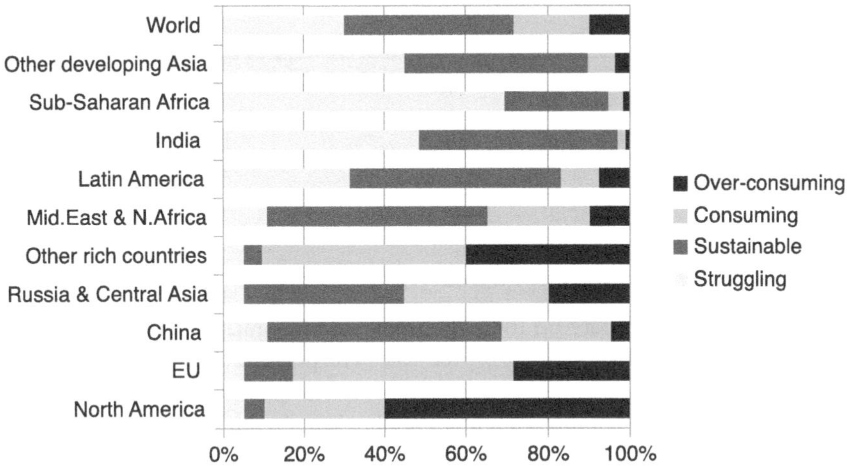

Figure 8.4 The shares of the four classes globally and across regions in 2013.

their lifestyles do not consume an excessive amount of energy or non-renewable resources. By uncovering this sizeable class of some 3 billion people falling between annual per capita income shares of around €700–6,000, we hope to shed some optimism on the otherwise gloomy prognosis for the future, namely that more than one-third of humanity seems to be able to live quite sustainably and decently. In reality, this class faces constant challenges with the lure of the 'consumer paradise' on the one hand, and their precarious existence on the lower ladders of power structures on the other. Both of these classes are also threatened by commodification, enclosures and dispossessions.

The number of people belonging to these classes and their relative share in the world and its regions is indicated in Figure 8.4. As issues such as basic needs and environmental sustainability cannot really be measured, the graph below and the numbers above should primarily be seen as an invitation for further debate rather than definitive outcomes.

Looking at the shares, we can see that North America is dominated by the over-consuming class, while in the European Union (EU) and other rich countries the consuming class is the biggest with a sizeable over-consuming population. The sustainable class has the largest share in Latin America, China, the Middle East and North Africa regions. In Sub-Saharan Africa, India and other developing countries in Asia the struggling class is the most numerous group.

One point worth noting here is that the regions we have found to be predominantly inhabited by members of the sustainable class bear a similarity to the outcomes of the Happy Planet Index by the New Economics Foundation. The top ten countries in their ranking, which is based on the efficient use of an ecological footprint for achieving reported life satisfaction and measured longevity, fall in the same regions. The countries are: Bangladesh, Colombia, Costa Rica, Ecuador, Mexico, Nicaragua, Panama, Thailand, Vanuatu and Vietnam (NEF, 2016).

Table 8.3 Schematic estimate of the gender division among the cultural classes.

	Male	*Female*
Over-consuming and Consuming class	2/3	1/3
Sustainable class	1/2	1/2
Struggling class	1/3	2/3

3.3 Gender and the income-based classes

Within the current debate on the Anthropocene and climate change mitigation, gender issues undoubtedly play a central role. The presentation of the four classes above does not take account of gender in precise terms, as the income statistics used did not readily encompass gender-specific data. As this is difficult to find, we will proceed to discuss the gender aspects of the classes using some rough estimates.

In Table 8.3, we present a scheme for the gender division of the three classes. Our estimate is that two out of three members of the over-consuming class are male, and similarly two out of three members of the struggling class are female. The sustainable class has an equal share of both genders.

The purpose of this scheme is to highlight the fact that the consumption patterns in classes differ considerably in gender terms. This has to be kept in mind when thinking about the transformation agendas for more sustainable futures.

Male-dominated over-consumption is causing significant hardship among the women of the struggling classes. It is the poor women in developing countries who bear the brunt of environmental degradation. These women typically lack access to essential resources, but at the same time they are responsible for food, fuel and safe water supply. Environmental loss and degradation considerably increase women's workloads in obtaining these essential resources (Hemmati and Gardiner, 2002, p. 24).

Gerd Johnsson-Latham has studied the issue of gender and consumption and made pertinent observations. Even though the family is often taken as a single socio-economic unit, she observes that it seldom represents a balanced distribution unit and the differing access to resources and consumption is most pronounced in poor families. She concludes, 'If women's consumption levels were to be the norm, both emissions and climate change would be significantly less than today' (Johnsson-Latham, 2007, p. 50).

4 Class-wise transition and transformation scenarios

Using the classes established above, we next present different transition scenarios for each one. The best ideas for moving towards more sustainable and socially equitable futures in the Anthropocene/Plutocene would have a far better impact when applied to a class-based understanding of society and political alternatives.

Consideration of the Plutocene makes *degrowth* the obvious future scenario for the consuming and over-consuming classes. For the struggling class, *empowerment* is an appropriate response, while the sustainable class can continue in a *steady-state* fashion.

4.1 Degrowth for the over-consuming and consuming classes

For the members of the over-consuming class, an immediate degrowth scenario (here mainly referring to a decrease in material consumption) is needed in order to reduce their ecological footprint to an acceptable level. This would most likely also lead to a contraction in their monetary wealth/income as measured in GDP terms because phasing out fossil fuels would reduce energy input into the economic process considerably. Such a degrowth scenario is being welcomed by an increasing number of scholars and actors. Proponents of degrowth argue that the current economic growth is unsustainable over the long term because it depletes natural resources and destroys the environment, and because it fails to help populations improve their well-being significantly. The challenge is to devise degrowth policies that would be equitable and that would bring about the changes in a democratic and incremental manner, rather than through collapse and inflicting an unfair burden on the least powerful (see e.g. D'Alisa et al., 2015).

Immediate degrowth measures aimed at the richest 0.7 billion or 10 per cent of humanity would be the first priority. Such an approach has been advocated by Hervé Kempf (2008), for example. In a similar vein, Shobil Chakravarty et al., (2009) have argued that in the case of the climate, reducing the CO2 emissions of the most polluting billion would take climate protection forward in a just and significant way.

Proposals addressing over-consumption by the rich also include establishing a maximum income through high progressive income tax rates or laws limiting the highest salaries in comparison with the lowest ones, for example in the ratio of 5:1 or 10:1. On the resource use side, helpful economic instruments would be various kinds of luxury tax that would progressively increase the tax on energy or other material use.

For the consuming class, a gentle degrowth scenario is appropriate. The measures would be similar to those presented above, but would be introduced mainly after there has been a breakthrough with the immediate degrowth of the over-consuming classes.

At the societal level, attaining degrowth would imply a major transformation from plutocratic fossil capitalism to an eco-sufficient, democratic and egalitarian society. It is beyond the scope of this chapter to describe such transformation in detail. Suffice it to say that society has to be liberated from the growth imperative that is part and parcel of the capitalist world system. This would mean transitioning from hierarchies to equality, from competition to cooperation, from growth to sufficiency and from violence to peace. In other words, peaceful coexistence with fellow humans and non-human nature (cf. Ulvila and Pasanen, 2009).

4.2 A steady-state for the sustainable classes

For the sustainable classes, a steady-state scenario embracing the economics of permanence would be the most appropriate. Such communities and societies would continue to change and evolve, but within the current level of environmental impact and by maintaining further improvement in human dignity for all, right down to the last person, in accordance with the last-person-first principle.

The phrase *steady-state economy* originates from ecological economics, most notably the work of Herman Daly. The idea carries connotations of constant populations of people and constant stocks of capital. It also connotes a constant rate of throughput, namely energy and materials used to produce goods and services. Steadiness duly implies stagnation. In the short run, mild fluctuations in population and throughput are normal, with the aim of stable equilibrium in the long run (Daly, 1977; Czech and Tietenberg, 2007).

An older definition of a similar idea was provided by the Gandhian economist J. C. Kumarappa in 1948 with the idea of an *economy of permanence* as the desirable societal goal for a liberated India. Observing the 'natural economy', Kumarappa noted that nature ensures the cooperation of all of its units, each working for itself and in the process helping other units to get along with each other. When this transpires harmoniously and violence does not break the chain, an economy of permanence ensues. Its highest form is the economy of service which 'functions neither for its present need nor for its personal future requirement, but projects its activities into the next generation, or generations to come, without looking for any reward' (Kumarappa, [1948] 1997; see also Lindley, 2007, pp. 4–7).

As the sustainable classes also have a case for achieving a fairer share of power and resources, the agenda regarding this group includes respect, protection and promotion. Thus far, this sizeable class has been ignored to a large extent in the debates about environmental sustainability because the focus has been on over-consumption on the one hand, and poverty on the other. It is high time this middle sector received appropriate positive attention and became an acknowledged source of inspiration and learning.

If we accorded greater recognition to the ways of living of the sustainable classes, we might begin to see that the good life might be something quite different from the image produced and portrayed by the entertainment and advertisement industry and experienced by the over-consuming classes. The members of the sustainable class should, therefore, be considered experts and contemporary examples and role models for living well within one's fair and sustainable share of environmental space.

A meaningful task ahead would be to conduct a global mapping of presently sustainable livelihoods and ways of living in the sustainable classes. We should have clear ideas and definitions of the typical occupations, resource bases, housing arrangements and other features of such communities. Many people in the sustainable classes probably earn their living directly from the land through gathering, farming and animal husbandry; in addition, there is probably small-scale artisanal production and the provision of non-industrial services. It would also be important to study the cultural dynamics of the sustainable classes, such as how members of this class perceive the attractions of the consumer culture, what their resilience capabilities might be in dealing with environmental disaster, what potential threats would cause a member of the struggling class to fail and so on.

4.3 Empowerment for the struggling classes

For the struggling classes, the case would be primarily for an empowerment scenario. The current hunger and poverty within the struggling classes is clearly a symptom of powerlessness. Successful transformation would call for a situation where the poor would have the right to natural resources that they depend on, the right to have basic needs met through their own efforts whenever possible and the right to an equal say in matters that affect their lives through the political process. If all these positive changes take place and some people find their income increased, thereby also raising the GDP, then that growth would be justified.

A last-person-first principle in economics would be of paramount importance for the empowerment of the struggling classes. Current planning and understanding is overly focused on national or regional averages, leaving the conditions of the weakest sectors of society in the dark. The central principle in last-person-first economics is encapsulated in Gandhi's maxim that the measure of a society can be determined by the way it treats its weakest members. In this way, societies would strive not for the growth of national GDP or its per capita average, but for the well-being of the last person, exemplified by the lowest 10 per cent. To this end, (re)allocating resources from the top to the bottom and thereby reducing inequalities would be the appropriate process.

Since the members of the struggling classes are predominantly women, the role of women's movements is of prime importance. One of the demands of such movements is to gain recognition and respect for the reproductive work done in households and productive work done by women in the informal sector, both of which are currently ignored in GDP calculations.

The popular movements of the struggling classes have provided detailed suggestions for transformations that would enhance the power and resources of the people in these classes, thus creating a more sustainable world. Such movements include the Via Campesina of rural workers and small farmers, the World March of Women, which unites feminist groups and actions across the world, Friends of the Earth International, which addresses environmental concerns and represents future generations in this sense, and War Resisters International, which promotes peace and non-violence in many facets of society. The movements of indigenous people also fall in this category.

When enhancing power in any group, the first step is to recognize the rights of the poor. *The right to food* and a dignified place in society are primary basic needs, which require attention first and foremost. This is also an issue of the customary *right to the natural resources* of the local environment, such as common forests and lands, the *right to vote* freely for a preferred, freely chosen candidate and the *right to information* about policies and programmes that will affect the lives of all those concerned. Since most members of the struggling class are female, all of these rights are of particular importance for women.

The end of violence against members of the struggling class is also essential, whether it concerns the beating or harassment of women, atrocities committed against minority groups or genocidal processes inflicted on indigenous people. Since compensation for people facing forced evictions by development projects has proved to be non-existent or inadequate, communities should also have the right to reject such projects.

When it comes to the sharing of resources, *land reforms* are highly topical. For the struggling members of rural communities, even a small plot of land for a dwelling and a kitchen garden makes a great difference. In the urban context, giving title deeds to families that have built their huts on common lands (squatters in slums, that is) would be one place to start.

4.4 On making the transformations a reality

One could easily dismiss the presented scenarios as wishful thinking because the current megatrends point in totally different directions. Growth in income and wealth are dominant aspirations in all classes. Even billionaires exert a great deal of energy in accumulating ever more wealth as a means of showcasing their professional excellence. At the same time, the age-old teachings of many philosophies and religions about simplicity or frugality being the surest route to contentment and even salvation are by and large dismissed.

Nonetheless, we can envisage transformations taking place, not least because current multi-faceted crises concerning the environment, inequality, economic stability and the meaning of life have all reached critical points. The irreversible environmental damage related to economic growth and the increase in population are reaching such a level that notions of endless growth and accumulation are being questioned. This could develop into a cultural transformation whereby economic progress as the *leitmotif* of humanity is supplanted by the idea of a good life within a safe and just environmental space. Such a sufficiency revolution is perhaps already in the making.

Yet cultural change would be necessary but insufficient since we also live – perhaps primarily so – in a political system. Capitalism and plutocracy have led us to the Plutocene and will not be able to provide the way out. An alternative would be to move more towards an ecological democracy (cf. D'Alisa et al., 2015; Shiva, 2016). Popular demands to phase out corporate power and the influence of finance capital from political decision-making at all levels have become visible, for example through the Indignados and Occupy movements. A transformation from plutocracy to democracy would readily be welcomed by today's marginalized majorities, such as the poor, women and people of colour.

Although the aspirations of the struggling and sustainable classes include increased consumption, their material realities make it easier for them to demand and realize a sustainable society. People who have not cultivated a dependency on private motoring, frequent flying and spacious housing can more easily imagine and demand a society where they are not the norm but, rather, unacceptable behaviour that needs to be more or less phased out.

In an ecological democracy, we would expect limits on both extraction and consumption of natural resources, and systems that gear their mobilization to fulfilling basic 'needs', while restricting the use of 'wants' in a communal fashion. Fair distribution of work in institutions controlled by people instead of capital, such as cooperatives, small-scale family enterprises and public production would liberate human energies for satisfactory engagement, instead of consumerist living. Combined with sufficient basic social services and security elements, a good life for all could be a real possibility.

5 Conclusion

One of our main concerns regarding the Anthropocene concept and narrative, besides the growing criticism levelled at its analytical incorrectness, is whether its conceptualization of the 'human species' narrative and the drivers behind anthropogenic changes to the biosphere can foster the necessary political action to do something about this negative development. Here, it is worth keeping in mind that the current political space and climate in which the discussion on the Anthropocene is taking place is *post-politics* (Lövbrand et al., 2015), where discussions on societal and environmental issues have become to an ever greater extent de-politicized, where power, conflicts and contradictions are swept under the rug, and the focus is on quick techno-fixes instead (see e.g. Kenis and Lievens, 2015). The generic 'we', so typical in post-politics, insinuates that we, humanity as a whole, are all in the same boat (or lifeboat), that we are all equally responsible as a species for the global environmental changes and that we will be equally affected by these changes.

In this chapter we have argued that a class analysis might help in re-politicizing the debate on ecological sustainability and social justice, with an emphasis on the massive environmental damage caused by the wealthy minority. Understanding our era as the Plutocene could foster political analysis, which could improve the chances of challenging the vested interests and business-as-usual attitude, which stand in the way of moving towards a post-fossil economy and degrowth and post-growth futures. This could help in reducing the negative effects brought about by the Plutocene/Anthropocene era.

The transformation agenda we have presented in this chapter points in different directions for different classes. This begs an obvious question: even if we agree with the approach, how could such major changes take place within a relatively short timeframe?

Our view is that cultural and political change is likely to happen when the members of the classes that have the most to gain from the transformations to just and sustainable futures rise up and force these changes. For this reason, we should take a keen interest in the popular movements of the struggling and sustainable classes. An important contemporary gathering place for such movements is the World Social Forum process, where many members come together and energize each other around the slogan 'Another World is Possible'. The non-hierarchic structure of the 'open space' created by the forum and the minimalist joint agenda of non-violence and rejection of neoliberal corporate capitalism resonate well with the content of this chapter. Added to this, recent large gatherings and movements with a clear focus on re-politicizing the debate on societal and environmental issues and calling for real democracy are significant landmarks in such processes (e.g. the climate justice movement, Kenis and Mathijs, 2014; and the 15M or Indignados movement in Spain, e.g. Swyngedouw, 2014; Asara and Muraca, 2015).

The looming environmental crisis and the inadequate responses to date can easily engender an atmosphere of hopelessness and even despair. However, in the round of dialogues in East Africa, South Asia and Northern Europe, there has been very little pessimism in the air. We hope to leave readers of this chapter with this optimistic spirit. Focusing on life itself gives us answers and resources to imagine and build a sustainable future for all. To this end, we have suggested alternatives constituting a thorough cultural and societal transformation for each of the four classes.

Transformation towards sustainable futures should be seen as a journey leading to something clearly better than what we have now. There is no need to be fearful or anxious. Embracing degrowth should be an empowering experience for the over-consuming classes, as by giving up unnecessary but environmentally and socially costly luxuries one can discover much more valuable things in life. Moreover, lending support to, and calling for, political and structural transformations towards sustainability will be saluted by the world majority and future generations. In short, there are plenty of rewards in store in the sustainable futures.

Bibliography

Abdallah, S., Michaelson, J., Shah, S., Stoll, L. & Marks, N. (2012) *The Happy Planet Index: 2012 Report. A Global Index of Sustainable Well-Being*. London: New Economics Foundation.

Asara, V. & Muraca, B. (2015) Indignados (Occupy). In: D'Alisa, G., Demaria, F. & Kallis, G. (eds) *Degrowth: A Vocabulary for a New Era*. London: Routledge, pp. 169–171.

Baskin, J. (2015) Paradigm Dressed as Epoch: The Ideology of the Anthropocene. *Environmental Values*. 24, 9–29.

Bentley, M. D. (2003) Sustainable Consumption: Ethics, National Indices and International Relations. Unpublished Doctoral Dissertation. Paris: American Graduate School of International Relations and Diplomacy.

Castree, N. (2014) The Anthropocene and the Environmental Humanities: Extending the Conversation. *Environmental Humanities*. 5, 233–260.

Chakravarty, S., Chikkatur, A., de Coninck, H., Pacala, S., Socolow, R. & Tavoni, M. (2009) Sharing Global CO2 Emission Reductions Among One Billion High Emitters. *Proceedings of the National Academy of Sciences*. 106(29), 11884–11888.

Chancel, L. & Piketty, T. (2015) *Carbon and Inequality: From Kyoto to Paris Trends in the Global Inequality of Carbon Emissions (1998–2013) & Prospects for an*

Equitable Adaptation Fund. Available from: www.parisschoolofeconomics.eu/en/news/carbon-and-inequality-from-kyoto-to-paris-chancel-piketty (accessed 5 December 2015).

Crutzen, P. J. & Stoermer E. F. (2000) The Anthropocene. *Global Change Newsletter.* 41, 17–18.

Czech, B. (2000) *Shoveling Fuel for a Runaway Train: Errant Economists, Shameful Spenders, and a Plan to Stop Them All*. Berkeley: University of California Press.

Czech, B. & Tietenberg, T. (2007) Steady State Economy. In: Cleveland, C. J. (ed.) *Encyclopedia of Earth*. Washington, DC: Environmental Information Coalition, National Council for Science and the Environment. Available from: www.eoearth.org/article/Steady_state_economy (accessed 20 November 2015).

D'Alisa, G., Demaria, F. & Kallis, G. (eds) (2015) *Degrowth: A Vocabulary for a New Era*. London: Routledge.

Daly, H. E. (1977) *Steady-State Economics: The Economics of Biophysical Equilibrium and Moral Growth*. San Francisco: Freeman.

Di Chiro, G. (2016) Environmental Justice and the Anthropocene Meme. In: Meyer, J. M., Gabrielson, T., Hall, C. & Schlosberg, D. (eds) *The Oxford Handbook of Environmental Political Theory*. Oxford: Oxford University Press, pp. 362–384.

Durning, A. (1992) *How Much is Enough?: The Consumer Society and the Future of the Earth*. New York: W.W. Norton & Company.

Hamilton, C. (2013) *Earthmasters: The Dawn of the Age of Climate Engineering*. New Haven, CT: Yale University Press.

Heede, R. (2014) Tracing Anthropogenic Carbon Dioxide and Methane Emissions to Fossil Fuel and Cement Producers, 1854–2010. *Climatic Change*. 122, 229–241.

Hemmati, M. & Gardiner, R. (2002) *Gender and Sustainable Development*. World Summit. Papers of the Heinrich Böll Foundation, No. 10. Berlin, Heinrich Böll Foundation. Available from: https://web.archive.org/web/20130228132818/www.worldsummit2002.org/publications/wspaper10.pdf (accessed 20 November 2015).

Hornborg, A. (2001) *The Power of the Machine: Global Inequalities of Economy, Technology, and Environment*. Walnut Creek, CA: AltaMira Press.

Hornborg, A. (2015) The Political Ecology of the Technocene: Uncovering Ecologically Unequal Exchange in the World-System. In: Hamilton, C., Bonneuil, C. & Gemenne, F. (eds) *The Anthropocene and the Global Environmental Crisis: Rethinking Modernity in a New Epoch*. London, Routledge, pp. 57–69.

Johnsson-Latham, G. (2007) *A Study on Gender Equality as a Prerequisite for Sustainable Development*. Report to the Environment Advisory Council. Available from: https://web.archive.org/web/20090219062029/http://genderandenvironment.org/admin/admin_biblioteca/documentos/rapport_engelska.pdf (accessed 5 December 2015].

Joutsenvirta, M., Hirvilammi, T., Ulvila, M. & Wilén, K. (2016) Talous kasvun jälkeen (Economy after Growth). Helsinki: Gaudeamus Helsinki University Press.

Kempf, H. (2008) *How the Rich are Destroying the Earth*. Totnes: Green Books.

Kenis, A. & Lievens, M. (2015) *The Limits of the Green Economy: From Re-inventing Capitalism to Re-politicising the Present*. London: Routledge.

Kenis, A. & Mathijs, E. (2014) Climate Change and Post-politics: Repoliticizing the Present by Imagining the Future? *Geoforum*. 52, 148–156.

Korten, D. C. (1994) *Sustainability and the Global Economy: Beyond Bretton Woods.* People Centred Development Forum. Available from: http://livingeconomiesforum.org/1995/bretton (accessed 3 April 2016).

Kumarappa, J. C. ([1948] 1997) *Economy of Permanence.* Varanasi: Sarva Seva Sangh Prakashan.

Lindley, M. (2007) *J.C. Kumarappa: Mahatma Gandhi's Economist.* Mumbai: Popular Prakashan.

Lövbrand, E., Beck, S., Chilvers, J., Forsyth, T., Hedrén, J., Hulme, M., Lidskog, R. & Vasileiadou, E. (2015) Who Speaks for the Future of Earth? How Critical Social Science Can Extend the Conversation on the Anthropocene. *Global Environmental Change.* 32, 211–218.

Malm, A. (2013) The Origins of Fossil Capital: From Water to Steam in the British Cotton Industry. *Historical Materialism.* 21, 15–68.

Malm, A. & Hornborg, A. (2014) The Geology of Mankind? A Critique of the Anthropocene Narrative. *The Anthropocene Review.* 1, 62–69.

Meadows, D., Randers, J. & Meadows, D. (2005) *Limits to Growth: The 30-Year Update.* London: Earthscan.

Moore, J. W. (2014a) *The Capitalocene, Part I: On the Nature & Origins of Our Ecological Crisis.* Available from: www.jasonwmoore.com/uploads/The_Capitalocene__Part_I__June_2014.pdf (accessed 20 November 2015).

Moore, J. W. (2014b) *The Capitalocene, Part II: Abstract Social Nature and the Limits to Capital.* Available from: www.jasonwmoore.com/uploads/The_Capitalocene___Part_II__June_2014.pdf (accessed 20 November 2015).

Moore, J. W. (2015) *Capitalism in the Web of Life: Ecology and the Accumulation of Capital.* London: Verso.

NEF (2016) *The Happy Planet Index 2016: A Global Index of Sustainable Well-Being.* London, New Economics Foundation. Available from: http://happyplanetindex.org/s/NEF_HPI-BRIEFING_WIP.pdf (accessed 10 August 2016).

Norgaard, R. B. (2013) The Econocene and the California Delta. *San Francisco Estuary & Watershed Science.* 11, 1–5.

Norgaard, R. B. (2014) Escaping Economism, Escaping the Econocene. In: Schneidewind, U., Santarius, T. & Humburg, A. (eds) *Economy of Sufficiency: Essays on Wealth in Diversity, Enjoyable Limits and Creating Commons.* Wuppertal, Germany: Wuppertal Institute for Climate, Environment and Energy, pp. 44–52. Available from: http://wupperinst.org/en/publications/details/wi/a/s/ad/2473 (accessed 20 November 2015).

Norgaard, R. B. (2015) The Church of Economism and Its Discontents. *Great Transition Initiative.* Available from: www.greattransition.org/publication/the-church-of-economism-and-its-discontents (accessed 20 March 2016).

Nurmela, J. & Mäenpää, I. (2014) Perustarpeet rasittavat ympäristöä eniten. *Tieto&Trendit.* 6, n/a. Available from: http://tietotrendit.stat.fi/mag/article/92 (accessed 25 December 2015).

Oxfam (2015) *Extreme Carbon Inequality.* Author: Timothy Gore. Available from: www.oxfam.org/sites/www.oxfam.org/files/file_attachments/mb-extreme-carbon-inequality-021215-en.pdf (accessed 20 March 2016).

Ruddiman W. (2003) The Anthropogenic Greenhouse Era Began Thousands of Years Ago. *Climatic Change.* 61, 261–293.

Satterthwaite, D. (2009) The Implications of Population Growth and Urbanization for Climate Change. *Environment & Urbanization.* 21, 545–567.

Shiva, V. (2016) Responding to the New Nature. *Boston Review*. Available from: https://bostonreview.net/forum/new-nature/vandana-shiva-vandana-shiva-response-new-nature (accessed 20 March 2016).

Shiva, V. & Turhan, E. (2016) *The Earth and the People are not Inputs to Your Capitalist System, Sorry Sir! An Interview with Vandana Shiva*. Available from: http://entitleblog.org/2016/03/08/the-earth-and-the-people-are-not-inputs-to-your-capitalist-system-sorry-sir (accessed 20 March 2016).

Steffen W, Crutzen P. J. & McNeill J. R. (2007) The Anthropocene: Are Humans Now Overwhelming the Great Forces of Nature? *Ambio*, 36, 614–621.

Swyngedouw, E. (2014) Where is the Political? Insurgent Mobilisations and the Incipient "Return of the Political". *Space and Polity*. 18(2), 122–136.

Swyngedouw, E. (2015) Foreword: Apocalypse Now? From the Marketisation to the Politicisation of the Environment. In: Kenis, A. & Lievens, M. (eds) *The Limits of the Green Economy: From Re-inventing Capitalism to Re-politicising the Present*. London: Routledge, pp. ix–xv.

Ulvila, M. & Pasanen, J. (eds) (2009) *Sustainable Futures: Replacing Growth Imperative and Hierarchies with Sustainable Ways*. Helsinki: Ministry for Foreign Affairs of Finland.

Wiedmann, T. O., Schandl, H., Lenzen, M., Moran, D., Suh, S., West, M. & Kanemoto, K. (2013) The Material Footprint of Nations. *Proceedings of the National Academy of Sciences*. 112(20), 6271–6276. Available from www.pnas.org/content/suppl/2013/08/28/1220362110.DCSupplemental/sd01.xlsx (accessed 10 August 2016).

Worldwatch (2004) *State of the World 2004*. Washington, DC: Worldwatch Institute.

9 Conceptualizing worker agency for the challenges of the Anthropocene

Examples from recycling work in the Global North

Eeva Houtbeckers and Tiina Taipale[1]

1 Introduction

> My pure and authentic view is that this system is collapsing. Full stop. – And I'm concerned how much pioneer structures have time to make it from there [in time] *before* it collapses when we are really very screwed.
>
> (Reuse Informant 1, Interview 2013)

The notion of the Anthropocene conveys an agreement among scientists that we have entered a new geohistorical epoch, during which human activities have remarkable impacts on ecosystems (Crutzen, 2002). A rapid climate change combined with the fragmentation of species is predicted to result in mass extinctions, possibly including the human species, and the collapse of the ecosystem (Barnosky et al., 2012).

The harmful effects of humans on the ecosystems have been revealed in recent geological studies (Waters et al., 2016). It is said that the Anthropocene is manifested in the complex cause-effect relationships of everyday living on planet Earth. The omnipotence of human agency seems to go beyond our comprehension and the scope of human action (Latour, 2014). Instead, we are left with a fundamental question of what to do with this knowledge about the ongoing – and already materialized – collapses, and how to proceed in reorganizing human activities (see e.g. Swyngedouw, 2013).

In this chapter, we tackle this broad issue by focusing on *work* in order to imagine changes in the social and economic patterns that reproduce the Anthropocene. We have four starting points related to work. First, we view our social and material realities as constructed and maintained by human activities, and that many of these activities we refer to as work (Grint, 1991, pp. 7–8). Carrying out tasks related to basic needs, such as food, housing, moving and caring, requires work, as does bettering the quality of life and living conditions. Moreover, work also affects 'more-than-humans', such as plants, animals, the biosphere and geology.

1 Authors in alphabetical order.

Secondly, most contemporary societies have increasingly become 'paid work societies', in which waged work is the principal means of making a living (Standing, 2010, pp. 38–39). This differs from arrangements in which people satisfy some or most of their basic needs independently of earning a wage. In addition, the division of labour between different professions, most of which require a specialized education, characterizes industrialized contemporary societies. Professional and waged work structures the course of people's lives, defining not only their income level, but to a great extent their social status and lifestyle.

However, it is feared that the necessity to create paid work for an increasing number of humans becomes ecologically impossible under the current mode of production, which is based on an unsustainable use of fossil fuels and other natural resources (Latouche, [2007] 2009). The fact that people need to earn a living through waged work creates a need to generate economic growth, since a lack of growth in the contemporary economic models leads to unemployment, which is considered socially and politically unsustainable (Antal, 2014). However, the efforts to decouple economic growth and ecological impacts have been insufficient (Antal, 2014). The problem is exacerbated by technological progress contributing to increasing productivity of work, combined with global market policies emphasizing deregulation and the flexibilization of labour markets. These trends result in the decreasing security of paid work and undisturbed income (Nierling, 2012). Instead of developing new kinds of socio-ecological policies that would contribute to long-term global social and ecological justice, under the contemporary political doctrine the focus is on sustaining economic growth to stimulate employment and job creation at the national level. Hence, there is a call to reorganize work and work systems at various levels, ranging from global labour market policy regulations to the way we understand work (Standing, 2010; Nierling, 2012; Antal, 2014).

Thirdly, workers, who for their part reproduce and contribute to the paid work society, can themselves act as change agents in the transformation of work. Although work in contemporary paid work societies is organized to a large extent by the logic of production and managerial control (see e.g. Standing, 2010, p. 21), workers have had, and still have, a significant role in shaping working patterns (but the degree surely depends on the context). The diverse and interdisciplinary field of labour studies, ranging from labour history to industrial relations, has discussed the role of workers' movements and organizations in societal transitions (see e.g. Zeitlin, 1987; Grint, 1991, pp. 152–198). Alarmingly, recent research has described the ways in which neoliberal politics and managerial practices have weakened collective interests by establishing global production, or destruction networks (Rainnie, Herod and McGrath-Champ, 2011; Herod et al., 2014). In many contexts, this has largely broken down the power of traditional labour movements and organizations (Chhachhi, 2014).

Accordingly, new prominent ways of social resistance and protests have emerged to draw attention to the different social problems and injustices related to the flexible use of labour and 'capital hopping to cheap labour sites'

(Chhachhi, 2014, p. 897). These range from campaigning for better working conditions in countries with low labour costs, to protest movements of the un- and underemployed in countries that have been industrialized for a long time. Some of these protests have already highlighted that exploitation of the workforce goes hand in hand with exploitation of the environment and joined forces with environmental movements. Thus, there is hope that new kinds of counter-capitalist movements and organizations will be formed, which could overcome the tendency of plural solidarities hindering collective class-based action (Burawoy, 2010).

Fourthly and finally, we are aware that not all forms of worker agency are concerned with ecology, nor is all of the so-called green behaviour self-evidently concerned with social justice or democracy. That being so, combining these agendas has been portrayed as a fruitful way to challenge the contemporary trends, as indicated by writers such as Naomi Klein (2015). Therefore, it is important to outline a proposal for a *worker agency* that builds on both the social and ecological critique of neoliberal capitalism and advances the principles of democracy as well as ecological and social justice.

To better understand the role of work and worker agency in maintaining and changing the paid work societies and influencing the Anthropocene, we draw from previous literature on industrial and global capitalism. In this chapter we examine *how workers can challenge the contemporary organizing of work and respond to the challenges of the Anthropocene*. The previous literature on labour studies provides insights into this question by arguing that worker agency is always embedded in socio-material conditions (Coe and Jordhus-Lier, 2011, p. 216). Accordingly, various forms of *labour agency* exist, which inspire resistance to and the modification of global structures (ibid.). We add to this literature by studying *employee agency* including employee resistance (Parker, 2006) and employee green behaviour (Norton et al., 2015). By combining the literature on labour and employee agency – with different historical roots and conditions – we develop a new category of worker agency to address the challenges of the Anthropocene. Hence, we map examples that could challenge the contemporary dynamics between capital and (human) labour, as well as between capital and the more-than-humans.

In order to examine the embeddedness of worker agency, we present findings from two qualitative studies on the recycling work in the Global North, the parts of the world with the highest income per capita. Specifically, we show how actors reflect on their own agency and position in the global production and destruction networks, which they recognized and found unsustainable. We describe the forms of worker agency found in these organizations, and how this worker agency is embedded in local and state governance systems, as well as in the production and destruction networks. We conclude that the concept of worker agency has the potential to address some of the challenges of the Anthropocene in the studied sites, as well in general.

2 The Anthropocene and worker agency

It is suggested that the contemporary geological epoch that follows the Holocene should be named the Anthropocene, because this portrays the multitude of contemporary human effects on our planet, including the loss of biodiversity, increasing CO2 emissions and the increased use of toxic substances (Crutzen, 2002; Waters et al., 2016). These effects strain the capacity of planet Earth to sustain human and more-than-human life (Rockström et al., 2009). The Anthropocene offers a new geological perspective that shows the effects of human agency on the balance of ecological systems (Crutzen, 2002) and positions humans as one of the many species affected by human activities (Gibson-Graham and Roelvink, 2010).

Stating the cause-and-effect relationship in this way highlights the moral question of the responsibility of humans (Latour, 2014). In addition to humans, various agents of the so-called natural world have an impact, but these are increasingly understood to be beyond human control due to the deepening ecological crisis (ibid.) and of minor importance in relation to the anthropogenic forcing (IPCC, 2014). Taking the Anthropocene seriously should lead to rethinking the notions of power, social order, critique and political struggle that relate to the time of modernism (Latour, 2014). Consequently, the concept of the Anthropocene brings forth the force of human effects on the ecology and signifies that the human agent has become global in its reach (for a critical discussion of such agency, see the previous chapter).

It goes without saying that in order to survive as a species, humans must engage with their environment to produce a means of survival and well-being, which entails work. What activities count as work depends on the social and historical context (Grint, 1991, p. 7). In this chapter, we use three related concepts: work, labour and job. *Work* is understood here as a general term referring to those efforts that are put in to accomplish something (Grint, 1991, pp. 7–8). *Labour* is used to highlight the interests of the workers and wage earners in relation to the interests of the capitalists or capital itself. Labour has also been used to refer to things 'pertaining' to labour, manifesting, for instance, in the labour movement, as well as policies, organizational principles and legislation on labour (Random House, 2010). Labour also refers to controlling, organizing and arranging wage labour and paid work; the latter is also referred to as *jobs*.

In order to address how workers can challenge the contemporary organizing of work and respond to the challenges of the Anthropocene, we review previous studies on labour and employee agency (summarized in Table 9.1). In other words, we outline the different kinds of worker agency that could challenge the inequities and ecological consequences associated with contemporary free market capitalism. We take into account that workers are citizens of states, in which social rights are to a large extent bound to one's labour market position and capacity to work (Kettunen, 2010; Standing, 2010). The transformation to new ways of working is affected by these factors.

Capitalism is to a great extent the dominant mode of production in the industrialized world and it dictates how work is done and valued. Next we present previous studies that have documented, for instance, the effects of free market capitalism on working conditions. We then present previous research on how workers can influence and advance the negotiations between capital and workers, which affects human-nature relations and the challenges of the Anthropocene, *within* the current practices with historical roots.

2.1 The conditions for labour and employee agency

In the era of national industrial capitalism (see Sennett, 2007; Standing, 2010), industrialization and the spread of market mechanism were followed by the 'labour question'. Social movements built a new kind of class awareness and formulated the collective interests of workers in relation to capitalists. Eventually, labour interests became institutionalized in labour market regulation and social democratic politics, through which states attempted to balance interests between workers and capital. These policies then led to establishing paid work societies, where wage earning and the right to work formed the core principles of social order and social rights (Kettunen, 2010, p. 22; Standing, 2010, p. 38).

However, economic development and the rising levels of welfare had some paradoxical results in relation to worker agency. Rising levels of education and income resulted in narrower professional and employee interest groups, which eroded class-consciousness and solidarity, and replaced labour with the concepts of 'employee' and 'consumer' (Jacoby, 2004, p. 213). The gradual change of thinking from labour to employees was (and still is) also reflected in the way 'employment' relations and resistance replaced 'industrial relations' and 'labour resistance' as targets of politics, management and education.

Since the 1980s, economic globalization has gained momentum. The transformation towards opening up economies was accompanied by neoliberal policies and managerial paradigms, free trade and the flexible use of workforce. Backed up by the development of communication technologies, these together created conditions in which transnational corporations flourished (Rainnie et al., 2011). The forms of networked organization, based on efficient subcontracting structures, that were adopted are described as the thriving force of globalization, as transnational corporations have been able to take advantage of the international labour market and 'new spatial division of labour' through this economic restructuring (ibid., p. 162).

Various ideological and related power shifts paved the way for the transformation of national capitalist systems into free market capitalism. The nation states were reframed as competition states (Cerny, 1997) vying for investments and production by offering competitive terms, including qualified and attractively priced labour. The reframing meant that states started to withdraw from some of their former ways of adjusting the imbalance between capital and labour; namely by cutting down on welfare policies or replacing them with 'workfare' policies (Jessop, 1993; Kananen, 2012). The interests of capital were often portrayed in terms of requirements of the economy and as universal. Unlike before, when negotiating different interests of labour and capital was understood to contribute to society, workers are increasingly seen to have a 'biased interest', which compromises national competitiveness (Kettunen, 2010, pp. 39–40).

The emphasis on flexibility and the 'race to the bottom' with falling labour costs have resulted in growing unemployment, lack of job security and increasing inequality. This has made work an unreliable source of income, resulting in increasing difficulties in maintaining one's right to work and sense of belonging (Frayne, 2015). One consequence of these developments is the spread of new forms of social unrest, exemplified by the creation of such movements as Occupy and Indignados (Lewis and Luce, 2012; Antentas, 2015). Thus, the 'labour question' has become topical again (Chhachhi, 2014).

This has given rise to new kinds of counter-capitalist responses, which call for understanding the changes in social relations while reorganizing work. Recently, labour geography has drawn on the literature on global production networks to discuss the conditions and possibilities of labour agency in the globalizing economy (Coe and Jordhus-Lier, 2011; Rainnie et al., 2011). These studies emphasize the importance of labour for the functioning of the production network. Moreover, they describe the uneven development resulting from production organized in global networks, which can be used to 'reveal the variegated landscape of agency potential across different sectors' (Coe and Jordhus-Lier, 2011, p. 221).

According to Coe and Jordhus-Lier (2011, p. 216), some actions and agents have more impact than others, because agency is embedded in the 'social relations that condition their potential'. In other words, labour agency is always embedded in socio-material conditions. When labour agency is defined primarily as a collective effort to advocate and protect the interests of labour vis-à-vis the interests of capital, *employee* agency is mainly comprised of individual agency. According to the work of organization scholars on employee resistance (Parker, 2006) and employee green behaviour (Norton et al., 2015), workers have agency not only as labour (positions vis-à-vis capital) but also as employees. Partly due to control systems, such as the Human Resource Management (HRM), which emphasize normative commitment and fit between employee-employer values, people increasingly relate to their work as employees and try to shape the world through their own work organizations (see e.g. Fleming, 2012; Ramarajan and Reid, 2013).

However, this does not necessarily mean actively engaging with reshaping the conditions and power relations of work organizations, but reshaping the goals and ways of working *within* organizations. It follows that adequate forms of worker agency for the challenges of the Anthropocene are based on the understanding of the power dynamics between workers and capital (labour agency), as well as agency as employees informed by this knowledge. In other words, instead of arguing for a certain kind of labour or employee agency to be the most fruitful way of transforming production and economic systems to operate within the limits of Earth´s ecological boundaries, we offer a framework that maps the different forms of worker agency already in place. These different forms of agency range from traditional trade movements to new kinds of employee behaviour. More efficient ways to act can surely be found by understanding how these embedded forms of agency inform each other of the structures and consequences of free market capitalism.

2.2 Worker agency's role in dealing with the challenges of the Anthropocene

Following Coe and Jorhus-Lier (2011) and Katz (2004, cited in Coe and Jorhus-Lier, 2011), we have categorized various potential forms of socio-materially embedded worker agency in Table 9.1, namely resilience, reworking and resistance,

Table 9.1 Integrating labour and employee agencies to develop a worker agency.

Forms of embedded activities	*Worker agency*	
	Labour agency	*Employee agency*
Resilience Helping human individuals and groups to get by Helping more-than-humans to get by	• Developing welfare policies • Collectively organizing social and economic solidarity • Self-sustaining local communities and alternative organizing	• Nurturing solidarity • Fighting careerism • Developing greening work practices (for example, green office behaviour)
Reworking Challenging social relations Reworking human-nature relations	• Aiming at decent work • Quality green jobs policies • Recognition of civil and care work • Incorporation of interests of un(der)employed • Building professional communities among self-organized groups	• Developing professional and organizational moral codes for sustaining solidarity • Supporting organizational democracy • Introducing new sustainability practices • Aiming at strong employee green behaviour (contributing to change in production patterns and values)
Resistance Direct challenges to social relations Game-changing human-nature relations	• Labour internationalism (building solidarity between workers across geographical scale) • Building alternative economies and organizational logics (solidarity economy, local economies, cooperatives, circular economy) within ecological limits • Basic income policies	• Using insider information to alter the logic of production • Aligning forces with consumer campaigns and social movements • Abandoning work and alternative work • Self-employment and social enterprise

from least to most influential in order to change social and human-nature relations. Based on these categories, we outline some examples of labour and employee agency before turning to our empirical illustrations.

2.2.1. Worker agency and resilience

Agency contributing to resilience consists of small acts that enable 'individuals and groups [to] cope with everyday social realities but do not change existing social relations' (Coe and Jordhus-Lier, 2011, p. 216) and offer support for those with scarce resources, like little specialized education or assets. Thus this kind of labour agency is seen to consist of mobilization of social support, such as assistance by local labour organizations in times of hardship. Such peer or network support might temporarily protect individuals and groups from commodification, here understood as one's ability to protect oneself from becoming marketized, and having oneself or one's labour power sold and bought for poor wages and in poor conditions, without means to avoid others' control over one's life (Standing, 2010).

Institutional safeguards were built in to the capitalist social or welfare models, advanced in Western democracies in the 1900s, to offer social protection, regulation and redistribution and to protect workers from commodification. The building of these safeguards was attained by labour agency, reworking and resisting exploitation of labour. While this social protection has weakened and changed because of the increasing emphasis on flexicurity and workfare, new ways of offering social protection have been emerging. These include local initiatives and movements of un(der)employed, which offer help in different forms, such as food aid or urban gardening. As employees and professionals many individuals do and can contribute to resilience by building strategies of peer support and solidarity. This might entail resisting overreaching managerialism and protecting occupational praxis in conditions where economic performance measures are implemented. Strategies that support various 'stakeholder groups' in more vulnerable conditions may also be useful, such as participating in company organized volunteering.

As Michael Burawoy argued (2010), the contemporary advancement of capitalism and its capacity to break free from attempts to embed markets in society is characterized by a deepening commodification of nature. This is evident in the way water, land and even air, through carbon trading, are increasingly becoming commodities through their privatization. Both the older, as well as the newer, traditions of labour agency try to counter-balance this development by contributing to 'resilience', here understood as action that aims to alleviate the effects of destructive work and production on the environment. This is evident in the ways labour organizations have been committed to advancing 'greener workplaces' and 'green office' policies and practices. This also is the case with individual employers and employee groups, who commit to green practices at work, such as recycling or using public transport. Still, these forms of agency do not aim to rework or resist the commodifying logic.

2.2.2 Worker agency and reworking

Reworking concerns the efforts to materially improve worker conditions, in a way that challenges social relations, but does not really undo them (Coe and Jordhus-Lier, 2011). In the spirit of employee green behaviour (see Norton et al., 2015), we suggest that employees can rework contemporary production models by adopting green careers or green employee behaviour, finding and developing less resource intensive ways of doing their work. More efficient reworking might develop professional or organizational moral practices advancing ecological and social sustainability.

We suggest that alongside green employee behaviour, forms of traditional labour agency could be resurrected especially across different sites in the production network, such as campaigning for green work and decent working conditions and pay, and revitalizing notions of solidarity and organizational democracy. These forms of labour agency could inform adequate forms of employee agency, especially to be resilient in relation to outsourcing, careerism and other company politics contributing to social and ecological injustice at the organizational level, as well as across the production network. They could be combined with new forms of emancipatory and counter-capitalism agency from precariat and unemployed movements (Chhachhi, 2014). These might include alternative organizing, such as community cooperatives and local support programmes. Employees who resist current ways of organizing production by refusing to work could play a significant role in developing such alternatives.

2.2.3 Worker agency and resistance

Resistance consists of direct challenges to the dominant social relationships and is by nature game changing (Coe and Jordhus-Lier, 2011). This includes attempts to regain control over production and reproduction as well as to reshape the dominant capitalist in favour of the workers. Examples of such resistance could be measures belonging to the alternative economies project and include non-capitalist forms of organizing production and labour time, such as cooperatives and alternative currencies (Gibson-Graham, 2008).

There have been hopes of global counter-movements to challenge the way contemporary capitalism breaks free from mechanisms and to make the economy serve the society again. According to Burawoy (2010, pp. 306–307), two kinds of counter-movements have been postulated. The first pins its hopes on labour internationalism, which 'tries to link working classes across factories, localities, nations, regions and the world, united by their common exploitations'. The second pins its hopes on common resistance by various groups (farmers, the unemployed, environmental groups), who experience commodification at dispersed local sites. Burawoy calls for a global counter-movement drawn together by the experiences of commodification, especially the degradation of the environment affecting both rich and poor nations.

Wider socio-cultural changes are called for in order to find sustaining ways of living. As discussed in the previous sections, 'good jobs', which form the basis of income and self-value in wage societies, are becoming rare. New forms of resistance and agency are evoking the question whether employment can still be held as a prerequisite for full social citizenship, as it was constructed to be in social capitalism (Standing, 2010; Chhachhi, 2014). This is important, since creating jobs for all can also turn out to be ecologically devastating. Thus, new forms of worker agency include revoking discussions over the role of paid work in society. Promoting alternative ways of securing social citizenship rights, such as basic income, could replace the 'right-to-work' principle characterizing both social and free market capitalism. These could also create space for more ecological ways of working, since people would not be forced to do 'whatever' to earn a living. This could be achieved by advocating policies based on a holistic understanding of work, which would also recognize different forms of unpaid work, such as do-it-yourself work, voluntary work and family work (Nierling, 2012). Thus, instead of maximizing economic growth and profits, the objective of policy would be to achieve a good life by, inter alia, empowering individuals and communities.

Employee agency for resistance can be informed by both of the above-mentioned forms of labour resistance. Employees, especially those working in multinational companies or internationally networked organizations, can advance labour internationalization by insider knowledge and aligning forces with consumer campaigns. Employees can also refuse contemporary forms of waged work by committing to low-income and ecological lifestyles, or by organizing alternative working sites, such as social enterprises or cooperatives. They can call for new kinds of policies also via traditional workers' unions. Employees can also aim at agency by contributing to game-changing human-nature relations, without commitment to labour resistance. These forms of employee agency could cover commitment to advancing new technologies or business models that would replace the current ones with others that sustain instead of consume humans and more-than-humans.

3 Two empirical studies on recycling in the Global North

Developing worker agency requires understanding the connections between different production sites and the processes of commodification of people and the more-than-humans. In order to empirically grasp the potential worker agency and its embeddedness in the global production/destruction networks, we provide evidence of two sites, where we conducted participatory observation and interviews (Pink and Morgan, 2013) during 2011–2014. These sites are Finnish examples of labour and employee agency in production and destruction networks operating in the Nordic welfare context. In this context labour has been protected from commodification by establishing welfare policies, giving people opportunities for social income, and protecting them from vulnerability in relation to capital. This development places Finland and other Nordic countries in the top positions of country comparisons (Czarniawska and Sevón, 2003). However, the situation is gradually changing as social security has increasingly become workfare based.

These two settings used recycled materials in commodity production. Recycling and waste management have been seen as sectors in which there are possibilities for job creation (ILO/UNEP, 2012). Owing to accumulative awareness, waste is increasingly being used again, for instance in the production of new commodities. We examined self-employment for reusing materials and rehabilitation work organized by the municipality.

The first site studied was 'Reuse', a limited-liability company established in 2007 by two craftswomen with a background in the clothing sector. Their service included modifying used clothing according to customers' wishes. In addition to giving themselves employment, they aimed to find solutions to the increasing textile waste problem in developed countries. The most important objective was to reduce the use of virgin materials, which meant all the materials they used had been used before. They also aimed at high-quality design and durable clothing. These objectives made the site interesting as the recycling emphasized various elements of responsibility – social, ecological and also aesthetic. In addition, the site was an example of self-employment, which is increasing in Finland due to unemployment and outsourcing (Pärnänen and Sutela, 2014).

The second site studied was 'Renew' established in 1997 and coordinated and owned by the municipality. In the space of a few years, the cooperative-like workshop, which consisted of around 40 highly qualified artists and artisans, slowly transformed to become a producer of a 'rehabilitation service' for more than 500 people a year producing design items from recycled materials. In general, rehabilitation work in Finland organized by local authorities is a proactive social policy measure targeted at decreasing long-term unemployment. The Act on Rehabilitative Work Experience of 2001 formed a part of the tool kit of so-called 'activation policies'. Activation policy entails increasing the convergence of employment and social welfare policies and implies conditionality of social assistance and employment benefits (Keskitalo, Ala-Kauhuluoma and Mannila, 2002; Kananen, 2012).

We followed the two sites during 2011–2014. The empirical material consists of ethnographic interviews and participant observations in situ (Table 9.2).

Table 9.2 The empirical material of the study.

Organization	*Established*	*Owners*	*No of workers (paid, volunteers or rehabilitated)*	*No of informants*	*Interviews year (no)*	*Observation visits year (no)*
Renew	1997	Munici-pality	Approx. 500	9	2012 (3) 2013 (8)	2012 (12) 2013 (12)
Reuse	2007	2	Approx. 8	1	2013 (3) 2014 (1)	2011 (1) 2013 (2)

The analysis process included reading the interview transcripts and field notes in order to trace the personal reflections of the people studied. We understand that the people we have followed are able to reflect on their work (Hitchings 2012) and treat interviews as constructions developed by the interviewee and interviewer (Alvesson 2011).While conducting our analysis we paid special attention not only to the forms of agency but also to the factors that condition this agency. Based on the literature presented above and our sense of the empirical material, we developed themes to follow, namely material realities, the position of people and the activities taking place in related networks. These broad categories proved to be useful for organizing the empirical materials and people's reflections on their work. Finally, we used these themes in presenting examples of *reworking* the human-nature relation, *resilience* in social relations and *resisting* commodification and changing human-nature relations, which are discussed in the next section.

4 Embedded worker agency and recycling work in the Global North

The sites analysed represent different sides of the recycling work in the Global North. Both Reuse and Renew reflect how worker agency is embedded not only in the changed logic of production, but in the 'local and non-local systems of rules, norms, customs, legal structures and regulatory mechanism', which shape the behaviour of workers and employers (Rainnie et al., 2011). Work is disappearing in manufacturing sectors, such as clothing, and for the low-skilled workforce and craftsmen in general due to globalization and automation. Combined with neoliberal policies underlining individual responsibility, this has led to a workfare instead of social services, and to the rise of self-employment instead of employment. National and local authorities have created specific labour market positions for educated clothing artisans and the unemployed. Next, we present some examples of worker agency (Table 9.1) met in the sites studied.

4.1 Reworking human-nature relations

Both Renew and Reuse reworked the contemporary human-nature relations (Table 9.1). They aimed to extend the use of materials, to prevent waste production, and to promote ecological sustainability. Both organizations also fostered traditional craftsmanship skills. Thus, the use of recycled material was related to the nurturing of skills and activities, which are increasingly seen as outdated in the cheap-commodity production world.

The two fieldwork sites aimed for small-scale serial production, using recycled materials, and enabling design, creativity and meaningful work. From 2005 onwards, the work in Renew was increasingly centred on small-scale production made from recycled material:

> When I started in my post in 2005 many workshops still used plenty of new materials. They bought silver for the jewel workshops and tinkering materials

> from a retail shop for other workshops. So I just started to push that we should find alternative materials, like for this sheet fabric that we used for making bags. That was my ideology, and on the other hand it is about costs. All that we can save from the materials, we can use for other things in the rehabilitation, for excursions and so on.
>
> (Renew Informant 1, Interview 2013)

At Reuse, they considered that minimizing the clothing waste was their duty:

> This type of service concept [including taking in materials and reusing them according to customers' wishes via employing craftspeople] exists nowhere else in Finland.
>
> (Reuse Informant 1, Interview 2013)

The systematic use of recycled materials required management of various kinds of networks to access materials and balance the different interests. The owner-manager of Reuse sourced materials from several locations. In addition to sourcing materials from large recycling organizations, she tried to gain access to large clothing manufacturers:

> The owner-manager hosts visitors to discuss co-operation. The visitors are fascinated by the products being sold in the space. They stop in front of a rack full of clothes made out of colourful printed fabrics. Are they really materials someone considered waste? Yes. The owner-manager explains that they came from a large Finnish clothes manufacturer, which was at first positive giving their production waste for Reuse. But when presenting the designs to the decision-makers, they wanted to protect the prints. She suggested Reuse would use only the blank parts. Eventually, they considered it too difficult to sort the waste. The cooperation ceased and the leftover parts continued to go to waste. The visitors are shocked. She continues: 'I try to stab every potential place. This is a preaching job. But not to worry, [there exists] already six years of preaching.'
>
> (Reuse Informant 1, Observation 2013)

The Renew workshop itself hosted different workshops, which produced material for each other. This material itself drove the design processes and made possible the use of the skills and creativity of the supervisors, many of whom were highly educated artist or artisans. Apart from the availability of the material, the nature of the rehabilitation work in Renew enabled the designing of products because they were easy to make:

> It forces your imagination to work, that we get this material, and we think what this could be used for. – Like this inner tube from bicycles, we had too much of it on the bicycle reparations, and now we have many products made out of it.
>
> (Renew Informant 1, Interview 2013)

Materials were also gained from firms, other municipality operators, such as hospitals and schools, and private agents. They worked to guarantee a flow of materials and it seemed to pay off:

> Then we have found all these alternative materials, and we also get them as donations. We have a good reputation because we use these recycled materials and have such nice recycled products, and that has brought about this virtuous circle, we get this material, and we are known, and we are offered materials.
>
> (Renew Informant 1, Interview 2012)

The ability of Renew to establish relations with commercial corporations, which offered certain sets of materials, enabled corporations to use the cooperation to build an image as a responsible organization. Thus, one could claim that Renew was one knot in the sustainability-branding network.

4.2 Resilience in social relations

As indicated above, the use of recycled materials is labour-intensive. Thus, it invites people to develop win-win solutions that target both ecological and social effects; engaging unemployed people or professionals to handle used materials and recycle them into new commodities.

Based on our analysis, the recycling of materials led easily to the forced 'recycling of people'. In general, the clothing and craft sectors in Western societies are in crisis because the work has been moved to countries with lower wage levels. Yet in Finland, the institutions keep educating young people as dressmakers and artisans while many fresh graduates end up unemployed or are employed in different sectors from those in which they are qualified:

> A teacher is visiting the owner-manager to agree issues concerning a new intern. The teacher is fascinated by the working conditions and the atmosphere in the atelier. She asks an older intern about the possibility to continue there after graduation. The intern replies: 'Currently, there are no jobs anywhere'.
>
> (Reuse Informant 1, Observation 2013).

The quote above shows the paradoxical nature of the everyday work of dressmakers. While ateliers keep on running with limited turnover and staff, interns keep coming monthly and eventually they graduate. The competition for the limited number of positions is stiff. Yet, the majority of graduates would like to work in the sector. This has resulted in the rise in self-employment. In Reuse, they realized quite soon that it was not possible to increase the business without implementing a series production approach to clothing reuse:

> We had no possibilities to employ anyone – so for almost three years I run it [an employment model that was developed].
>
> (Reuse Informant 1, Interview 2013)

The model, developed in collaboration with employment authorities, engaged young unemployed professionals, who enjoyed working with recycled materials and ecological design. They were able to enjoy social security while sewing garments for piecework pay at Reuse, which was deducted from their unemployment benefit. All were glad that this model enabled young professionals to maintain their expertise and engage in ecological dressmaking.

As explained before, Renew operated around rehabilitation work. It also intervened in the life of the unemployed, a measure that was supposed to activate and support. But if one chose to not take the measure, one's employment benefits were refused:

> You can't just quit here, you will lose your benefits. So this is like a forced marriage. That is why we aim to make this as painless and enjoyable as possible, so that it would not feel like forced labour.
>
> (Renew Informant 1, Interview 2012)

The organizers emphasized that using recycled materials was part of the strategy to make this experience as pleasant as possible to the people 'under activation':

> First and foremost we are an organizer of rehabilitation work. But if we would be working with new materials, then we would probably be packing some products to boxes, which would not offer much feelings of achievement. But this kind of selling and creating new things and design, working with recycled materials adds all this.
>
> (Renew Informant 1, Interview 2012)

This can be seen as employee agency, which is informed by labour resilience tactics: the commodifying elements of rehabilitation were recognized and to some extent counter-balanced by aims to make work activities meaningful. The 'need' for activation was reevaluated every three months and the maximum stay was limited to two years. This meant that the workers (clients) changed continuously, even though some of them would have really liked to continue. But also a vast number of the instructors were contracted from the pool of unemployed artists or artisans and given two-year contracts, though many of them would have liked to have had longer contracts. This made operating the workshops challenging:

> Now we – have made rules, processes and descriptions of how we work, so that when people change, the operations would not change. – And it is very important here – we have had 580 people on rehabilitation this year, out of which around 350 were new ones. And half of the instructors change every year. So if all the operations would change as well . . .
>
> (Renew Informant 1, Interview 2013)

In general, there was an agreement among the instructors that working on handicrafts and design-jobs was therapeutic. While working with their hands on something beautiful, people could also talk to others, find comfort and share experiences. As far as the instructors were concerned the aesthetics of the work at Renew compensated for the low pay and temporary contracts. Many also shared the commitment to ecological and social sustainability and they tried to advance these principles, which is aligned with employee agency to rework human-nature relations (Table 9.1). Still, both production-wise and organization-wise, Renew sustained its operations by having specific labour market conditions that were ensured by law. This pushed people to a certain status and to have certain obligations. This gave rise to many questions about agency formation and its limitations.

Due the lack of resources, both Reuse and Renew had to build on a very specific workforce whose skills were not wanted in the labour market. Although the aim was to alleviate people's situation, this was not always achieved, mostly because they were unable to offer long-term support. At Renew, the awareness of worker agency increased, especially among instructors, many of whom were employed on pay subsidy on short-term contracts. Some seemed to seriously question not only their work content, since they were not experts on evaluating it, but also the key elements of the Renew brand, i.e. the use of recycled materials:

> One of the instructors wants to discuss the new bags given to customers at the Renew shop. It is a vinyl-sized bag, made out of a certain kind of plastic, received from a company. The plastic goes through a lot of workshops, from construction, where it goes through pressure cleaning, to a workshop where it is cut, and to crafts, where it is washed with small washing machines, to dressmaking, where it is sewn. The material is easily broken, so at home 'the customer just dumbs it to trash'. The instructor doubts this can really be sustainable compared to the fact that the firm could in the first place recycle the material properly.
>
> (Renew Informant 2, Observation 2013).

4.3 Resisting commodification and changing human-nature relations

The case of Reuse can be interpreted as a site where two employees (later founders) *resist* the current anthropogenic and anthropocentric production logic by refusing to contribute to this production model as employees. Their refusal led them to self-employment and contributing to an alternative production model. However, this resistance was not care-free:

> What annoys me in these large recyclers – is that they have *no* intentions to develop their own activities. They are satisfied with an income flow. It's very market-oriented. It's a shame because they should be targeting environmental issues instead of higher revenues.
>
> (Reuse Informant 1, Interview 2013)

Despite the fact that Reuse sourced materials from large recycling organizations, the owner-manager was not happy with the recycling system. Her annoyance was intensified because of the discrimination against selling recycled materials:

> So fewer people consider – when they visit the non-profit organizations [second-hand shops] they think it is pricy but fewer know that they pay no value added tax [on sold clothing]. And we [as self-employed] need to do this.
> (Reuse Informant 1, Interview 2013)

Her implicit view was that Reuse functioned on the fringe with little support. The Reuse team attended clothing fairs side-by-side with other clothing producers in order to present their products and their ecological thinking. However, often they were the odd one out at events, where new collections were presented every season. People in Reuse considered this practice unethical:

> Overall – ecological and ethical thinking do not belong to fashion business. – They are two different worlds. And if someone goes there and says they represent design that is like ecological, the prefix is, *I'm a freak*. But then I open my mouth and [demonstrate that] I know what I'm talking about so they need to accept that, damn, apparently that person is *serious* with that thing [ecological issues], not a butterfly.
> (Reuse Informant 1, Interview 2013)

Thus, events with an ecological focus were their own territory. In fact, the owner-manager was actively involved in organizing a large annual recycling event, which hosted numerous actors involved with using recycled materials in design.

There were signs of resistance at Renew. When addressing worker agency and resistance, it is important to consider that not all people in the same organization have the same agency. Based on everyday discussion at Renew, the change of personnel created hierarchies and reasons to protest. Interestingly, questioning the logic of Renew led to a call for permanent instructor positions. The instructors then had to compete against each other for the positions. Eventually, some refused to do so and left – abandoning work at Renew, thus abandoning work in the organization (Table 9.1). However, there were also examples of people aligning their actions with the expectations of Renew and even developing them further, because they shared the 'spirit' of recycling and sustainability.

5 Embedded worker agency and the challenges of the Anthropocene

Our research portrays two socio-materially embedded attempts to organize work in new and greener ways including various degrees of worker agency. To some extent these are positive examples, since they contributed to sustainability (in terms of recycling) and, at least temporarily, to a better life for those citizens with scarce resources. The problem seems to be that in the current economic climate the social, ecological and economic value of such work is neglected and at the same time the actual social and ecological costs of globalized production models are downplayed. In such a framework it is difficult to sustain the novel ways of working described above as a long-term solution for the people involved. Thus, instead of feeling they were being offered emancipation and social protection, people at Renew were still left feeling 'lacking' and in need of control measures. Similarly, at Reuse the resistance via worker agency was limited to few with a possibility for limited and unstable income.

Despite these limitations, bringing labour and employee agency together as worker agency means potentiality for novel solutions (Table 9.1), as also demonstrated by the organizations studied. The potential of *resilience at the organizational level* is the nurturing of solidarity either in self-managed organizations or as employees. This potential is amplified by the expectancy of increased recycling work in the Global North. Previous research on global destruction networks have indicated that in the Global North recovery processes tend to be capital-intensive, while they are labour intensive in the Global South (Herod et al., 2014). Our empirical sites in the Global North portrayed how an un(der)employed workforce did the labour-intensive tasks related to recycling materials instead of capital-intensive investments. This finding complements previous research on the nature of recycling work in the Global North. Interestingly, the production models studied were made possible because of formalized employment policies and structures created by the state in its endeavour to find solutions to unemployment and social exclusion. This 'recycled labour' model offers a non-permanent solution for the un(der)employed worker. Such temporality combined with the loss of waged work in all spheres of working life (Standing, 2010, pp. 38–39) may lead to increased concerns about un(der) employment and could create a favourable sounding board for solidarity.

For *reworking* within the production network, an organization's position in the global production and destruction networks is also relevant for the emergence of new worker agency. Renew and Reuse became part of such networks through their commitment to the use of recycled materials, which came from firms operating on both the national and international level. Thus, recycling materials also has a reputation value. This is evident in the way large established organizations gave their waste to Renew and Reuse and bought themselves a 'responsible aura'. Likewise, for Renew and Reuse it was very important where the used material came from since the conscientious customers could question any unethical sourcing. This tendency results in a situation in which people involved in work processes have access to knowledge that might be partially narrated or hidden. It seems that this knowledge on the activities taking place in various networks could increase worker agency, which transcends the organizational boundaries. Such production-related information could be used to affect other agents in the production and destruction networks. In the era of citizen consumerism, combining this kind of worker agency with consumer campaigning could lead people to reflect on how the values created by different forms of work could be distributed in a just manner.

Resistance, involving direct challenges to social relations and game-changing human-nature relations, seems to require broad and orchestrated collective activities. Worker agency in such instances means aligning forces with others nationally and internationally. While this may sound grandiose, it seems that the self-employed dressmakers at Reuse had a potential for it and, at times, delivered such worker agency. They attempted to resist by using insider information to change the means of production in the clothing sector. They aligned their aims with increasing consumer awareness of ecological consumption and used self-employment as a means to deliver services. Their resistance was aimed at transformative human-nature relations. Yet, during the time of the study, such evidence was marginal.

6 Conclusion

Work can be understood as a channel which leads us to discuss the Anthropocene, because the reorganization of work around global production networks affects more and more workers, leaving them in vulnerable and precarious labour market positions. Our observations led us to consider as the position of 'last resort', in which people end up with unemployment, activation or self-employment. Yet, the examples described are not that far removed from the flexible workforce management doctrines used in all contemporary organizations, which also seem to increasingly 'recycle' people and commit to few.

We conclude that workers can challenge the contemporary organization of work and respond to the challenges of the Anthropocene by developing a sort of worker agency that brings together the intertwined labour and employer agency (Table 9.1). While labour agency has its roots in industrial capitalism, employee agency is more to do with contemporary efforts to make capitalism more responsible. The development of an influential worker agency requires an understanding of both labour and employee agency, and may take any of the three forms of action in Table 9.1, namely resilience, reworking and resistance.

To respond to the challenges of the Anthropocene, for example by mitigating the anthropogenic climate emissions, we need to understand the relationships between changes in the organization of work and changes in human-capital-nature relationships. To be able to rework human-nature relationships as an employee, one has to have a job or resources for self-employment. People without a job have fewer possibilities for such agency, unless they create a sense of collective agency as unemployed. Yet, the sense of agency of self-employed or un(der)employed people has not been encouraged in the contemporary political doctrine. Potential worker agency, the potential to rework or resist the prevailing human-nature relations, is hindered if narrow employee group interests are advanced without the awareness of collective labour interest. Thus, the relevant issue remains: how to support the emergence of worker agency, consisting of labour and employee agency, in relation to employment and un(der)employment?

The feeling of worker agency and the reflections of the self-employed or un(der)employed may increase the transformative power of work. In comparison to the networks that exist to discuss global trade and finances, there seems to be a lack of global networks for such discussions on worker agency. However, the notion of the Anthropocene may enable a creation of such trans-local networks, reflections on worker agency and the global peaceful coexistence of capital and workers on planet Earth.

Bibliography

Alvesson, M. (2011) *Interpreting Interviews.* Los Angeles: SAGE Publications.

Antal, M. (2014) Green goals and full employment: Are they compatible? *Ecological Economics.* 107, 276–286.

Antentas J. M. (2015) Spain: The indignados rebellion of 2011 in perspective. *Labor History.* 56(2), 136–160.

Barnosky, A. D., Hadly, E. A., Bascompte, J., Berlow, E. L., Brown, J. H., Fortelius, M., Getz, W. M., Harte, J., Hastings, A., Marquet, P. A., Martinez, N. D., Mooers, A., Roopnarine, P., Vermeij, G., Williams, J. W., Gillespie, R., Kitzes, J., Marshall, C., Matzke, N., Mindell, D. P., Revilla, E. & Smith, A. B. (2012) Approaching a state-shift in the biosphere. *Nature.* 486, 52–58.

Burawoy, M. (2010) From Polanyi to Pollyanna: The false optimism of global labor studies. *Global Labour Journal.* 1(2), 301–313.

Cerny, P. G. (1997) Paradoxes of the competition state: The dynamics of political globalization. *Government and Opposition.* 32(2), 251–274.

Chhachhi, A. (2014) Introduction: The 'Labour Question' in contemporary capitalism. *Development & Change.* 45(5), 895–919.

Coe, N. M. & Jordhus-Lier, D. C. (2011) Constrained agency? Re-evaluating the geographies of labour. *Progress in Human Geography.* 35(2), 211–233.

Crutzen, P. J. (2002) Geology of mankind. *Nature.* 415(6867), 23.

Czarniawska, B. & Sevón, G. (2003) Introduction: Did the Vikings know how to organize? In: Czarniawska, B. & Sevón, G. (eds) *The Northern Lights: Organization Theory in Scandinavia.* Malmö and Oslo: Liber, pp. 9–16.

Fleming, P. (2012) The birth of 'biocracy' and its discontents at work. *Research in the Sociology of Organizations.* 35, 177–199.

Frayne, D. (2015) *The Refusal of Work: The Theory & Practice of Resistance to Work.* London: Zed Books Ltd.

Gibson-Graham, J. K. (2008) Diverse economies: Performative practices for other worlds. *Progress in Human Geography.* 32(5), 613–632.

Gibson-Graham, J. K. & Roelvink, G. (2010) An economic ethics for the Anthropocene. *Antipode.* 41, 320–46.

Grint, K. (1991) *The Sociology of Work: Introduction.* Cambridge: Polity Press.

Herod, A., Pickren, G., Rainnie, A., & Champ, S. M. (2014). Global destruction networks, labour and waste. *Journal of Economic Geography*, 14, 421–441.

Hitchings, R. (2012) People can talk about their practices. *Area.* 44(1), 61–67.

ILO/UNEP (United Nations Environment Programme) (2012) *Working Towards Sustainable Development: Opportunities for Decent Work and Social Inclusion in a Green Economy.* Geneva: International Labour Office.

IPCC (Intergovernmental Panel on Climate Change) (2014), *Fifth Assessment Report.* Available at: www.ipcc.ch/report/ar5 (accessed 1 June 2016).

Jacoby, S. M. (2004) *Employing Bureaucracy: Managers, Unions, and the Transformation of Work in the 20th Century.* London: Psychology Press.

Jessop, B. (1993) Towards a Schumpeterian workfare state? Preliminary remarks on post-Fordist political economy. *Studies in Political Economy*. 40, 7–39.

Kananen, J. (2012). Nordic paths from welfare to workfare: Danish, Swedish and Finnish labour market reforms in comparison. *Local Economy*, 27(5–6), 558–576.

Katz, C. (2004) Growing up global: economic restructuring and children's everyday lives. Minneapolis, MN: University of Minnesota Press.

Keskitalo, E., Ala-Kauhuluoma, M. & Mannila, S. (2002) *An Evaluation of a Proactive Social Policy Reform and Local Activation Practices in Finland*. Helsinki: STAKES.

Kettunen, P. (2010) The sellers of labour power as social citizens – a Utopian wage work society in the Nordic visions of welfare. *Workfare and Welfare State Legitimacy. NordWel Studies in Historical Welfare State Research*. 1, 16–45.

Klein, N. (2015) *This Changes Everything: Capitalism vs. the Climate*. New York: Simon & Schuster.

Latouche, S. ([2007] 2009) *Farewell to Growth*. Cambridge and Malden, MA: Polity Press.

Latour, B. (2014) Agency at the time of the Anthropocene. *New Literary History*. 45(1), 1–18.

Lewis, P. & Luce, S. (2012) Labor and occupy Wall Street: An appraisal of the first six months. *New Labor Forum*. 21(2), 43–49.

Nierling, L. (2012) 'This is a bit of the good life': Recognition of unpaid work from the perspective of degrowth. *Ecological Economics*. (84), 240–246.

Norton T. A., Parker, S. L., Zacher, H. & Ashkanasy, N. M. (2015) Employee green behavior: A theoretical framework, multilevel review, and future research agenda. *Organization & Environment*. 28(1), 103–125.

Parker, M. (2006) The counter culture of organisation: Towards a cultural studies of representations of work. *Consumption, Markets and Culture*. 9(1), 1–15.

Pärnänen, A. & Sutela, H. (2014) *Self-employers in Finland in 2013 [Itsensätyöllistäjät Suomessa 2013]*. Helsinki: Statistics Finland.

Pink, S. & Morgan, J. (2013) Short-term ethnography: Intense routes to knowing. *Symbolic Interaction*. 36(3), 351–361.

Random House (2010) *Webster's College Dictionary*. New York: Random House.

Rainnie, A., Herod, A. & McGrath-Champ, S. (2011) Review and positions: Global production networks and labour. *Competition & Change*. 15(2), 155–169.

Ramarajan, L. & Reid, E. (2013) Shattering the myth of separate worlds: Negotiating non-work identities at work. *Academy of Management Review*. 38(4), 621–644.

Rockström, J., Steffen, W., Noone, K., Persson, Å., Chapin, F. S., Lambin, E. F., Lenton, T. M., Scheffer, M., Folke, C., Schellnhuber, H. J., Nykvist, B., de Wit, C. A., Hughes, T., van der Leeuw, S., Rodhe, H., Sörlin, S., Snyder, P. K., Costanza, R., Svedin, U., Falkenmark, M., Karlberg, L., Corell, R. W., Fabry, V. J., Hansen, J., Walker, B., Liverman, D., Richardson, K., Crutzen, P. & Foley, J. A. (2009) A safe operating space for humanity. *Nature*. 461(7263), 472–475.

Sennett, R. (2007) *The Culture of the New Capitalism*. New Haven, CT and London: Yale University Press.

Standing, G. (2010) *Work after Globalization: Building Occupational Citizenship*. Northampton, MA: Edward Elgar Publishing.

Swyngedouw, E. (2013) Apocalypse now! Fear and doomsday pleasures. *Capitalism Nature Socialism*. 24(1), 9–18.

Waters, C. N., Zalasiewicz, J., Summerhayes, C., Barnosky, A. D., Poirier, C., Gałuszka, A., Cearreta, A., Edgeworth, M., Ellis, E., Ellis, M., Jeandel, C., Leinfelder, R., McNeill, J. R., Richer, D., Steffen, W., Syvitski, J., Vidas, D., Wagreich, M., Williams, M., An, Z., Grinevald, J., Odada, E., Oreskes, N. & Wolfe, A. P. (2016) The Anthropocene is functionally and stratigraphically distinct from the Holocene. *Science*. 351, aad2622.

Zeitlin, J. (1987) From labour history to the history of industrial relations. *The Economic History Review*. 40(2), 159–184.

10 From exploitation and expansion to evolutionary coexistence

A new realism for life beyond the Anthropocene[1]

Karl Johan Bonnedahl

1 One more such victory and we are ruined

For most of its history, mankind constituted a relatively insignificant category of life on Earth. Our abilities and activities were few, and the space and resources beyond our local dealings appeared infinite. In recent history, this has changed at an accelerated pace.

The human-nature relation is basically determined by an interplay between technology, the economy and our numbers (e.g. Chertow, 2001), and we can take the latter as an indication of the massive change in our ecological equation. At the onset of the modern era, the time of Galileo, the global human population equalled that of today's European Union (EU), and not until 1804 did it reach an estimated 1 billion (UN, 1999). The next billion now takes about 12 years. Compared to the year when the author of this chapter was born, the global net population has increased by the amount of the current nine most populous states: China, India, the USA, Indonesia, Brazil, Pakistan, Nigeria, Bangladesh and Russia (and if you read this one year after it was written, you can add a new Iran or Germany (UN, 2011, 2015a)). That is equivalent to an additional 1.3 new human and social worlds, and an economic expansion far greater than that (roughly 40 times in current prices, and five times in constant prices). Obviously, no new biophysical world has appeared during the same period, statistically only slightly longer than half of the lifetime of a well-nourished Westerner with good access to advanced health care.

On the contrary. Signs of a shrinking resource base and ecosystem capacity become increasingly plentiful. The societal body is growing but it cannot change its costume, which is the core of the sustainability problem: the possibility of continued survival with a high standard of living – and, on top of that, our desire for 'progress' or 'development' – is threatened by the depreciation of environmental qualities and functions. Such an intertemporal view of the sustainability

1 This chapter is based on the author's book titled *Från ekonomiskt till hållbart, från exploatering till samexistens* published by Studentlitteratur (2012).

problem cannot, however, be separated from ethical issues today; not least the exploitation and extinction of other species and the satisfaction of basic needs for the planet's many underprivileged humans.

On the contrary again. Most often, a deterioration of conditions hits the weakest hardest, and who knows what our priorities will look like if we understand that the space for human expansion on the planet is running out, and the corresponding room for manoeuvre – choice – is shrinking, making adaptation under a tyranny of the circumstances as necessary as it will be unpredictable?

Our economic language, with its theories, models and claims, normally gives a completely different story from the one above. It is a story about a continued, perpetual drive along the illuminated highway of development, which has growing economic value and consumption as its main ingredients. This myth of victory, for our technology, organization and production, and for us as a species, is on the front cover of the human story on Earth. The competing story is that a pyrrhic victory has been won at the cost of the future. Not only have we consumed the Earth's non-renewable stock and marginalized other species, we have also chewed from the processes that enable life, the ones that produce what we see as 'natural resources' and silently absorb the residual waste of human activities.

Conflicts between these two stories are the subject of this chapter. One explanation as to why conflicts still exist, in spite of the knowledge we possess, is that the economic language, way of thinking and field of science originate in times when an increased exploitation of nature and expansion of societies were possible – due to available space, capacity in the ecosystems and immense quantities of stored fossil energy.

Now, the same ideas and methods, including versions that emphasize green-tech, eco-efficiency and compromises between economic and ecologic sustainability, are becoming our misfortune. Lack of knowledge or practical solutions, in terms of the next generation's green-tech, more efficient taxes, etc., are not the major obstacles on a path towards sustainability. Rather, it is our lock-ins into structures, patterns of thought, lifestyles and privileges; all largely represented and upheld by mainstream economic conceptualization. Hence, a planet without capacity for further exploitation and expansion is in radical need of new ways of thinking. It needs an economy built on realistic scientific assumptions and active ethical standpoints.

2 Stages of development and different types of realism

Now when the concept of sustainable development has been around for more than a quarter of a century, and been crowned by global Sustainable Development Goals, it may be understood as a challenge to conventional views on development. That would be fully logical. 'Sustainable' should refer to something being unsustainable, and what would that be if not our conventional dealings?

However, mainstream sustainable development does not question the fundamental traits of the unsustainable society; dominant ideas and structures concerning, for example, ownership, production and trade, with consumerism and growth as key features. As it aims to add, but not to subtract, it presents a version 3.0 manual for the modern human society, after the early modern era (or the long enlightenment; Liedman, 1997) and industrialism. While development 1.0 brought liberation from superstition and empowered humans, it also provided an ethical and intellectual starting point for a radical strategy of planetary exploitation and expansion. The human order was separated from the order of God, and scientific inquiry provided a means for technological innovation, societal progress and domination.

The second phase, development 2.0, brought liberation from scarcity and hard labour (still just a promise in large parts of the world), but it also magnified our resources for exploitation, conversion and domestication of nature, not least through new technology and fossil energy. Now, a third version, development 3.0, labelled sustainable development, is said to liberate us from poverty and environmental problems – but without disturbing prevailing interests in society. In relation to nature, exploitation should be careful and efficient, consumption ethical and businesses green.

Not surprisingly, so-called sustainable development has failed: ecological balance has not been reached, not even in a strictly anthropocentric sense, where all 'natural resources' are destined for human service. The failure was signalled as early as the famous Brundtland Report, which with an optimism neighboring sheer ignorance proclaimed that limits are not determined by nature but by technology and social organization, and that these 'can be both managed and improved to make way for a new era of economic growth' (WCED, 1987, p. 24).

'Natural' limits are certainly not fixed, and human skills and choice are key in both how to use and how to value a tree, a piece of land or an animal. However, the denial of an active role for nature in value-creating processes which dominates the discourse on development and progress is, to say the least, unrealistic.

Still, 'realism' plays a major role in our failure to approach sustainability. This discourse and the attempts, rhetorical or practical, take place in a social setting where interests and privileges are real, in the sense that they are both perceived and matter as social phenomena, but also in that they provide real obstacles to change. In our realities, we are more occupied with our social positions than with conflicts between our society and its environment. That is one of the reasons why nature is on the losing side in social gatherings at the highest level, such as the United Nations Framework Convention on Climate Change (UNFCCC) climate summits, or when we decide how to spend a normal day.

Such a socially realistic but ecologically dysfunctional approach manifests as the conventional guiding model for how to understand sustainable development: as the trinity of social, economic and environmental sustainability. Often this is illustrated as communicating, overlapping circles, with the presumption that perspectives and values from the three spheres can and should be compared and negotiated. This model, which also obscures differences between what to sustain and what to develop (Kates, Parris and Leiserowitz, 2005), can lead us away from extreme forms of economism and exploitation, where we do not even pretend that there are social and environmental values worth their own story. However, it is

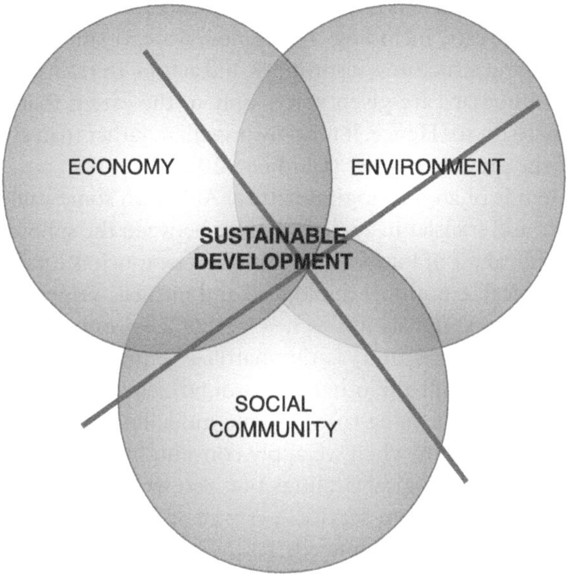

Figure 10.1 The misleading trinity model of sustainable development. Please forget it.

not only without relevance for sustainability; it is misleading and provides an important obstacle if we sincerely want progress in this direction.

The conventional model has of course been debated and criticized (e.g. Giddings, Hopwood and O'Brien, 2002; Robinson, 2004; Redclift, 2005) but the trinity, or the three pillars, still dominates the discourse. It is reflected in the most influential business perspective and reporting system on sustainability (the Triple Bottom Line and the Global Reporting Initiative) as well as in national and international sustainability agendas and policies (UN, 2002, 2015b). Its power rests in its conservatism; legitimizing prevailing interests and systems which are expected to reform themselves (Banerjee, 2003). Among the most obvious problems, one is practical, leading to the model's weakness as a normative guide. In the real world, the pretended equality between the three parts is overruled by power differences between stakeholders; for example, corporations vs. environmental non-government organizations or rich vs. poor. Established discourses and measures from the economic sphere also have an advantage over claims from challenging perspectives, making us understand and promote, for example, consumption, private ownership and growth rather than idleness, communitarianism and sufficiency.

While this problem of normative weakness manifests itself today, involving actors and interests that are present, and actually or potentially able to argue, it leads us to an inter-generational type of problem. A priority of 'here and now' over actors and interests in other places and times is a natural outcome of the behaviour of any biological creature: a normal survival strategy is to cater for our own needs before we consider other goals. The model above, however, presents the situation as one of negotiation between interests, including intertemporal negotiation, yet it is placed in the hands of existing structures, institutions and actors. In reality, nature, other species and unborn humans are given voices only to the extent that actors within the system choose to do so. Hence, it is no surprise that, rather than change, we see consolidation of the prevailing order (Gardiner, 2011).

A third type of problem is of an ontological nature. Although some values are possible to communicate and transfer in a relevant sense between the spheres, like the commercial and social values of lumber and its products, much is fundamentally different (like aesthetical, emotional, biological and intrinsic values relating to what we often see as lumber). Translating such 'social' or 'environmental' value to a common unit misses the point, and, as the matter is generally to translate other value to economic value (not the other way around), such processes subordinate social and environmental value to economic modelling and valuation. Hence, we must be careful not only when we apply conventional measures such as environmental taxes in our ecological dealings but also when using concepts such as 'natural capital' and 'ecosystem services', as well as when we talk about market demand as if we were dealing with needs.

This means that the trinity model, while possibly contributing to some reform, conserves the superiority of established economic perspectives, with instrumental and commercial views on entities in society and nature. As the simplest alternative we must understand 'social' as the sphere of human goals: What do we – understood in a broad and just way – want from life, society and the planet?

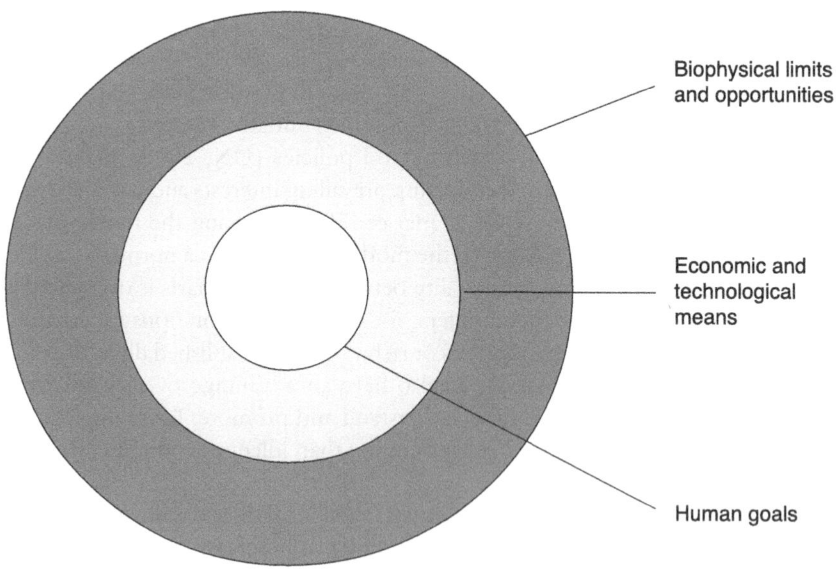

Figure 10.2 Development 4.0: sustainable development as anthropocentric realism.

'Environmental' must signify the framework of such goals: Within which limits can we manoeuvre and try to reach human and societal goals such as health, housing and happiness? Finally, the 'economic', together with technology, should be purely a sphere of means, not one of goals. Hence, and in contrast to most of the similar alternative models that have been presented, the economy is not placed at the centre but, also for pedagogical reasons, given a mediating role. This gives us an equally simple, but more realistic and relevant, model for sustainable development.

3 Heading towards a tyranny of the circumstances

We will return later to a crucial problem with the more realistic development model presented above, its purely anthropocentric point of departure, but any major influence on our societies comes from the more problematic trinity model. The modern 'Western' society resides somewhere between development 2.0 and 3.0, where some good examples, plans and a lot of rhetoric are what comes closest to the latter. As we also want to exploit the Arctic, clear forests for farming, continue to drill, blast and dig for fossil energy, destroy marine ecosystems through commercial trawling and continuously increase consumption and economic throughput, we also have a firm foothold in the industrial perspective on nature and development. Although its main architects have been found in the West, industrialized exploitation is now a foundation for societal progress globally. It builds our cities, paves our roads, gives us employment and fills our dinner plates. It just has not reached everyone yet. In practice, our plans and actions resemble the economics of imperialism, but also in a technological and cultural sense (cf. Banerjee, 2003), in which we steadily 'go further west', to new minerals, forests or any resources or pieces of land that we perceive are needed by us as individuals, companies or societies.

Hence, the degree of the real and desired influence of the sustainable development discourse can be questioned. Since the Brundtland Report's political compromising with reality, we have had continued economic growth on the global scale, but not in a way that was new in relation to the ecological challenges or the distribution of wealth. The world GDP more than doubled over the 25 years that followed the report – as it did the 25 years immediately prior to the report (Maddison, 2011). Whereas some environmental indicators have improved, others have appeared or deteriorated, but, more importantly, total ecosystem pressure has continued to increase.

Although inappropriate indicators of economic wealth or activity (not least GDP) still dominate as measures and objectives in society, the world has seen an amelioration in some indicators of real human welfare (categories such as health and education). As a proof of the so-called trickle-down effect, this is however far from satisfying as it has come at the cost of the massive unsustainable exploitation of Earth. We tend to focus on the effects of this (such as climate change or depletion of resources) but we should also recognize ourselves on the causing side. Estimations of the biomass of species can serve as illustration: while the total human biomass quadrupled over the twentieth century, the corresponding mass of wild terrestrial mammals fell to half, and 'by 2000 the zoomass of all wild land mammals was only about a tenth of the global anthropomass' (Smil, 2011, p. 618). The estimated mass of domesticated animals was approximately 24 times larger than the mass of wild terrestrial animals. In spite of this massive exploitation and domestication of nature, the number of people in extreme poverty exceeds the total global population at the dawn of industrialization, and for those that like to value people as equals, it is disturbing to see the extreme imbalances in economic wealth and power (Oxfam, 2016). Using the economic language, we can conclude that both the effectiveness and efficiency of the human processes involved in 'development' have been poor: heavily borrowing from the past and consuming the future, the whole production system is bankrupt, and our combined economic efforts are allocated towards the preferences of the already wealthy.

In sharp contrast to mainstream economic descriptions declaring continuous increases in value (better products, higher profits, more advanced technology), the resource base has continuously been carved out through increasing pressure on nature's remaining stocks and reproductive capacity. Therefore, not only has our – at least rhetorical – quest for sustainable development failed; in the era of markets and consumer choice, our room for manoeuvre has become smaller. This is irrespective of what development model we subscribe to and what direction we would like to have for Spaceship Earth (cf. Boulding, 1965). We are approaching a point where we no longer make the important decisions. Great plans for prosperity, peace, democracy or any other human aim will be put in the background, while circumstances will make the choices for us. Paradoxically, these are circumstances that we cannot fully anticipate even though we are their main architects.

The closer we get to the point of this tyranny of the circumstances, the more our agendas will have to deal with adaptation to a series of negative events and processes which are hard to predict. They may appear as food security problems, lack of fresh water, obsolete infrastructure and physical planning, lack of relevant competences and educations, enforced re-evaluation of lifestyles, threats against democratic institutions, mass migrations, armed conflicts or other political, economic and social adaptation costs resulting from climate change, the extinction of species, lack of resources in both quantity and quality and the degradation or collapse of the ecosystem functions.

The roles on the causing side are certainly very unequally distributed between the rich and the poor. It is estimated that the USA caused 29 per cent of the cumulative global CO2 emissions 1850–2002 (Baumert, Herzog and Pershing, 2005), and, as another example, the richest 1 per cent in the USA, Saudi Arabia, Luxembourg and Singapore cause greenhouse gas emissions that are 2,000 times higher per capita than for people with the world's lowest incomes (Chancel and Piketty, 2015).

As a global human community, however, we share an unsustainable pathway, described in Figure 10.3. Through the strategy of exploitation and expansion, humanity is moving deeper into the funnel of Anthropocene. The 'floor' rises with the growing demand for 'natural resources' and the 'ceiling' falls as the

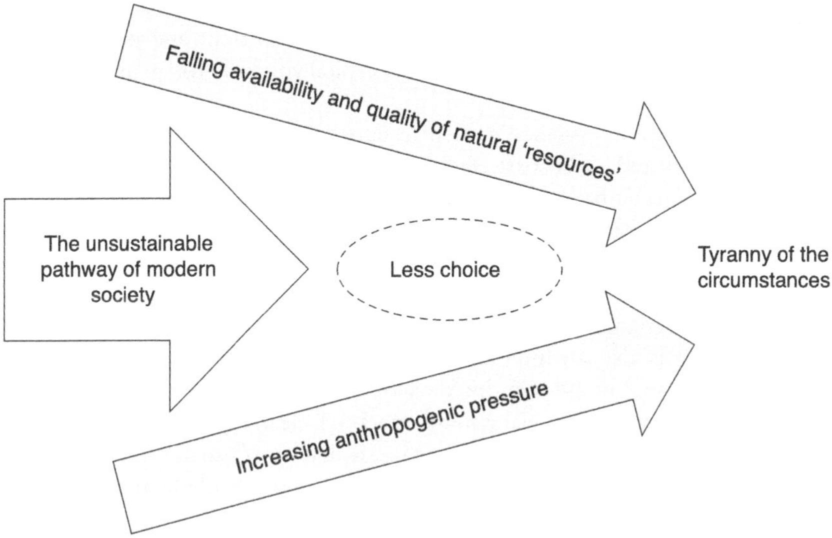

Figure 10.3 The tyranny of the circumstances.

anthropogenic pressure causes a decrease in the access to and quality of resources and space in nature. Mainstream development means eating ourselves deeper into the funnel, transforming 'natural capital' into food for the metabolism of our consumerist society.

As we approach the tyranny of the circumstances, we are likely to talk less about climate change mitigation and see more adaptation measures. In practice, we would get less focus on avoiding adjustments that threaten lifestyles or incur costs for national industries, and more focus on measures that are needed in order to handle the real problems that result from climate change (flooding, poorer harvests, invasive species, health problems, political conflicts). It is also likely that we will be forced to abandon our sophisticated attempts to determine suitable and efficient types of energy, taxes and subsidies to take us out of the fossil society, and instead acknowledge that we are in the middle of a combined energy, resource and climate crisis, which demands completely new perspectives and solutions, from the level of transportation and food habits to forms of governance and international relations.

These kinds of pressures for adaptation and change will accentuate some of the different preconditions between states, in terms of economic, technological and natural resources, and vulnerability in relation to climate effects, resource scarcity, etc. It will also accentuate differences in individual and socio-demographic factors, where one intriguing fact is that the social classes most responsible for the problems, also most catered for in terms of satisfaction of needs, are likely to also have the greatest resources for survival and continued prosperity. However, in this massive, multi-dimensional change, we cannot rule out revolutionary processes, where the institutional stability is challenged in many directions, affecting democracy, ownership and financial systems (Welzer, 2012). Rather, a planned adaptation and a smooth reform of the existing institutions and norm systems may be a more surprising outcome, and the capital you have today may be out of your hands tomorrow.

Climate change is a process of particular dignity as it is directly related to human economic activity and affects basically all systems; social, human-made and natural. While it is likely to hit hardest – when it comes to human societies – the ones with the worst starting point, climate change is very complex in terms of the relationship between acts and impact. While the causes are clearly anthropogenic, they are disconnected from the effects both in space and time, which makes apportioning responsibility particularly challenging (Gardiner, 2011). Bearing this in mind, climate change is also an important example of how knowledge has not led to sufficient action. Lifestyles in the 'developed' world, as well as the social organization (infrastructure, financial systems, markets), clearly qualify as unsustainable, but the general conclusion, again and again, is that most can continue as before: growth in population, global trade and tourism, car-oriented planning, excessive meat consumption and so on.

It is understandable that we wish to continue as before; to perceive, act and expect, as we are accustomed. However, claims about the feasibility, or even sustainability, of such conservatism lack empirical credibility and moral soundness. The conflict, and our choice of direction, can be illustrated by the ambiguity of the term 'possible'. For quite some time, we humans have mainly attached the question of what we can do with the upside of the possible, stretching the limits, and concluded that what we want and can, we also should. Science, technology and economic thinking have held central roles in these efforts (e.g. von Wright, 1989). Now, the challenges of sustainability tell us that this has not only been optimistic, but also thoughtless. What we want has to be related to the limiting side of 'the possible', what we can do within planetary boundaries, but also to what we ought to do, given, for example, the vast differences in welfare between people, the industrial treatment of animals and the massive loss of natural places, systems and species.

Hence, these two dimensions are strongly interrelated. The status of Earth and its ecosystems obviously influences how and to what level we can approach poverty reduction and related targets, particularly if we are unwilling to compromise any other resource-dependent targets (like the level of consumption among the already wealthy).

Until now, the modern society's relation to nature can be characterized as one of exploitation and expansion, leading to wealth and domination, but also taking us deeper into the funnel, where we threaten the resource base and quality of life for ourselves and other species. If we, as a global society, were now to aim for sustainability, we would add a lot of complexity to our understanding, adapt to a more realistic view of nature, and adopt a more conscious and inclusive ethics. Hence, the challenge contains far more than practical measures, such as through technological innovation. It is largely about proving that a new role for us as individuals, societies and species is possible. We will no longer eat, breed and expand as long as the habitat allows, until collapse, or will we?

A responsible conclusion must be to reasess many of the goals, which have guided us, and many of the means that we have used. This is not only valid for goals and means on the societal level, such as continuous economic growth, fossil energy and a resource allocation system built on power rather than needs. It is equally valid on the private level, affecting comfort, mobility and lust for high and varying consumption.

This leads us to the domain of economic language and thought, which provides a very influential perspective and frame of understanding for our ways of living and organizing; affecting our goals and means, and contributing significantly to the sustainability problems. In order to approach sustainability, we need substantial redefinitions within the economic language, as well as a new relationship between the dominant economic sphere and other spheres in society and life.

3.1 Economic, unsustainable thinking

Whereas conventional wisdom says that 'economic' corresponds to good management, efficient allocation of resources and a paradigm that has guided society during an era of impressive increases in wealth, this section presents the critical problems of the mainstream economic discourse. The first problem area selected is how the relationship between humans and nature is normally conceptualized. The superiority given to human-made systems leads to a second area of how humans are viewed. The reduction of values constitutes the third area, which relates to the role given to markets, particularly demand, as the fourth. Finally, the production side is treated by looking at the ideas about the efficient and growing creation of economic value. Through growth, a circle is closed: the content of growth is largely taken from the nature we first left, and growth also impacts on the nature we can never leave.

3.1.1 The separation from nature

As the possibly most evident flaw, mainstream research and literature in business and economics presents economic systems and relations as independent from, or superior to, nature. With occasional exceptions, where some representation of nature becomes an add-on (as with environmentally labelled products), this is also valid for economic practice, from policy level to individual consumer behaviour. Within business, we allow ourselves to deal with marketing, investment, product development, etc. without fundamentally connecting to – or even mentioning – each activity's base in natural systems and their repercussions on the same. An example is given through the table below, displaying parts of a review aiming to investigate whether the natural environment appeared in business school literature. Three indicators were chosen: (1) emissions and waste, where high awareness could be expected both in business and academia due to visibility, costs and regulation, (2) climate change, which deserves attention in basically all sciences due to its implications, and finally (3) ecosystems and ecology, which could indicate more profound treatments but would probably be more demanding to include in this kind of literature. The selection of sub-disciplines was broad, but excluded specific areas such as environmental economics, corporate social responsibility (CSR) and business ethics (to which sustainability discussions mainly are assigned).

The normality of disregarding nature (or its implicit presence through an absurd belief in correct market prices on everything) is also mirrored in the 'best' books in Table 10.1. David Jobber gives nature 0.5 per cent of his book's content, as part of the marketing environment because '*Environmentalists* attempt to protect the physical environment ...' (Jobber, 2010, p. 81; my italics). In a subsequent section on 'Ethical Issues Concerning Products', nature is absent. The second book with a hit recognizes planetary resources as a subcategory under geographical factors witin the operative environment, but states that managers should decide on 'the location, quantity, quality, and availability of the world's resources, as well as *the best way to exploit them*' (Daniels et al., 2011, p. 64; my italics).

Table 10.1 The absence of nature in business school literature.

Title/area (author, year)	*Pollution, emissions and waste*	*Climate change, global warming*	*Ecosystems, ecology*
Accounting. An Introduction (McLaney & Atrill, 2010).	No	No	No
Contemporary Logistics (Murphy & Wood, 2011)	No*	No	No
Corporate Finance (Moles, Parrino & Kidwell, 2011)	No	No	No
Entrepreneurship & Small Business Management (Mariotti & Glackin, 2012)	No	No	No
Innovation Management and New Product Development (Trott, 2012)	No*	No	No
International Business: Environments and Operations (Daniels, Radebaugh & Sullivan, 2011)	No	Yes (pp. 222–225)	No
Introduction to Materials Management (Arnold, Chapman & Clive, 2012)	No*	No	No
Microeconomics (Gravelle & Rees, 2004)	No	No	No
Operations & Supply Chain Management (Verma & Boyer, 2010)	No*	No	No
Organizational Behaviour (French et al., 2011)	No	No	No
Principles and Practice of Marketing (Jobber, 2010)	Yes (pp. 83–85)	Yes (p. 81)	Yes (pp. 81–85)
Retail Management. A Strategic Approach (Berman & Evans, 2007)	No	No	No

*Mentioning waste, but only as an economic problem, e.g. as 'rejects, wasted movements, waiting time, over production, i.e. any activity that does not add value' (Trott, 2012, p. 136).

There is certainly some recognition of nature also in the mainstream, but but mostly only indirectly, channelled to economic actions through norms and regulation. The main categories in which nature can appear in economic decision-making as something other than an economic resource are:

- as resistance to exploitation, transformation and distribution, leading to costs for labour, machinery and energy;
- as scarcity, through lower quantities or qualities, for example decreasing availability of non-renewables like oil, or pollution of soil and water;
- through imposed costs, such as taxes on materials or emissions.

Economic decision-making is obviously not entirely economically rational and bounded by factors such as the above, but also affected by, for example, social pressures. All this has, however, proven inadequate for the preservation of environmental qualities (as it has for a fair distribution of welfare). Rather, the lack of realism in mainstream economic discourse is supported by policy and society at large through calls for growth and the hailing of hedonistic and ever increasing consumption. The unsustainable pathway is upheld by unsustainable understandings of which two stand out.

A primitive version of the first guides much of our practice, telling us that nature is infinite as a source and a sink. It is operational when tour companies chase the next unexplored beach, when municipalities decide on new, car-oriented shopping centres, and when we deny the problems of population growth. The more academic version of this understanding says that human-made and natural capitals are substitutable, as when aquaculture replaces marine ecosystems (Holland, 1997). This unsustainable ontology has a necessary complement in the (more axiological) understanding that value is not only determined by humans, but also created by humans. Neither the sun, nor photosynthesis, geology, soil or animals are given independent roles, but everything important is happening in society, driven and determined by economic processes and measures (cf. Georgescu-Roegen, 1975; Daly, 2005). This ignorance is reflected in everyday language, for example, when we talk about primary production or claim to be the producers of meat or oil. With this separation from nature, we claim that value appears and increases only when a natural entity enters and travels through human-controlled processes. Hence, to leave, use and change nature means creating economic value. As long as we keep this understanding, most of our efforts will accelerate ecological imbalances and be contrary to sustainable development.

3.1.2 Human liberation and new forms of dependence

Society's separation from nature is a radical outcome of the conventional 'development', relating to the first types of human liberation mentioned (from superstition and scarcity). Another type, science, technology and fossil energy have enabled liberation from the boundaries of our own nature. Georgescu-Roegen (1975) expressed this as transcending our biological limits through developing and becoming dependent on exosomatic instruments, i.e. tools that are not part of our bodies. Without the continuous development of such instruments and subsequent transformation of natural resources to machinery, infrastructure and so on, we would live in hardship and end our days long before we could spell 'pension plan'. It has, however, also caused major problems. Apart from ecological dilemmas such as habitat destruction and accumulation of waste, this process of producing economic wealth distances humans from (the remaining) nature. As one illustration, in order to see space as Galileo did at the onset of the modern era (basically its empirical starting point), we need 'undeveloped' areas: nature reserves, deserts, high mountains or deprived areas.

The example may also demonstrate how our 'addiction to exosomatic instruments' (Georgescu-Roegen, 1975) and distance to nature can be mutually reinforcing. This does not only signify that we get light pollution with economic development but also that we aim to solve problems through further control, transformation of nature and adding to the human-made capital. This approach includes solutions to ecological problems, meaning that we keep the toolbox that gave us the problems, locking our focus to the technology T of the IPAT formula. Hence, as we prefer nuclear power, genetically modified organisms (GMOs) and geoengineering over behavioural change, our actions are likely to imply positive feedback and augmented problems.

While it is intellectually dubious to believe that one approach can lead to two contradictory outcomes, it is understandable for psychological reasons. Together with the enabling fossil energy, exosomatic instruments define most of our capacity to shape life and society. As we have reduced our ability to identify and relate without all this 'capital', it is logical that solutions to various matters become energy and technology intense. A similar normality can be attributed to the economic perspective on the world, co-emerging with the above tendencies. It is reflected in the assumptions and values key to our understanding of our societies and life projects, and it appears reasonable that we try to defend these, together with accustomed priorities and privileges that largely rest on technology and economic power.

Hence, dependency and conservatism result from human liberation, of which we can also identify yet another type: disconnection from background and context. This 'liberation' from the collective is paradoxical as we in our specialized roles are more dependent than ever. Economic thought builds on a radical individualism (Ghoshal, 2005) where the roles and positions are defined through the system: for example, the producer, the consumer, the employer and the employee. The variations are vast but we are all atomistic parts of the same game and can share the same type of aspirations, not least to possess and consume. These are operationalized as preferences and demand, and assumed to be based in instrumentally rational behaviour, which motivates and guides society's economic efforts. As the economy's engine, individual aspirations to consume must, however, be infinite to avoid societal collapse.

This is clearly dysfunctional as we face the collective problems of sustainability. Theoretically, it may be plausible to curb environmentally detrimental behaviour through internalization, but pricing alone is unjust as it puts the poor out of the bad business first. Moreover, as long as self-interest weighted by purchasing power guides our dealings, we will not get decisions that favour common and long-term interests. Individualization and specialization have created functional rather than responsible relations, and while it was unproblematic at the time of Adam Smith, the ecological footprint is now a major problem, and not just a side-effect of our invisible hands.

3.1.3 Reductionism

As individual decision-making units (persons or organizations) are emphasized, the role of values and perspectives on other societal and planetary levels (such as humanity or all forms of life) is obscured. The number of relevant questions are reduced and focused around what I, or my decision-making entity, want. It is further presumed that these wants can be displayed and satisfied by markets, where both actors and what they bring are exchangeable. In practice, this is also a basis for the standardization of relations and their content, enabling the extreme division of labour in our advanced and complex economies.

A strong belief in the relevance of this reductionism is necessary for the system to make sense. Among the critical issues are the assumption that what we care about is possible to handle and compare in markets and the related approximation between wealth and welfare (with largely quantitative and qualitative features respectively). The assumptions and their practice give rise to a number of problems in the sustainability context, including displacement, exploitation and negligence.

Regarding the first, (a) values and preferences that cannot make an imprint on the economy's supply or demand side are economically irrelevant and will, without political measures, be left out of the conventional analysis. This includes many of the needs of deprived people. There are also (b) values that cannot be given proper economic valuation, such as the emotional value of places and the suffering of animals. Attempts within environmental economics partly fall into this category due to the incommensurability between, for example, emissions and profits in terms of time scales, as well as system levels. As we, nonetheless, tend to pursue common valuation and do so under the economic framework, (c) economic models displace other frames of understanding: life and entities in nature become resources and capital, subordinated into preservation or commercialization depending on how economic assessments capture human perceptions of utility. Further, the normative power of these descriptions gives (d) a dynamic aspect of displacement. Where prices, commercial messages and private benefit dominate in communication, it will affect perspectives, priorities and social interaction.

The second problem is the fact that economic reductionism has exploitation as its rationale. Subjects, objects and systems in nature are reduced to resources with values defined in the processes of production and consumption, with infinite growth and not satisfaction as an end, which further complicates the issue.

The rhetoric of efficiency is invalid as, when profitable, continued exploitation is an imperative. Hence, this instrumental view is incompatible with sustainability.

The third problem is that the reductionist approach hides values that are systemic or distant in time or space. In nature, systems and processes (such as climate regulation and nutrient cycles) have features and functions that cannot be properly treated through economic valuation of its parts. Rather, economic practice has proven that unsustainable exploitation is the norm. In social interaction, we can point at systemic negligence when perspectives become commercial and objectifying, and responsibilities are limited primarily to the benefit we seek through our own market activities (mainly rent or utility from consumption). A corresponding negligence over geographic distance is expected through specialization; awareness or concern about issues in the total economic network in which one is involved (e.g. mining, deforestation, animal maltreatment or child labour) is neither required, nor possible. Hence, responsibility will be primarily economic and functional, but the unsustainable direction of the modern society is equally caused by the failure of laws and social norms to counteract the exploitative economic mechanisms.

3.1.4 Demand as a guiding instrument

A form of reductionism worth its own story is the role of demand. Its presence is one of the modern society's strongest arguments for action, as it is assumed that through demand we get relevant signals about individual benefits that can be aggregated (again) to societal values. This does not only apply to fully commercialized activities but also to education, housing, transportation and so on. Hence, real or presumed demand is a decisive factor in deciding how societal resources are used and what the relationship between values in nature and human-made capital (including consumption) should be.

The excessive focus on demand found in an economically advanced society basically implies the general reductionist problems (above). More specifically, it displaces value that does not get a fair expression as demand. It favours the transformation of a mountain into a skiing resort and recognizes the need for transportation more than the need for a stable level of atmospheric CO_2. The dimensions in life that (can) become objectified, quantified and commercialized become more dominant and we get a systemic pressure for consumption and for the transformation of values in nature to commodities. Concerning negligence, the functional separation of the decision about what is needed may infuse a lack of responsibility among 'suppliers'. As such it is also rational to take part in the commodification and commercialization processes, as this is what generates rent. This influence means that demand is not only an expression of a 'sender', but the result of interaction between consumers and producers.

Given the key role of demand in the economic theory, and its power in society, it seems odd that its connotation is rarely discussed. When definitions are found, they can be 'desired or planned purchases' (Gravelle and Rees, 2004, p. 34) or something someone is 'willing and able to purchase' (Dolan, 1986, p. 55).

Implicitly, a direct relationship between demand, preferences and needs is assumed. The lack of problematization signifies a taken-for-grantedness; a normalization of a society revolving around commercial activities, presumably led by individual decisions. When liberal and consequentialist arguments are raised, they appear sound but cannot hide the decisive error: the relationship between demand and needs is sometimes weak, often negative.

Market demand is a function of preferences and purchasing power. While preferences may be positively related to needs, the opposite is the case for monetary possessions. When a person has more financial capital, we expect a larger proportion of basic needs to be satisfied, as some will be possible to satisfy through the markets. Still, and contrary to the idea of efficient allocation, the ability to give the market signals directing production efforts further towards one's wants rises with wealth. The most deprived, however, do not send any market signals showing that they are without proper housing, education, sanitation or food. Hence, the markets provide no supply. Finally, as the power of market demand is positively related to planetary exploitation (e.g. Chancel and Piketty, 2015), change in the norm of free-market decision-making is crucial if we want collective survival and not just short-term, individual wealth maximization.

3.1.5 Efficient and growing creation of value

Demand is obviously only one component of a more complex idea of value creation, still well understood through Smith's 'invisible hand'. Action driven by human self-interest will be coordinated in markets and both enable satisfaction in an efficient way and drive continuous increases in value. Another conventional way to promote this kind of understanding is through a 'value chain', containing functions and processes such as logistics, procurement and marketing but revealing no biophysical foundations or limitations. Although authors such as Porter and Kramer (2006) tried to add issues of broader societal relevance, this basic economic model, which drifts above environmental fundamentals and ethical concerns, remains an excellent illustration of the dominant and unsustainable economic theory and practice.

The problem is not only the alchemic character of this thinking, saying that we can create value independently of the biophysical circumstances. It is also a matter of confusing means and ends and a consequential imperative of growth that has turned into the blind devotion to 'more'.

Regarding the first, this value creation always uses 'natural resources', and whereas they are upgraded to goods and services in the economic system, the same process degrades their capacity for further use. With consumables and rent we get waste and diffusion (entropy), and environmental pressure is mounting at both ends of the process. Second, while the original alchemists had an idea about a higher end with their process (gold), the modern alchemists-economists strive for no final end but for more of anything that can be marketed and consumed. In this devotion to more, distinctions between preferences in terms of needs and urgency are left out, and instead of a sane view on the economy as a means to achieve certain qualitative ends, promoted by, for example, Keynes ([1930] 1972), the process has become an end in itself (Burenstam Linder [1969] 2007). The logic is contained within the economic idea of value creation which says that if we have what we call demand, and if a corresponding supplying process can run with profit, it should run. This is an imperative for growth, in which growth does not only become a measure of success but an end in itself: per definition, more output is better.

Still, output is just what it is – a hundred cars or boxes of oranges – and as such a measure of economic activity, whether the economic entity is preparing for war or for peace. Even if we were to accept its role as an indicator of wealth, output says nothing about distribution and little about welfare. Regarding the latter distinction, beyond a certain level of wealth economic processes give mainly relative value, as they feed social processes without final ends. While much of the explanation can be found in the role of positional goods (Hirsch, 1977) and hedonic adaptation, the empirics of this phony progress is expressed by the happiness–income paradox: at a point in time, happiness and income are positively related, but over time happiness does not increase as income goes up (Easterlin et al., 2010).

As we still play the game, a key element in 'production' is to produce the corresponding 'needs', by promoting the feeling of dissatisfaction and anxiety among people, who are promoted as 'consumers', possibly the most important role of humans in modern societies. This is fairly logical given the democratic suggestions of consumerism: everyone can share the same materialistic dreams. The real distribution of wealth is, however, dramatically unequal, and our quantitative measures misleading if we really are aiming for well-being.

The model is also fundamentally unsustainable as the imperative for growth pushes throughput upwards. The promise of efficiency is like a cat chasing its own tail (Sanne, 2006): we aim to create more processes and products that are ever more efficient; the T, which is never likely to reach the P × A in the IPAT equation. Even if it could, it wouldn't. The rebound effect strikes back as long as we keep the priorities and systems of consumerism and growth. Moreover, also when the ecoefficiency tail is held high, the ambition is normally only for relative improvements, typically operationalized as a quota between 'environmental' and economic measures (such as CO_2/GDP). These measures deal with productivity; how we get economic value from environmental pressure. They say nothing about ecological balance. For the latter we need the absolute version of an environmental pressure (such as emissions) and some estimation of the corresponding environmental capacity (to absorb emissions).

While there has been much talk about dematerialization, presumably linked to processes behind growth, the economies need huge amounts of fuel, minerals, concrete, wood and land. As an example from an economically advanced and by reputation progressive area, the EU generates about six tons of waste per person per year (EEA, 2010), a quantity that rises to an estimated 50 tons if all biomass, fuel and minerals are included in our material resource footprint

(Watson et al., 2011). Still, such a throughput measure does not capture our full imprint on land, water, air, ecosystems and biodiversity.

In our dealings with these sustainability problems, we have favoured economic measures and technology over, for example, changes in regulation or morals. As argued above, the excessive economic focus reinforces causes of unsustainability, and in addition to the need for reform in content, we have to change the economy's role. Following Keynes ([1930] 1972, p. 332), it would be splendid if economists had a role 'as humble, competent people, on a level with dentists'. Concerning technology, a similar change is needed as the ecological crisis is fuelled by 'the extraordinary acceleration of exosomatic mode of human evolution' (Giampietro and Mayumi, 1998, p. 22). Our excesses here take us further away from a balanced development *together* with our environment, from a coevolution which would be more generous to other forms of life and more promising for our own future. So far, development, under the strategy of exploitation and expansion, has led to complete human dominance of the planet, but at the cost of most forms of life and it now also threatens the quality of human life.

3.2 A very different way forward

3.2.1 Developing in coexistence

The much-needed reform of our economic thinking on the grounds just described could only marginally be met if based on an understanding in line with conventional sustainable development. Furthermore, a closer look at the presumably realistic alternative to the trinity model reveals that it is not. Even if we take the radical step of fully subordinating the economy and technology to becoming means, and, as such, means that do not support exploitative and expansionist goals, crucial problems remain in the development 4.0.

Keeping the purely anthropocentric perspective means keeping an instrumental view on the world. Everything is there for us, but now under sustainability restrictions. A new aim would be to find balance points below those where further consumption of Earth's capacities would lead to serious problems. This is unrealistic for both knowledge and governance reasons. With the anthropocentric instrumental view it remains rational to aim for high consumption levels, with some margin for the estimated risk of breaching a 'planetary boundary'. The knowledge needed to make such decisions is not available. The limiting complexity and unpredictability is well illustrated by uncertainties in today's estimations of tipping points related to climate change. Nor is it relevant to expect the creation of a global governance regime that would have the capacity and mandate to process such information and to make the relevant decisions. Among the obstacles are the goal conflicts and distribution issues involved, such as when risks and costs do not affect everyone equally, which is the normal situation.

Contrary to the optimistic expectations necessary for the development 4.0, much of real human interaction shows that we do not sacrifice today's local preferences for the benefit of others or the future, and that severe conflicts over resources are likely to magnify as circumstances become more acute. This insight should make us start at the other end, with a desired sustainable state, and not with today's priorities. Taking inspiration from Rawls' veil of ignorance (Rawls, 1972) and backcasting, we should ask what this would demand from us in terms of a worldview and strategy.

Instead of today's attempts to fine-tune our instrumental relationship with the planet, with greener consumption and ever more advanced technologies, the solution must be built on non-instrumentality; a relationship which pays much less attention to control, exploitation and consumption. Can we accept this? If not, we can conclude that 'sustainability' is therapeutic; a rhetoric making hedonists feel good, or as Herman Daly put it (1993, p. 439): we may well be chanting the mantra of sustainability to 'absolve us from our addiction to robbing the future'. Our capacity to argue is certainly superior to other forms of life, but we have not proven that we differ from other species in our ability to control our own expansion, in our unique biological position characterized by the absence of predators and capacity to consume basically everything, everywhere.

Realistic sustainability ambitions must aim directly at the causes of ecological imbalances, the roots of exploitation and expansion, and not just aim to curb their effects. In order to achieve this, we must focus not only on the non-consumerist values in our lives and societies, but also in the non-human world outside (including intrinsic values). Combined, these efforts could enable evolutionary coexistence, characterized by humans living and developing together with, and not only through, other forms of life. Here, evolution should not be understood as changes on the level of genes over generations, as in general biology, but rather as in ecological economics, coevolution between, for example, biophysical, biotic and cultural systems (Gual and Norgaard, 2010).

Although facts about degradation, eradication and limits to human expansion have to be taken much more seriously, evolutionary coexistence (which would be development 5.0) is not only a survival strategy for humans. It will be driven by a more profound valuation of life and aim for a qualitatively and ethically more advanced stage in development. In contrast, the modern consumerist society, obsessed by growth, has meagre roles for the planet's life, including its human masters. The explosion of material wealth enabled by fossil fuels and planetary overshoot may have temporarily blinded us, and it may be possible to recapture and turn into common sense the wisdom of persons like Keynes and Mill. Keynes commented on what we should leave behind: the love of money and accumulation of wealth, promoted by pseudo-moral principles and distasteful human qualities that we have given the position of the highest virtues (Keynes, [1930] 1972, p. 329). Commenting on what we could reach, Mill wrote that:

> a stationary condition of capital and population implies no stationary state of human improvement. There would be as much scope as ever for all kinds of mental culture, and moral and social progress; as much room for improving

> the Art of Living, and much more likelihood of its being improved, when minds ceased to be engrossed by the art of getting on.
>
> (Mill, [1848] 1926, p. 751)

Utopian or not, such possibilities for humans would be given through the quantitatively more restrictive and ethically more inclusive evolutionary coexistence strategy.

3.2.2 Change in economic conceptualization and practice

Based on the new sustainable development model, we could achieve the necessary reform of economic thinking. As key features, such reform logically follows and counters the flaws discussed above. Table 10.2 briefly presents the main traits of this reorientation towards scientific realism and a more inclusive ethics.

If we succeed in this change of understandings, and make today's economic mainstream into something extreme and unrealistic of the past, substantial change can also take place in the economic practice. There has never been a lack

Table 10.2 From economic to sustainable understandings.

Problem area	*Conventional economic understandings*	*Sustainable understandings*
The separation from nature	Nature is infinite or substitutable	We are dependent on nature, find value in non-transformed nature and are able to harm nature
	All values appear through social and economic processes	Human activities must harmonize with nature's processes and be contained within biophysical frames
	Using and transforming nature implies progress	Norms, regulation, measurement and reporting should support stewardship
Human liberation and new forms of dependence	Individual choice leads us right	Ideas of individual integrity must be aligned with our common challenges
	Exosomatic instruments can take us where we want	Our means should be contained within a strategy of coexistence
	Strong specialization possible as we share same aspirations	Governance structures must support collective goals
Reductionism	What we care about can be handled and compared on markets	The costs of degrading resources must be high, but more fundamental valuation should override pricing
	Our rationality is primarily instrumental	Rationality builds on values and not only means-end calculation
	Strict separation of functions and responsibilities is sound	Norms, contracts, regulation and pricing should align economic activities with their consequences

(continued)

Table 10.2 From economic to sustainable understandings. *(continued)*

Problem area	*Conventional economic understandings*	*Sustainable understandings*
Demand as guiding instrument	Market demand is a relevant indicator of needs	Demand is based on purchasing power, why needs must be advanced through new measures
	Demand is the main argument for action	Non-market values and expressions should be elevated in decision-making
	Demand directs society towards utility and efficient allocation	Market demand drives injustice and exploitation, and must be subordinated to social goals and planetary boundaries
An efficient and growing creation of value	Market activity based on self-interest drives continuous increases in value	Economic value creation crowds out or destroys other values, that is why market regulation as well as other spheres must be made stronger
	Perpetual growth is possible and required	Growth is environmentally destructive and as a goal unworthy of an advanced society
	Production and allocation is increasingly efficient	Progress must be related to absolute effects and capacities

of relevant ideas and examples, but they have been drowned and counteracted by the immensely successful economism of the fossil-based, consumerist modern era. It is suggested the new sustainable economic practice should be built on six categories of change under three main headings.

3.2.2.1 PRODUCTION AND CONTENT OF WELFARE

These efforts should improve the economy's relevance and respond to the questions of how (to produce) and what (to consume). The need for sustainable ways of producing goods and services corresponds to most of society's sustainability efforts today. Some 'greening' and eco-efficiency measures are necessary but the focus on relative improvements should be recognized as irrelevant, and new efforts must target absolute impacts and environmental capacities. Today's excessive production-side focus also takes attention away from fundamental change and leads to further degradation as it presupposes control, commercialization and consumerism. New measures must build on a less instrumentalist relation to the world. With coexistence as its aim, production is directed by mechanisms other than profit and demand, and uses means that are less technology oriented and built more on values and connection.

Sustainable consumption is also an area discussed in the mainstream, but we need more than change in content. The role of this activity category, and consumerism, must be toned down in society. This contains a huge potential corresponding to the new focus on qualitative development instead of growth. As far as content is concerned, long distance travel and the consumption of animals are obvious areas for cuts, and when time overrides money as 'currency', activities that promote health, aesthetics and social interaction will be favoured. As destructive consumption is income related, regulation (which includes quotas) needs to be used, both to reduce impact and make consumption fairer.

3.2.2.2 SPEED AND SCALE OF THE ECONOMY

These categories aim directly at aligning the economy to its environment and reducing the human footprint. To limit the pressure on nature's sources and sinks it is essential to reduce throughput. Here, efficiency is not enough, and the so-called 'circular economy' does not make ecologic sense if it avoids questioning the speed of throughput and the overarching goal of growth. Higher tax on virgin materials and land exploitation, restrictions on advertising and a financial system that cannot steadily expand credit to exploitation and consumption are among the measures that together with new norms support an economy with more sharing and repairing.

As the scale of our societies also determines the throughput and environmental impact, we must take this dimension seriously. Most importantly, the wealthiest's consumption should decline, but plans for lower global population and average imprint on nature (through consumption of e.g. land, materials and energy) should be made. The principal means is to replace our unworthy growth targets with intelligent and ethically relevant goals concerning the qualities of life, society and the environment. Practical measures will include physical planning that reduces transportation, and regulation that favours more common ownership and shared use of resources and products.

3.2.2.3 ORGANIZATION

Important efforts are also needed in order to promote ethics in the economy. One part of this is to connect people and organizations to the consequences of their actions; creating relationships that support responsible decisions by making needs and harms more comprehensible. This will demand more local and small-scale activities, more collaboration, but also organizational forms, contracts and trade regimes that do not excessively favour economic power or prioritize profits over fundamental human and environmental values. Institutions must also explicitly protect future values, for example, through nature reserves, strict emission caps and low (zero) discount rates.

Finally, we need to radically change the power money has in society and re-organize the economy towards basic needs. One way is to introduce new currencies and allocation mechanisms, for example time based, or including components of needs, caps or quotas. Market allocation could also be made more relevant if differences in income and financial wealth were reduced. And as perhaps the most difficult step, we need invigorated democratic decision processes in which local participation is contained within responsible global and intertemporal governance regimes.

4 Conclusion

It is time to accept that our success – the human expansion and almost complete dominance of Earth, as manifested in the term Anthropocene – is a threat, and that the causes of this threat are found in our own understandings and priorities. Present levels of control, domestication and exploitation contradict ecological balance, and a crucial part of the necessary change is the subordination of economic activities and systems under a realistic and ethically generous model for sustainability. Evolutionary coexistence forms such a model and could become a framework for sustainable human decision-making. Within this framework, the suggested changes in economic conceptualization and practice would form the basis for an economy which would serve the planet and its inhabitants over many generations instead of maximizing output and consumption for a temporary human elite.

The smaller role of human societies in terms of sheer size and dominance would be well compensated also with anthropocentric points of departure. When economic activity focuses on basic needs, quality of life and profound relations, well-being could be improved on material levels somewhere inbetween today's extremes. Finally, contrary to conventional 'sustainable development', the strategy of evolutionary coexistence gives human society a chance to survive and prosper in a just and peaceful way. To avoid the crises and conflict, which will intensify if we continue our journey towards the tyranny of the circumstances, we 'just' need to prove that we are morally and biologically apt to change.

Bibliography

Arnold, J. R. T., Chapman, S. N. & Clive, L. M. (2012) *Introduction to Materials Management*. Seventh edition. Upper Saddle River, NJ: Pearson Prentice Hall.

Banerjee, S. B. (2003) Who sustains whose development? Sustainable development and the reinvention of nature. *Organization Studies*. 24(1), 143–180.

Baumert, K. A., Herzog, T. & Pershing, J. (2005) *Navigating the Numbers. Greenhouse Gas Data and International Climate Policy*. Washington: World Resources Institute.

Berman, B. & Evans, J. R. (2007) *Retail Management. A Strategic Approach*. Tenth edition. Upper Saddle River, NJ: Pearson Education.

Bonnedahl, K. J. (2012) *Från ekonomiskt till hållbart, från exploatering till samexistens*. Lund, Sweden: Studentlitteratur.

Boulding, K. E. (1965) *Earth as a Space Ship*. Washington: Committee on Space Sciences, Washington State University.

Burenstam Linder, S. ([1969] 2007) *Den rastlösa välfärdsmänniskan. Tidsbrist i överflöd – en ekonomisk studie*. Stockholm: Ratio.

Chancel, L. & Piketty, T (2015) *Carbon and Inequality: From Kyoto to Paris. Trends in the Global Inequality of Carbon Emissions (1998–2013) & Prospects for an Equitable Adaptation Fund*. Paris: Paris School of Economics.

Chertow, M. R. (2001) The IPAT equation and its variants. *Journal of Industrial Ecology*. 4(4), 13–29.

Daly, H. E. (1993) Free trade, sustainable development and growth: Some serious contradictions – a review. *Population and Environment*. 14(4), 439–443.

Daly, H. E. (2005) Economics in a full world. *Scientific American*. 293(3), 100–107.

Daniels, J. D., Radebaugh, L. H. & Sullivan, D. P. (2011) *International Business: Environments and Operations*. Thirteenth edition. Upper Saddle River, NJ: Prentice Hall.

Dolan, E. G. (1986) *Economics*. Fourth edition. New York: Dryden Press.

Easterlin, R. A., McVey, L. A., Switek, M., Sawangfa, O. & Smith Zweig, J. (2010) The happiness–income paradox revisited. *Proceedings of the National Academy of Sciences*. 107(52), 22463–22468.

EEA (European Environment Agency) (2010) *The European Environment – State and Outlook 2010 (SOER 2010). Material Resources and Waste*. Luxemburg: Publications Office of the European Union.

French, R., Rayner, C., Rees, G. & Rumbles, S. (2011). *Organizational Behaviour*. Second edition. Chichester: Wiley.

Gardiner, S. M. (2011) *A Perfect Moral Storm: The Ethical Tragedy of Climate Change*. New York: Oxford University Press.

Georgescu-Roegen, N. (1975) Energy and economic myths. *Southern Economic Journal*. 41(3), 347–381.

Ghoshal, S. (2005) Bad management theories are destroying good management practices. *Academy of Management Learning & Education*. 4(1), 75–91.

Giampietro, M. & Mayumi, K. (1998) Another view of development, ecological degradation, and north-south trade. *Review of Social Economy*. 56(1), 20–36.

Giddings, B., Hopwood, B. & O'Brien, G. (2002) Environment, economy and society: Fitting them together into sustainable development. *Sustainable Development*. 10, 187–196.

Gravelle, H. & Rees, R. (2004) *Microeconomics*. Third edition. Harlow: Pearson.

Gual, M. A. & Norgaard, R. B. (2010) Bridging ecological and social systems coevolution: A review and proposal. *Ecological Economics*. 69, 707–717.

Hirsch, F. (1977) *Social Limits to Growth*. London: Routledge & Keegan.

Holland, A. (1997) Substitutability: Or, why strong sustainability is weak and aburdly strong sustainability is not absurd. In: Foster, J. (ed.) *Valuing Nature? Ethics, Economics and the Environment*. London: Routledge, pp. 119–134.

Jobber, D. (2010) *Principles and Practice of Marketing*. Sixth edition. Maidenhead: McGraw-Hill Education.

Kates, W. R., Parris, T. M. & Leiserowitz, A. A. (2005) What is sustainable development? Goals, indicators, values, and practice. *Environment: Science and Policy for Sustainable Development*. 47(3), 8–21.

Keynes, J. M. ([1930] 1972). Economic possibilities for our grandchildren. In: Keynes, J. M. *The Collected Writings of John Maynard Keynes. Vol. IX, Essays in Persuasion*. London: Macmillan Press, pp. 321–332.

Liedman, S-E. (1997) *I skuggan av framtiden. Modernitetens idéhistoria*. Stockholm: Bonnier Alba.

Maddison, A. (2011) *Historical Statistics of the World Economy: 1–2008 AD*. The Groningen Growth and Development Centre. Available from: www.ggdc.net/maddison (accessed 15 April 2016).

Mariotti, S. & Glackin, C. (2012) *Entrepreneurship & Small Business Management.* Upper Saddle River, NJ: Prentice Hall.

McLaney, E. & Atrill, P. (2010) *Accounting. An Introduction.* Fifth edition. Harlow: Pearson.

Mill, J. S. ([1848] 1926). *Principles of Political Economy.* London: Longmans.

Moles, P., Parrino, R. & Kidwell, D. (2011) *Corporate Finance.* European edition. Chichester: Wiley.

Murphy Jr., P. R. & Wood, D. F. (2011) *Contemporary Logistics.* Tenth edition. Upper Saddle River, NJ: Prentice Hall.

Oxfam (2016). *An Economy for the 1%. How Privilege and Power in the Economy Drive Extreme Inequality and How This can be Stopped.* 210 Oxfam briefing paper. Oxford: Oxfam International.

Porter, M. E. & Kramer, M. R. (2006) Strategy and society: The link between competitive advantage and corporate social responsibility. *Harvard Business Review.* December, 78–93.

Rawls. J. (1972) *A Theory of Justice.* Oxford: Clarendon Press.

Redclift, M. (2005) Sustainable development (1987–2005): An oxymoron comes of age. *Sustainable Development.* 13, 212–227.

Robinson, J. (2004) Squaring the circle? Some thoughts on the idea of sustainable development. *Ecological Economics.* 48, 369–384.

Sanne, C. (2006) *Rekyleffekten och effektivitetsfällan – att jaga sin egen svans i miljöpoliken. Rapport 5623.* Stockholm: Naturvårdsverket.

Smil, V. (2011) Harvesting the biosphere: The human impact, *Population and Development Review.* 37(4), 613–636.

Trott, P. (2012) *Innovation Management and New Product Development.* Fifth edition. Harlow: Pearson.

UN (1999) *The World at Six Billion.* New York: United Nations (Population Division).

UN (2002) *Johannesburg Declaration on Sustainable Development, World Summit on Sustainable Development.* New York: United Nations.

UN (2011) *World Population Prospects: The 2010 Revision.* CD-ROM edition. File 1: Total population (both sexes combined) by major area, region and country, annually for 1950–2100 (thousands). Estimates 1950–2010, April 2011. New York: United Nations (Department of Economic and Social Affairs, Population Division). Available from: http://esa.un.org/unpd/wpp/Excel-Data/population.htm (accessed 10 July 2011).

UN (2015a) *World Population Prospects: The 2015 Revision.* DVD edition. New York: United Nations (Department of Economic and Social Affairs, Population Division). Available from: http://esa.un.org/unpd/wpp/Download/Standard/Population (accessed 29 March 2016).

UN (2015b) *Transforming Our World: The 2030 Agenda for Sustainable Development.* New York: United Nations.

Verma, R. & Boyer, K. K. (2010) *Operations & Supply Chain Management: World Class Theory and Practice.* Florence: Cengage Learning.

von Wright, G. H. (1989) *Vetenskapen och förnuftet. Ett försök till orientering.* Stockholm: Månpocket/Bonnier.

Watson, D., Herczeg, M., Acosta, J., Wittmer, D. & Schütz, H. (2011) *Key Messages on Material Resource Use and Efficiency in Europe. Insights from Environmentally Extended Input-output Analysis and Material Flow Accounts.* European Topic

Centre on Sustainable Consumption and Production. ETC/SCP working paper 3/2011. European Environment Agency.

WCED (World Commission on Environment and Development) (1987), *Our Common Future*. Available at: www.un-documents.net/our-common-future.pdf. (accessed 1 June 2016).

Welzer, H. (2012) *Climate Wars: What People will be Killed for in the 21st Century*. Cambridge: Polity Press.

Index

For Product Safety Concerns and Information please contact our EU representative GPSR@taylorandfrancis.com Taylor & Francis Verlag GmbH, Kaufingerstraße 24, 80331 München, Germany